On the Road Again

On the Road Again

WAYNE ROSTAD

M&S

Canadian Cataloguing in Publication Data

Rostad, Wayne
   On the road again

ISBN 0-7710-7582-0

1. Canada – Biography.   2. Canada – Description and travel.   3. On the road again (Television program).   4. Rostad, Wayne.   I. Title.

FC25.R68 1996   971.064'8'0922   C96-931063-3
F1005.R68 1996

Wayne Rostad's song lyrics © Stag Creek Publishing, SOCAN.

The publisher acknowledges the support of the Canada Council and the Ontario Arts Council for their publishing program.

Typesetting by M&S, Toronto
Printed and bound in Canada

McClelland & Stewart Inc.
The Canadian Publishers
481 University Avenue
Toronto, Ontario
M5G 2E9

1 2 3 4 5   00 99 98 97 96

For all the people
who invited us into their homes,
who opened their hearts
and shared their stories

Contents

Acknowledgements / ix
Introduction / xiii

Dollard Marlow / 1
Common Questions / 17
Pig / 23
"What I Seen, I Seen!" / 35
Red-Wattle Lincoln / 41
Clarence the Caribou / 53
The Yellowknife Caper / 63
The Ruins of British Harbour / 73
Among the Missing / 86
The Coke Lady and the Pepsi King / 93
Gathering of the Gwich'in / 99
Bug-Eater / 119
Maman Louise / 129
Tale of Two Charlies / 138
Iceberg Ice / 155
Mile-Long Hill / 169
The Chignic Incident / 177
Teapot Mountain / 185
Life Is a Railway / 195
Flies and Turpentine / 213
The A320 Tour Bus / 228
The Garbage-Dump Millionaires / 233

The Arctic / 243

Skydive! / 271

Gas Leak at Bow Valley / 291

Wilma / 297

Shubenacadie Tinsmith Man / 311

The Promise / 321

Acknowledgements

Sitting down and writing a book about my "On the Road Again" travels was something I had never really considered until James Adams, a senior editor at McClelland & Stewart, wrote me suggesting I entertain the notion of doing just that. When I first read his letter I felt like a duck out of water. The idea was intimidating. While I had written songs for years and had a handle on television scriptwriting, I didn't know the first thing about writing a book. I told James I wouldn't even know where to begin. Still, he persisted and, in the end, I agreed to sketch a few sample chapters for him, believing that would be the end of it. Much to my surprise, James encouraged me to go for it. Well, James, I followed through on your suggestion and I must say I'm very happy I did. Writing this book has been a joy. Thanks for the kick start.

I must also express deep appreciation to Pat Kennedy, my editor. She took over where James left off when he moved on to the *Globe and Mail*. Pat guided me through the process of putting it all together, reining me in when she had to. Until I met Pat Kennedy, I thought a galley was a kitchen on a ship. She taught me a lot and made my job easier.

To Doug Gibson, publisher of McClelland & Stewart, a big thank-you for waiting so patiently for the finished manuscript. It took longer than I anticipated to complete, in fact a couple of years longer.

I must also acknowledge the fans of "On the Road Again." Without them there never would have been a television show to provide fodder for a book. Many of these dedicated viewers took the time and trouble to phone in story ideas, or stopped us in malls, on streets, and in airport terminals to tell us about someone they believed should be on our show. Many of those very ideas are in the chapters that follow. We thank all of them for their incredible support.

I want to thank my "On the Road Again" television family, a group of very talented people who have worked together for years. Second effort has been the motto of our whole team. To all the producers, executive producers, researchers, camera and audio crews, editors, and office support staff who have worked long and tirelessly on the program, I tip my hat. It is an honour to work with such professionals.

To CBC management, my thanks for your insight and support in putting a program like "On the Road Again" on the air and for your continuing encouragement over the years.

Thank you, Don Attfield, for opening that very first door and for believing that music and the lyrics of a song could help tell a story. Thank you to music producer and arranger Joe Turner for making those songs paint pictures.

Gerry Janneteau and Norm Bolen, thanks for believing in us and taking the show to the national level, and to Sheila Petzold and Sue Stranks for being there in the formative years as executive producers. It was an awesome task to put together the logistics of covering an entire country on a modest budget. You took the bull by the horns, and won. Hooray for all of you!

Paul Harrington, thank you for being there during the formative stages of putting this collection of memories together. Your insight was invaluable (as it always is). You are truly a friend.

The pictures in this book were taken by members of our talented team: first and foremost producer Andy Little, who just happens to be one heck of a fine photographer; producers Janet P. Smith and Jonathan Craven; audio man Mike Champagne; cameramen Gilles Guttadauria and Keith Whelan; and me. A few were provided by our show's guests themselves. Thanks, gang!

To my family and friends, who knew something was up when I started spending more time with my computer than I did with them. For their patience and encouragement, I am deeply appreciative.

Finally, I wish to acknowledge my wife, Leanne, who helped me find my "voice" and made sure I stayed true to it. She provided untiring support, once again reminding me why marrying her was so right. There is only one of her in the whole world and I wonder sometimes how I got so lucky. Thanks, Lee-Lee. This is one book you don't have to read. You know every word by heart.

Introduction

Sometimes the most wonderful things in life happen by accident, not design.

Back in the summer of 1980, I was working full-time as a country-music entertainer. One night, after I had performed at the National Arts Centre in Ottawa, a CBC producer by the name of Don Attfield came backstage to talk to me. He was looking for someone to replace the host of his television show "Country Report" and wondered if I would be interested in the job.

I had been in television twice before, and twice before I left it for music. While I was flattered by Don's offer, I had to tell him that, much as I would love to host a show like "Country Report," I had a new album to promote and had to go on the road. Besides, "Country Report" was a farm show that talked about things like soybeans and cattle prices. I was a long-haired guitar picker and I really didn't think his viewers would fancy the look of me. Still, Don insisted. If I was willing to just fill in until he found someone, he'd be happy – no more than two or three months.

A few weeks later, I agreed to do it – but only for a few months. Well, that was seventeen years ago and I'm still filling in.

You see, a wonderful thing happened. I fell in love with that little farm show. It turned out that roaming around the Ottawa Valley in search of stories was right up my alley. The stories we did fed the songwriter in me and my songwriting, in turn, became part of "Country Report"'s storytelling. I had, by accident, found the perfect career combination. Best of all, as a single parent, it allowed me to work close to home so I could raise my young son, Josh.

Over the next seven years, my hair got shorter and shorter as "Country Report" evolved from a farm show into a lifestyles show, forming the foundation of "On the Road Again." The pilot series aired on the CBC national network in 1987 and we've been going strong ever since, travelling to just about every nook and cranny in this country from sea to sea to sea, meeting Canadians in all walks of life, finding out what makes them tick and sharing their stories with the rest of the country.

It's been an incredible odyssey. Every member of our "On the Road Again" team is filled with a sense of joy doing this show. There isn't a day that goes by that I'm not thankful for the opportunity to do what I do. I have never been able to consider it a job. It's been more of a privilege. I don't think I will ever tire of exploring this great country of ours.

The mandate of "On the Road Again" is to bring the people to the people. The guests who appear on our show make that possible. I am grateful to all of them for inviting us into their lives. They are stars, each and every one. They have touched our hearts. They've made us laugh and they've made us cry. Most importantly, they have taught us what it means to be Canadian.

The chapters of this book revisit some of the places "On the Road Again" and its predecessor show, "Country Report," have taken me and help me relive some of the precious moments shared with the people who welcomed us into their homes. I've included a lot of behind-the-scenes stuff, because often the story behind the story is interesting, too. Sometimes, just getting to location is a story in itself. I have travelled to shoot sites in some of the most incredible fashions: by twin-track Bombardier snow machine across Great Slave Lake; by dog sled across Frobisher Bay; by helicopter to mountain tops; and by sailboat to abandoned and forgotten outports. I have been to the very last house at the end of the road; walked up the Rocky Mountains with pack goats; kissed a whale on the forehead in the Atlantic Ocean off the shores of Nova Scotia; flown to the Gulf Islands by sea plane to visit a Haida chief; and ridden a cablecar in Alberta, one hundred and fifty feet above a gorge across a thousand-foot expanse, to listen to a cowboy recite poetry. I have attempted to capture some of these experiences in the pages that follow. I wish I could have included them all. There are so many stories to tell. The ones I have chosen are only the tip of the iceberg.

Fortunately, I saved all the notes, letters, and pictures, research notes, producer's notes, newspaper clippings, and press articles for and about the shows over the years. I guess when you grow up without very much, you tend to be a pack rat. Well, this is one time my pack-rat nature paid off. It sure helped to have a basement full of boxes filled with memories.

This year marks the tenth anniversary of our television show, "On the Road Again," and I can't think of a nicer way to celebrate that than by publishing this book. I am thrilled to share these memories with you. Over the years I've been called a singer, a songwriter, a radio announcer, and a television host. But first and foremost, I am a storyteller. Here are a few tales from the road.

I hope you enjoy them.

Dollard Marlow

～

Dollard Marlow doesn't live on the Kaywood Road any more;
They took him to the city, to a government old-age home.
All of us, eventually, will wither and grow old;
Dollard Marlow doesn't live on the Kaywood Road any more.

– from the song "Dollard Marlow"

The old man who lived at the fork in the road was an ornery cuss. According to one of the locals, he was so ornery that the snow-plough operator had to lift the blade on his truck when he made the turn onto Dollard Marlow's road. The door of Dollard's cabin was only two metres from the edge of the road, and he sure didn't like the mess the plough made when it went by with its blade in the down position. Heaven help the ploughman who shoved dirty old road snow up against Dollard's door!

It wasn't just the mess, though. Dollard was a perfectionist who paid great attention to detail. The snowscape around his house was perfectly symmetrical. The snow, which fell from the roof in great heaps alongside the cabin walls, was meticulously squared with a shovel. It looked like the cabin was sitting inside a big white box, a box about a metre wider on all sides than the building itself.

He continued that squaring effect everywhere. A series of snowboxes bordered the walkways leading from his door. The path leading to the woodshed had them, as did the short one leading to the road. Even the portion of roadway left by the ploughman for Dollard to clear had perfectly squared snowbanks!

A third path wound its way down the hill from the cabin,

Dollard Marlow

Enjoying a visit with Dollard at the seniors' home at Notre-Dame-du-Laus

ending at Stag Creek, which circled the cabin and snaked off towards the township bridge. That path had several boxes in descending order of elevation. It was quite a scene: a log cabin set in a terraced winter landscape in the middle of the bush!

I heard another story about Dollard Marlow from Mona Monette, the proprietor of the local hotel in Brennan's Hill, a small hamlet in the Gatineau Hills, about sixty kilometres north of Ottawa. Dollard's place was twelve kilometres north of the inn. Mona told me that he often walked the entire length of dirt road from his cabin to the inn on Friday nights – rain, wind, sleet, or snow – to pick up a weekend case of beer. It was not uncommon to see him shouldering the case of brew back to his peaceful abode by the creek. Rarely did he accept a lift from people passing by, since there were far too many cottagers to suit his fancy and he had nothing nice to say to them anyway.

According to Mona, Dollard had been a conscientious objector, who took to the Quebec bush when Canada entered the First World War in 1914. He was not alone. There were other Quebecers at that time who felt the war was not their war and headed for the bush. In his nineties, Dollard was still living beside what once had been a footpath and was now a full-blown municipal road. And in winter that meant big, crude, noisy snow-pushers. No wonder he didn't like cottagers; if so many of them hadn't started to live full-time up the road at Lac St-Georges, another twenty kilometres to the north of Dollard's cabin site, they wouldn't have needed those big machines to keep the road open. Without them, at least in the wintertime, life would have been the way it was when he first picked his tranquil creekside retreat – quiet. My interest in Dollard grew with each story told to me. How, I wondered, could anyone have survived all these years, alone, so far back in the bush.

The year was 1972. It was winter, and I had been working at the Brennan's Hill Inn for several months. I had a three-piece band and we were the weekend entertainment. "On the Road Again" was very much in the future. Fifteen years in the future. However, when I look back, I realize it was a time in my life that was actually grooming me for my future role in television. The Gatineau Hills were the perfect place to be. They were full of fascinating people, and not only was I filled with the curiosity of a young city man turned country boy, I was also a songwriter who wanted to write songs about people. I noticed that, when people talked, Dollard's name kept coming up. I figured it was only time before our paths would cross.

Even my friend Rae Parker had met Dollard. Rae was living in a shack, as many of us "back-to-the-landers" did in the 1970s, not far from Brennan's Hill, and he once ran across the hermit woodsman along the Kaywood Road. He was pretty sure the old "centenarian," as Rae called him, lived in a log cabin, but he didn't know if it was the one at the fork. Although their encounter was brief, Rae came away mesmerized. He couldn't forget Dollard's eyes.

"They were incredible," he said. "The old boy is right out of a movie. Might be a song there for you."

"Could be," I replied. "I'd better meet this man."

A few months later, in March, while performing a snowy Sunday-afternoon matinee with my band at the inn, I met a fun-loving, boisterous man who had the same surname as Dollard. He introduced himself to me as Tommy Marlow.

"Are you related to the old fellow who lives up the Kaywood Road?" I asked.

"You mean my uncle?"

"I think his name is Dollard."

"You mean Adelord." It was clear by the tone of Tommy's voice that I had the wrong name.

"So, Adelord is his real name?" I exclaimed.

"He's my father's brother. Adelord is my uncle."

Tommy went on to explain how, over the years, the anglophones of the region had coined the name Dollard. Tommy's father, Louis, was living in an old log house in the small village of Fieldville, eight kilometres south of Dollard's place. Like his older brother, Dollard, Louis built his house back in the early 1900s. Louis was now in his eighties – Dollard, in his nineties.

"Louis spells his last name differently than Dollard does," Tommy continued.

"Really?"

"He spells it *Marleau*. All the other brothers spell it *Marlot*."

"How many other brothers are there?" I asked.

"There were seven boys . . . and two girls."

"Why different spellings?"

"It gets worse than that," Tommy went on. "When the great-grandfather came here from France, he spelled his name *Morlot*. After he got off the boat, somebody changed it to Marlot. On top of that, some anglophones wrote it down as Marlow. What a mess, eh?"

"No kidding," I replied. "What else can you tell me about Dollard?"

"The old man? He's giving my cousin, Charlie, a pretty rough time. They can't keep Adelord in the old-age place. He runs away all the time."

Tommy went on to explain how Dollard's memory had been slipping in recent years, and Charlie, Dollard's nephew, worried about the old man hurting himself. He thought his uncle should live out his remaining years in a senior-citizens' residence, and had recently put him in one at Gracefield, a small community north of Dollard's place.

"The cat was the last straw."

"The cat?"

"The cat. The old man can't see any more. Cataracts. He's

damn near deaf, too. One day, he puts wood in the big wood stove and shuts the oven door. He didn't notice the cat was inside the oven having a snooze. Then he lights the fire and sits down to have a smoke."

"He locked the cat in the oven?"

"Tight as a drum, sir. Lucky for the cat, Charlie just happened by to check on the old man. Apparently, it was a hell of a scene – screamin' cat and smokin' fur. The old man was completely unaware of it all. He was just sitting at his table by the window, watching the world go by, drawing on his pipe. At first, Charlie had no idea where the cat was. When he opened the oven door, he didn't really expect to find anything in there. That cat streaked by his face like a singed duck in full flight. Damn near ripped Charlie's face off!"

"Where is he now?" I asked.

"The cat?"

"No. Dollard."

"He's back at the cabin. He ran away from the old-age home at Gracefield. Came home straight through the bush, fourteen miles."

"Through the bush alone?"

"This is the second time! Adelord knows the hills up here like the back of his hand. For him, going home through solid bush is like you going for a Sunday stroll."

"Hard to believe a man in his nineties could do that."

"That's because he's contrary as old hell. He wouldn't even sleep in the old-people's place. He went outside when it was too hot and slept under a tree in the back yard. They almost shut the home down when someone reported to the government that one of the residents at the home was sleeping outside. They stopped him for a while, but what could they do? They couldn't tie him to the bed. And they had a heck of a time getting his axe away from him."

"His axe?"

"Yes, He took it to the home with him. He wanted to keep it in his room. He loved chopping firewood."

"Would Dollard accept a visitor?" I asked. "I'd like to see him."

"It depends. Sometimes he's all right, sometimes he wants nothing to do with you. I guess it's a question of whether he takes a liking to you or not."

"Would you mind if I dropped in on him?" I asked. I guess I figured that, if one of Dollard's relatives said it was okay, it would give me a visitor's permit to enter Dollard's world.

"It doesn't matter to me. Do what you want. Just take your time. Move slow. Don't talk like somebody from the city. They move too fast in the city. He doesn't like that."

I thanked Tommy for his conversation and shook his hand goodbye. He had a great, infectious laugh. I watched through the window of the Brennan's Hill Inn as he climbed on his farm tractor for the drive back to Fieldville. He brushed the snow from the seat, sat down, turned the key, and fired up the old diesel.

What a wild way to get around, I thought. A farm tractor! Mona told me later that the tractor was Tommy's only vehicle. His licence had been taken away many, many moons ago and this was it – his ticket to the hotel and home again – a big, red Massey-Ferguson. I heard that, on some nights, after prolonged libations at the inn, patrons of the hotel would walk out to the parking lot in the wee hours of the morning to see Tommy off. They loved to see him climb up on "Big Red" and would cheer as he roared up the dirt road leading over the steep hill behind the inn on his way back to Fieldville. But this was Sunday after-noon, and Tommy was drinking coffee, and my own glimpse of Tommy weaving homeward on his tractor would have to wait. What I decided couldn't wait any longer, however, was my meeting with Dollard Marlow.

After Tommy faded from sight over the crest of the hill, I

walked over to my drummer, Billy Carew. I told him about this
old man I wanted to visit back in the bush and recounted what I
knew about him, including Tommy's story about the cat. Billy
roared! He immediately understood my fascination with this
hermit character.

"Would you like to come with me today after the matinee?" I
asked.

"Would I ever!" he said. "Are you sure I won't be in the way?"

"No. Not at all."

We had one more music set to do, and we didn't waste any
time getting it done. Billy and I left as soon as it was over. We
wanted to make sure we had enough light left in the day for
our visit.

The woodpile by the back shed, that's the work of his withered hands;
The home he built out of local pine when he was a young man.
Now they've got him in that city compound, till he breathes no more;
I wonder, Lord, would he rather die along the Kaywood Road?

Some things are etched forever in the heart and in the mind.
That late winter afternoon, when Billy and I arrived at that fork
in the road, the sun was just falling behind the trees and the long
winter shadows were settling on the scene below us. The road
dipped down to the right at the fork, descending to the bridge. It
was just as I had pictured it. But what we saw on the other side of
the bridge completely took our breath away.

"My God, Bill. Look at that!"

At the top of the opposite rise, no more than two metres
from the edge of the road, stood the most beautiful little cabin
in the world. Dollard's cabin. No wonder he hated snowploughs!
We could see quite readily that, if they didn't lift their blades,
they would bury his doorway. The cabin was postcard-perfect.

It had a blue hue to it. The paint on the soffits and eaves, once a lively blue, had faded to almost nothing, but there was still enough colour to be caught by the sun. A long, twisting ribbon of smoke curled from the black stovepipe protruding through the tin roof. But the most amazing thing of all was the snow surrounding Dollard's house. It was exactly as I had heard it described, a perfectly terraced landscape! Bill started laughing in amazement.

"I don't believe this!" he said. "The old man does this?"

I was laughing by now, too.

"Unbelievable!" I said. "I know people who don't even bother to shovel their sidewalks."

We drove ever so slowly down toward the bridge, our eyes drinking in the scene. We could clearly see the path leading down to the creek. It stopped at the edge of the bank where a portion of ice on the creek surface had recently been disturbed. The creek was obviously Dollard's water source, and he had no doubt filled his pails that very morning.

As our car pulled up to the front of the cabin, I noticed the frail figure of a man in the woodpile rows to the left. The rows were impeccable; there wasn't a stick out of place. Dollard didn't acknowledge our arrival, which didn't surprise me. After all, his back was to us, and I remembered Tommy Marlow telling me Dollard was almost deaf. We parked the car on the road, away from his front pathway, remembering how ornery he was about vehicular traffic.

"Should we say hello?" I asked, hesitantly.

Dollard was a very small man, only about five-foot-two. He was turning slowly as we approached him, his arms laden with sticks for the fire. I hoped he had heard the crunching snow under our feet, and wouldn't be too taken aback.

"Hello," I said. "*Bonjour*. Monsieur Marlow?"

Despite our caution, he was momentarily startled. He stared at my cowboy boots – my very large cowboy boots. He was extremely bent and it took considerable effort for him to look up, so I quickly lowered my six-foot-four frame to his level and looked him in the eyes for the first time. Rae was right; they were incredible eyes, faded blue like the blue paint on the eaves of his cabin. But those blue eyes still danced, despite the off-white cataracts which veiled them.

"May I help you?" I offered.

"*Qu'est-ce que tu dis?*" he asked. His voice was not sharp or unkind. He simply did not understand English.

"May I help you carry the wood in . . . the wood . . . inside?" I motioned with my arms for him to transfer the load from his, and then I pointed to the cabin.

He had an incredible face, the kind lifted from a storybook. It was a thin, lean face, with the lines of ninety years of living written all over it, and a great drooping moustache that hung down to the bottom of his chin on both sides of his mouth. His breath had condensed, then frozen, on the handlebars of the moustache, making them look like walrus tusks.

"*Je ne comprends pas,*" he said, assessing my own face. He still didn't understand why we were there.

"We came to visit you . . . *une visite, avec vous!*" I was speaking much louder now, remembering that Dollard was hard of hearing.

Dollard smiled. He obviously didn't understand my French any better, but at least this time he smiled. Once again I pointed at his armful of wood and made motions of me carrying. At last, he understood my offer. Still smiling, he handed the load over to me and started walking towards his cabin, beckoning us to follow. At the corner of his cabin he stopped, pausing for the longest time, touching the pine logs, as if inspecting their condition.

"*C'est moi qui fait tout ça,*" he said, pointing to the walls. He was proudly announcing that it was he who had done all this work.

He ran his withered old fingers over the dovetail cuts he had made at the corners, interlocking cuts, which held the logs of the cabin together.

"*Tout seul . . . je fais ça tout seul.*" He wanted us to know that he did all this work alone. He was so proud of his cabin.

They weren't big logs – only about fifteen centimetres around – but they had survived many cold Gatineau winters and continued to shield him from the cold.

"*Viens dedans. Du thé. Du thé.*" It was more than I had hoped for. Dollard was inviting us in for tea!

The doorway was very small, but it was more than large enough for Dollard. Billy and I had to stoop to enter. Once inside, we noticed that he lived in a world of grey. Here, there were no traces of paint. Everything was natural wood, faded and aged like the old man himself. He took off his heavy wool overcoat and motioned for us do the same. I noticed that his pants were wool, too, thick, heavy grey pants into which he had tucked what once was a bright red flannel shirt. There was no belt, just a huge pair of suspenders holding everything together. I thought to myself that this grey actually had more depth or range of colour than most houses I had been in. There was no pretence here, no attempt to cover with paint and gaud the sins of inferior carpentry, or to make something homemade appear storebought.

"*Prends une chaise, ici . . . ici.*" He motioned for us to sit at his table while he tended the fire.

"So, this was the stove that almost cooked the cat," I chuckled quietly to myself.

Dollard lifted the feeder lid and proceeded to poke the ashes with the butt of a fresh stick. Then he loaded two others into the firepot. Everything he did was in slow motion. There was no sense of city hurry here. Time was something he had lots of.

"Billy, look at this table. See these marks? This is the corner he does all his work at."

The table had hundreds of little knife cuts at the corner

nearest the stove. I fancied that Dollard either whittled things or cut his daily bread there. Dollard joined us at the table after setting the kettle on the wood stove to boil.

"*C'est très belle*," said Billy. "*La table*. It's very nice."

I asked Dollard what make the knife cuts by pointing to them and making cutting motions with my hand.

"*Avec un couteau?*" I queried.

"*Oui. Un couteau*," he replied.

He went on to explain that he used the table for a bit of everything – bread-cutting, whittling – in fact, the whole beautiful tabletop was one giant kitchen cutting-board and toolshop workbench.

In the hour that passed, not a lot of anything was spoken so much as communicated. We laughed a lot. He was really a kind old man, not ornery at all. We laughed over tea, did a lot of pointing and gesturing at things, and laughed some more. The tea was something else. It was genuine "Stag Creek Country Tea," made with water drawn from the creek that very morning. No store-bought mineral water in the world could have rivalled its taste.

Finally, it was time to leave. Billy and I still had the Sunday-night shows to perform back at the inn. We thanked Dollard for his hospitality and attempted to express how flattered we were at having been invited into his world. I promised him that Billy and I would return for a visit some day.

Driving back to the hotel, neither of us spoke a word. We just glanced at each other a few times and smiled or laughed. We knew we had experienced something special. We had been privileged to enter Dollard's world, a world of beautiful simplicity, far removed from the trappings of modern society. His was a world of self-reliance, and his persistence to survive was impressive. I was so moved by his achievement. Mainly, though, I was filled with what Dollard exuded most – a quiet sense of peacefulness. That night, Billy and I did the evening portion of our show at the inn, and I can't remember all the songs I sang, but I know most of them were pretty mellow. My mind was preoccupied with the beginnings of the song I was already composing about Dollard.

I remember, Dollard shared a pot of Stag Creek Country Tea,
He poured himself a shaky cup, then one for Billy and me.
In leaving, we promised him we'd come again, for sure,
But Dollard Marlow doesn't live on the Kaywood Road any more.

I never did get back to see Dollard in his cabin home. Shortly after our visit, his nephew, Charlie, moved his old uncle again – this time to the town of Notre-Dame-du-Laus, a lot farther up the line. There would be no more hikes through the bush. It saddened me to hear the news. I knew he wanted nothing more than to live and die by the banks of his beautiful Stag Creek. I heard that, when the time came for him to go to Notre-Dame-du-Laus, he left his axe behind on the chopping block between those perfectly straight rows of firewood.

But although I couldn't visit him at the cabin, I did manage to see him one last time, at the seniors' home in Notre-Dame. The song I had written about him after he was taken from his cabin home that last time was being featured in the pilot for a national television show. My producer, Brian Lebold, wanted a few still photographs of the old man he had got to know through my song, so photographer John Galt and I paid him a visit. Dollard was now ninety-six and, like my friend Rae, I was now calling Dollard the Centenarian and was rooting for him to reach the magic one hundred!

Once again, Dollard and I laughed a lot. John snapped merrily away. Once again, the old man stole my heart.

"Wish I could take you home, Dollard. Wish I could take you home."

I guess Progress teaches all of us, we must pay its price,
Electric lights are practical but a lantern sure is nice,
Don't trust your neighbour out of fear that he will get you first,
And don't dare die until you've checked with the city officials first.

Two years later, in 1980, while I was vacationing in Fiji, I received
a phone call from Canada in the middle of a raging hurricane.
The resort manager sought me out in my room, telling me to
come quickly, that there was an important call from Canada in
the office. It was George Voisine, my business partner, who had
financed my first album, *Writer of Songs*; it included the song
about my old centenarian friend.

"George?" I could hardly hear him with the wail of the wind
penetrating the shutters. "What's wrong?" I asked.

"Dollard Marlow passed away, Wayne. I thought you would
want to know."

"When?"

"Two days ago. I've had a heck of a time trying to find you."

It was the strangest feeling in the world. Here I was, halfway
around the world, in the middle of a hurricane, hearing sad news
of Dollard's passing. The old boy had almost made the one hundred mark. He was ninety-eight.

Dollard now is crying out for the only life he knows,
Cursing modern progress that took away his home;
But someday soon his soul will come back to that cabin door,
And stare upon the pavement they've laid on the Kaywood Road.
No, Dollard Marlow doesn't live on that dusty road any more.

About a year after Dollard passed away, I returned to his cabin.
The door was off its hinges, and someone had literally ripped the

floorboards out. The tidy little world of grey that I remembered so fondly was now a world of disarray. The furniture was gone, including the table at which we had sat and had tea. Upstairs in the tiny loft, a pair of heavy grey trousers, like the wool trousers I remembered him wearing during that winter visit, lay rumpled in the corner. The woodpile was gone, too, and there were beer bottles strewn about; locals or cottagers had stopped to rummage, taking everything except their own garbage. I sat there listening to Stag Creek burbling by the cabin and to the birds singing around me. I imagine Dollard had done that a few times in his lifetime here.

I was happy when I heard that the cabin eventually ended up at Dollard's nephew's place. Charlie decided that, before the entire cabin disappeared in pieces, he would move it to his farm and put it to use a couple of kilometres down the road from where Dollard first erected it, "*tout seul.*"

Dollard remains an important part of my life. I still sing his song at my concerts and I still love to tell people about the day we sat and shared tea in his creekside cabin. One day in 1990 I received a phone call from Joe Carty, an old friend of mine who lives in the Gatineau Hills. Earlier that week, he had listened to a radio interview I did with an Ottawa radio station. He heard me talk about my album and my favourite song on it – the one about Dollard Marlow. He listened to the story about Dollard's world of grey and the lines cut on the table at which we sat. Joe had bought a table from an acquaintance that seemed awfully similar to the table I was describing in the interview. By the time I finished telling my story on the radio, Joe knew that he, in fact, had Dollard's table.

"That table was mine until I heard someone describe it who obviously loved it a whole lot more than me," Joe said. "I want you to have it, Wayne. No charge."

Today, Dollard's beautiful old table sits proudly in our living

Common Questions

～

In the ten years I have hosted "On the Road Again," I have met a lot of people with questions about the show. The one I'm asked most often is: "Where do you find your story ideas?" Some ask it differently: "Where do you find all those crazy characters?" Still others ask: "How do you manage to keep coming up with such wonderful people?"

Well, it isn't easy. This is a big country, and it's no mean trick finding them. They're out there all right, in every city, town, village, and out-of-the-way nook and cranny. The trick is flushing them out.

Of course, some stand out more than others. For example, there's "Sluggo," the Winnipeg resident who stands at busy downtown intersections, like Portage and Main, balancing things on his face – chairs on his chin, stepladders on his forehead, and big, sharp butcher knives on the bridge of his nose. Him, you don't miss! Actually, when he balances a knife between his eyes, you hope *he* doesn't miss!

Sometimes, people call us at the office to offer story ideas. We never know what to expect.

"Would your show be interested in meeting some real Quebec cowboys at the big annual rodeo in St-Tite, Quebec? It's the biggest one in the province; two hundred and fifty thousand people come for it, and we're a village of only four thousand. Not bad, eh?"

"Hello, this is Charlie McCarthy from Crosby, Ontario. We have a dog that climbs trees. His name is Champ. Goes up trees just like a cat. Comes down head first, flat out, on the run. What are the chances of getting Champ on your show?"

Keith Whelan ready to roll

Cameraman Tom Sharina (centre) hugs the mountainside to get a shot

Cameraman André Villeneuve and producer Janet P. Smith, leaving port, en route to the open sea

When I'm on the road, people stop me at airports, in restaurants, and on the street to offer me story ideas; some even manage to find my home phone number – I'm not sure *how* they find it, but I never refuse to talk to them. In addition, our CBC office in Ottawa now has a 1-800 number – 897-0230 – that we show in the closing credits of our program, along with instructions on how to reach us on the Internet by simply keying otra@ottawa.cbc.ca. Every call, every note, every letter and e-mail message that comes our way is important to us.

It works something like this. "On the Road Again" has two full-time researchers: Ruth Zowdu, who joined us in the fall of 1987, and Louisa Battistelli, who became part of our "family" two years later. They are our miracle-workers. Two people, covering an entire country! It still astounds me how they do it.

Ruth and Louisa might receive information by mail from a viewer who tweaks their curiosity, or see something in one of the many weekly newspapers sent to our office from communities across the country. Once their attention is grabbed, the first thing our dynamic duo does is get on the phone to do preliminary research. If they are sold on the notion of doing a story after they get off the phone, they take it to our executive producer. If the executive producer is also convinced it's a good story, it's put in our active file, until several other stories are found in the same region. Our executive producer then assigns the entire group of stories pertaining to that region – sometimes seven or eight of them – to one of our show producers, who flies out and does several days of extensive field research on them. Once home, that producer sits down with the executive producer and they determine *which* three or four stories we should do in that region and *when* we should do them. Then, a crew is booked, travel plans are put in place, and I'm given my marching orders for that week. *C'est tout!*

We've had great luck with this system. Almost every story we decide to do gets done and goes to air. Even when things go wrong in the field and a story is cancelled because of sickness or bad weather, something often comes up that fills the hole. Our profile of Newfoundland artist Ed Roche, and our subsequent journey to the beautiful island outport of British Harbour, is an example of a last-minute replacement that worked very well. Thank you, Ed Roche!

It is a lot easier today to put together a season of shows than it was the first year we went to air nationally. That first year, 1987, was a little intimidating to say the least. We were given approval by head office to do a season – a thirteen-week pilot series called "Out Your Way with Wayne Rostad." The trick was finding the formula for doing it. When do we travel? How do we travel? How much time will we need to edit? Where do we start looking for story ideas? The map on the wall looked awesome. "Country Report," the local CBC show from which "On the Road Again" was developed, covered a radius of about one hundred and sixty kilometres around Ottawa. The national show would have to consider every back road and every community in the entire country!

So, that first year, we went to our CBC regional stations – Halifax, Regina, Victoria, and so on – asking their news and current-affairs departments for any local stories they had done over the years that might fit a national lifestyle show like ours. They were all very helpful and managed to give us a few suggestions that fit the bill – enough, at least, to get our season started. But to finish the season, we had to keep digging. Every producer working with the show was reading, searching, calling around for stories. Sheila Petzold was the executive producer for that pilot series, and people were bouncing in and out of her office as if they were on pogo sticks! Sheila was really fired up to meet the challenge, as we all were. It was an exciting time for us; we were taking on the country and loving it!

And then, the most wonderful thing started to happen. By the end of our first season, mail was pouring in from across the country – great mail. Story ideas were starting to come from the viewers themselves! We opened and carefully read every piece of mail sent to us. Who better to give direction to our show than the viewers? They knew who deserved credit in their community, who would touch our hearts, and who would tickle the funny-bones of the nation.

"How would you like to meet the 'Cougar Lady' here in British Columbia? She's a crack shot with a rifle," wrote one of her neighbours.

"We have a couple of great ladies here on Prince Edward Island you should really have a look at. They're a comedy team who call themselves Bridget and Cicily. Have you heard about them?" wrote another.

And still another letter said, "My uncle, Albert Johnston, just finished building a rock wall out here near Smiley, Saskatchewan. It's nine feet high, twelve feet wide, almost a mile long, and doesn't go anywhere. It took him twenty-five years to build it – just for something to do. Would your program be interested in meeting him?"

Thankfully, our viewers haven't stopped writing. And we haven't looked back since. To this day, a lot of the stories you see on our program come from them.

I'm often asked: "Of all the shows you've done, which one is your favourite?" It's a fair question, but it's not easily answered. So many stories have touched me in so many different ways. I have sat in quiet wonder, been made angry, and laughed till my stomach hurt – and I've been moved to tears more than once. I am absolutely flooded with memories every time that question comes up. It's a hard one to nail down. I guess the best answer lies in the chapters of this book.

There is one other question I get almost every time I meet someone. "Do you enjoy doing your show as much as you appear to on television?"

That one is easy. All you have to do is read my smile.

Jack Semler shaking hands with Pig

Pig

Once upon a time, there were three little pigs. One little pig lived in a house of straw. The second little pig lived in a house made of twigs. The third little pig lived at Jack Semler's place near Perth, Ontario, and caused quite a stir in the community.

We found out about Jack's pig from one of his neighbours. He told us it wasn't your average pig-in-the-pigpen kind of pig. It was a pet pig. In fact, it was a very *large* pet pig – a thousand-pound, or four-hundred-and-fifty kilogram, porker who actually lived in the house with Jack, leading the life of Riley and being catered to royally.

In June of 1981, I drove out to Jack Semler's hilltop farm with my producer and crew. Back then, I was hosting CBC Ottawa's "Country Report," the regional rural lifestyles show which, in a few short years, would become "On the Road Again." The crew was in a particularly good mood. Gail Hannah-Norton, a free-spirited woman with a wonderful, infectious laugh, was producing the shoot that day. André Villeneuve, a talented francophone in his late twenties, who always brightened your day with his big, boyish smile, was our cameraman, and Mike Champagne, also in his twenties, was handling audio. It was a beautiful sunny morning, and we knew if wasn't going to be a run-of-the-mill kind of day. We were about to spend this one with Jack Semler's pig.

Jack sounded like an interesting character. We were told he had three loves in his life. One was horses, specifically, equestrian jumpers. He kept several jumpers at his farm and regularly put them through their paces in a riding ring set up adjacent to the barn. He also loved exotic woods. He had set up a nice little business at the farm called the Semler Hardwood Company, offering wood from around the world for sale. The third love in his life was Pig. Jack often drove into the village of Perth, fifteen kilometres east of his farm, with his rather large pig sitting in the back seat of his 1971 Cadillac.

Perth is a lovely community seventy kilometres from Ottawa. And while most of the six thousand residents were amused by the sight of a pig sitting in the Cadillac, some were quite concerned about Jack's state of well-being. Remember, this was long before pot-bellied pigs became fashionable, and long before Babe the pig was nominated for an Oscar.

We arrived at Jack's farm about nine o'clock. There was a huge sign by the laneway entrance: "The Semler Hardwood Company." We drove past long, low-lying sheds on our left that housed the exotic woods Jack offered for sale. On our right was his equestrian ring, with various jumps, fences, and barricades set up. I noticed horses off in the field on the other side of the ring, two dark bay-coloured ones and two big dapple-greys. They looked like hunter-type horses, basically big draft horses that excelled at jumping. Jack's farmhouse, which was at the top of the lane on a little knoll, was actually more like a great bungalow, with a huge walk-around verandah. Beyond the house were several outbuildings and an enormous barn. There was a fence beside the barn with a large hole cut out of it in the shape of an arched doorway, with a sign above it that read: "Pig Crossing."

Jack answered Gail's knock on the door. He was not a very large man, only about five-foot-seven. Although he was in his sixties, he still had dark hair that was just a little grey at the temples. He welcomed us in and, in a thick Czechoslovakian accent, asked if we would like a shot of cognac. We all politely declined, knowing that cognac and shooting just don't mix that early in the day. Cognac was another of Jack's loves – mind you, a distant fourth to horses, hardwoods, and Pig.

"So, you've come to see Pig," he said.

"We sure have, Jack," Gail replied. "This is André and Mike, and you may have seen this guy on 'Country Report' . . ."

"Yes, you I recognize," he said, smiling up at me from the doorway.

"Hello, Jack," I said. "Nice spot you have here on the hill."

"Hello, Wayne. Come in, gentlemen, please, come in.

When I shook his hand I noticed he only had two fingers on his right hand.

"This is my two-finger shake," he said good-naturedly. "It's also good for measuring cognac. When someone wants two fingers, they get it," he laughed. "Actually, I lost most of my hand in the war."

Jack had been a bomber gunner with the RAF in the Second World War, and he lived through a terrible crash after being shot down in the skies over Europe. He was lucky to survive. He spent eight months in an army hospital recuperating. To this day he walked with a cane and moved about with a fair degree of discomfort.

"I've learned to live with my aches and pains," he said. "My horses are my therapeutic exercise."

Because of his war injuries, Jack had developed a unique way of getting on his large horses, and was quite proud of it.

"Look here, through the window," he said, pointing out a set of stairs leading up to an elevated platform beside the riding ring. "I bring my horse alongside that platform and make him stand while I climb the stairs to mount."

"How many horses do you have?" I asked.

"Four. I have four horses and my old dog," he replied. "And Pig."

"That's the one we've come to see," I said. "Where do you keep Pig?"

"Oh, she's in her house – the pig shed," he said. "I had to move her out of this house a couple of years ago."

"Gail told me Pig used to live in the house, with you," I said.

"Yes. From when she was a little baby – until she almost burned my house down."

We were all ears.

Jack recounted the story of how, a few years before, a neighbour bequeathed him a baby pig as a gift. A tiny, wonderful little pig.

"They're very cute, you know, pigs, when they are small. They're very cute, with a squiggly little tail, and tiny little hoofs. They're very pink."

Jack sounded like he really loved the little gift pig.

"It was a great companion," he said. "Pig used to have the run of the house. She could go anywhere she wanted. She was very clean. If she had to go – you know, poop, or something – she always went in her box."

I was sort of glad about that, because I couldn't imagine having a pig in my house if it *didn't* go in its box.

"Why didn't you give her a name when you got her?" I asked.

"It never dawned on me to give her a name. She was a pig. I said, 'Hello, Pig,' and ever since I have just called her Pig."

Jack told us how, in the beginning, he would always give her a nibble of this and a nibble of that. Whatever Jack was having for supper, Pig had for supper. Pig sampled it all – Swiss steak, mashed potatoes, Scotch on the rocks – every culinary delight imaginable.

"Pig really got excited when I would call her for something to eat," he said.

"Little wonder. With a menu like that, I'd come running, too!" I laughed.

"The trouble was, I gave her too much. She's much bigger than a normal pig, you know. That's because of all the food."

"One day," Jack recounted, "I called Pig to come have some Italian spaghetti and crusty French bread. 'Here, Pig, Pig, Pig. Here Pig,' I called. Whenever she heard me call her like that, she knew it was suppertime. So, on this particular day she's really in a hurry – because she liked spaghetti a lot – and she came running around that corner over there, where I used to have a big wood stove, and she knocked that big stove right off its base. I had a fire burning inside the stove and everything, so there were smoke and ashes and cinders everywhere."

Jack had us roaring.

"What happened? Did the house catch fire?" we asked.

"There was just a small fire, there beside the stove. It burned the floor. Fortunately, the local fire department managed to save the house and there was very little damage."

"And Pig? What did Pig do?" I asked.

"She ate her spaghetti. Then I threw her out."

I could only imagine how the boys must have howled in the firetruck on the way back to the station. At any rate, that was the end of Pig's life in domestic splendour. She was exiled to her new domain: the pig shed.

It was a great story. Jack may have banned Pig from the house, but he was quick to add she had the run of the farm outside.

"Come. Come now, and I will introduce you to Pig," he said.

We gathered ourselves together and walked outside into the sunshine. As we turned the corner of the house, we saw a big Cadillac convertible sitting abandoned in the grass. A tarp lay over the roof of the car, protecting it from the weather. The old machine had seen better days.

"Is that the car you used to drive Pig around in?" I asked.

"Yes, that was her 'Pigmobile,'" Jack said.

"How did you get her in, let alone keep her in?"

"I just opened the door, and she would sit there in the back."

"She never tried to jump out?"

"No, she loved it!"

"It doesn't look like you use the car any more," I said.

"It runs beautiful," Jack replied. "It's just that the rear suspension is shot. Pig did that. Too heavy, I guess."

Jack motioned to a shed a metre or two from the Cadillac.

"That is Pig's house," he said, pointing proudly with his cane. Jack was delighted with the notion of a television show taking such keen interest in his pet.

Now, before I describe meeting Pig, I'd like you to think about pigs for a minute. Not a little pink-porker pig, the kind we've all seen on a table with an apple in its mouth, and not your everyday, visiting-the-farm-next-door pig. I want you to think BIG pig – bigger-than-any-pig-you-have-ever-seen-on-the-face-of-the-earth pig.

Jack pulled the door of the shed open and called inside.

"Here, Pig, Pig, Pig. Here Pig," he called, as he threw some grain in a feed-bin adjacent to the door.

There was a deep, throaty, rumbling response from within the dark confines of Pig's world. Off in the blackest corner, an awesome grey blob started to move. It got up on its feet and lumbered over to the feed-bin and began to eat. She ate with great ferocity. Not only did Pig look huge, she looked dangerous. Jack scratched her back. She was enormous! I stand six-foot-four, just shy of two metres, and my long legs put my belt about forty-four inches from the floor – over a metre. Her back came just about up to my belt. She was almost up to Jack Semler's armpits. In a matter of seconds the grain was gone.

"Wow!" André exclaimed. "That was fast."

"Not only fast," I replied. "Imagine if you had had your hand in there. You'd have no hand left."

"That's right. Look what she did to me!" Jack joked, holding up his hand with the missing fingers good-naturedly for us to see. "That's the real reason I threw her out."

"Speaking of throwing her out," Gail said, "can we get her out of this shed into the light for André to shoot her?"

"Shoot her? What do you mean shoot her?" Jack laughed.

"Tape her," Gail said, correcting herself. "Shoot her with the camera."

"Sure," Jack said. "No problem. Pig comes out every day, anyway. We can bring Pig out."

Jack pulled the gate enclosing the feed-bin aside and said: "Come on Pig, Pig. Come on, Pig."

Now, I never thought I was afraid of pigs, but when Jack opened that gate, and Pig made a move towards the open door, I could tell it didn't matter to her if something stood in her way. She was going out that open door, now! She wasn't stopping for anything or anyone. The crew and I didn't just move aside, we literally climbed over each other. She rolled by us like a slow-moving freight train loaded with lumber.

Once outside, Pig appeared quite calm. In fact, she looked almost friendly. There was a sense of majesty about her. André set up his camera and began rolling, as Pig wandered to and fro in the barnyard. Mike prudently covered the pig-crossing hole in the fence after Jack explained that it was the gateway to a mud pond that Pig relished. Her daily ritual was to go off to the pond and return covered in thick, black muck. We would shoot that scene later.

By the time lunch hour rolled around, Pig had become quite comfortable with us. Gail had picked up some box lunches for us to eat picnic-style on a blanket spread out on the ground in Jack's yard.

"Kentucky Fried Chicken!" she announced, pulling a KFC bag from the front seat of the truck.

"What! No ham sandwiches?" André joked.

"Now, how do you think Pig would feel about us eating one of her little relatives?" Gail quipped back. "Got to think of our guest. She's got feelings too, you know."

We also knew our guest had one heck of an appetite, and we watched Pig with bated breath as Gail took the chicken out of the box and placed it on the paper plates on the blanket to see whose lunch – if not everyone's – Pig would determine was hers.

We were lucky. It turned out that at high noon Pig had another ritual: napping for an hour in the soft, cool earth under the porch surrounding Jack's house. So, in spite of the food in our hands, Pig waddled off around the corner of Jack's house to her favourite spot of shade under the porch overhang. Within seconds we could hear her snoring peacefully, dreaming whatever pigs dream. While we ate our lunch, Jack slept, too, in the bedroom directly above Pig's napping spot – just as you'd expect buddies would do.

After lunch, we sat around the table waiting for Pig and Jack to wake up. They seemed to love their naps.

"Just like a dog, eh?" Mike said, casting a glance in Pig's direction.

"Yes," I replied. "Jack says they're very much like dogs, only even more intelligent."

"But," Gail chipped in, "when you play with a dog and the dog rolls on top of you, you can at least push him off. What would you do with Pig?" she laughed.

One funny thought led to another. We imagined what it would be like to live in an urban world where it was fashionable to keep pigs as housepets, as fashionable as it was to keep dogs and cats and singing canaries.

"Think about it," André said. "There you are in front of the fireplace with a beautiful woman, listening to the sound of the crackling fire and the grunting of your pet pig. How romantic!"

"Or imagine a three-hundred-pound pig with a diamond collar and gold-plated leash coming off the elevator in a luxury condominium," Mike laughed.

"Now, seriously," Gail said finally, putting her producer hat on, "before our guests are finished with their nap, what do we get Wayne to do with Pig?"

"Why don't I interview Pig?" I suggested. "It might be funny if, by coincidence, she grunts after being asked a question. Edit two or three questions and grunts together and we might have something." No one really had a better idea, so we decided we'd try the scene and maybe get lucky.

Jack finished his nap and joined us at the table. We told him of our planned interview with Pig and said that we needed his advice on a couple of things.

"Number one," said Gail, "is, how do we get her to wake up? She hasn't so much as grunted in nearly an hour. And second, how can we get her to stand still while Wayne asks her a few questions? It might take four or five minutes."

"Both of these things will be easy to do," Jack replied. "Could I ask one of you to fetch a bit of grain from Pig's house for me, please? There's a pail right on the floor by the door."

Gail walked over to Pig's house, filled the small pail with oats, and brought it back to Jack.

"Now to answer your first question . . ."

Jack had to do no more than rattle that little grain bucket and Pig came galloping around the corner of the house. This time, she was a *fast*-moving freight train loaded with lumber. She galloped right up to where Jack had dropped a little pile of grain and hit the air brakes. Not only did Jack get her up from her nap, we now had her undivided attention. She wasn't going anywhere as long as there was grain around.

After André established his camera position, we sprinkled a little grain on the ground and, right on cue, Pig came over to the very spot where André wanted her to be. I got down on one knee beside Pig, draped my arm over her back, and began chatting with her. I kept trying to find something funny, something workable, for our television show, but the grunts weren't on cue. It simply didn't look like two people having a conversation. While I was pondering how to make it work, I scratched her side with my hand. She didn't like me doing that. She squealed and ran away from me. She ran three or four metres, stopped, and came back to her grain on the ground beside me. I tried it a second time, and again she squealed and ran off.

"Perfect!" I said. "André, roll on this, if you don't mind. I think I have something."

"Well, Pig," I said, as André rolled tape, "it sure is nice living out here in the country, isn't it? Yes, sir, you sure are lucky, Pig. With somebody like Jack looking after you, you never have to worry about being in the *freezer*, do you?"

As I said the word "freezer," I scratched Pig, and, on cue, she squealed and ran off. It was a take. We now had the formula for putting together a running gag.

For part two of our gag, I apologized to Pig for using the word "freezer," scratched her on cue, and off she went again. She *hated* being scratched on the shoulder. We did one or two more "freezer" scenes and had what we wanted. It looked so convincing on television that I'm sure some viewers believed Pig actually understood the word and its implications.

The story of Jack Semler's pig turned out to be a favourite with viewers that season, and we received a lot of positive comments and good mail because of it. In 1985, four years after airing it, we received a phone call from a distraught neighbour, informing us that Jack Semler's pig had died. I remember feeling some concern for Jack, because I knew how much he loved Pig, so we decided to call him. As it turned out, he was very philosophical about it all. Though a little sad, he wasn't devastated. When I asked him what happened, he told me that Pig got into some fermenting apples piled in a neighbour's yard and she ate a ton of them. Well, the alcohol content in those fermenting apples was simply too much for Pig to handle. She went into cardiac arrest and died. Jack found her in the morning with a smile on her face from ear to ear. She now lies buried not far from the mud hole she loved to wallow in.

As soon as the news of her death reached our "Country Report" office, Don Attfield, our executive producer, instructed me to take a cameraman, find a tranquil spot out in the country, and eulogize Pig. He felt our viewers would be interested, so off we went to a quiet side road a short distance outside of Ottawa. I had never eulogized a pig before, least of all a pig that drank itself to death. We were in tears – but not from grief. I couldn't keep a straight face. We laughed so hard we fell to our knees. I think it took us sixteen takes before we had one that we could air.

There is a happy ending to this story, though. A few months

after Pig's parting, Jack went out and bought another pig. Today, it lives in the same pig shed that Pig lived in, and I'm told it's as fat and healthy as Pig was, and goes for a walk every day, just like Pig did, down to the mud hole. And not surprisingly, Jack simply calls it . . . Pig.

Herbie Butts, as pictured in the <u>Carleton Place Review</u>

"What I Seen, I Seen!"

❧

I don't believe Herbie Butts was lying the night he sighted the kangaroo,
Old Herbie said it was no dream.
He said, "Boys, what I seen, I seen!"
Well, I believe what Herbie "seen" was a kangaroo.

– from the song "Kangaroo"

Herbie Butts was a small, wiry man. He had a great sense of humour. When he smiled, you wondered what was going on behind those deep mischievous eyes of his. When he talked to you, he'd stand there with both hands in his pockets. His pant cuffs were often turned up smartly and, although he wore a belt, he wasn't dressed unless his suspenders were on, too. He spent most of his life working on the railroad. When he retired, he and his wife, Keitha, and their ten children rented an old farmhouse in Lanark County. Their home was just down the road from Hannahs' General Store in beautiful Watson's Corners, Ontario.

Now, Hannahs' General Store was about all there was in Watson's Corners. Except for people buying groceries or someone pumping gas, there wasn't a heck of a lot going on. Oh, there were a few houses at the crossroads – about a dozen families lived there – but that was it. Though it was within commuting distance of Ottawa, it was really worlds away from the hustle and bustle of the big city. Yes, sir, life in Watson's Corners was bee-buzzin', dog-barkin' quiet until the day Herbie Butts made an announcement. He'd seen a kangaroo!

Herbie was cutting wood in the fall of 1973 when he heard a commotion at the edge of his land. "I looked up and saw the dogs

were chasing this thing out of the bush. It came along and sat on
the rock. I said to myself, I never saw an animal like this before.
But I knew what it was. It was a kangaroo!"

Well, the news of a kangaroo sighting near peaceful, pastoral
Watson's Corners rocked the very foundations of Hannahs'
General Store. The locals were spellbound. And before you could
say "Boing," the press showed up. Television reporters combed
the woods around Herbie's farm looking for the kangaroo. They
drove all around Watson's Corners, through the crossroads, out
of town, and back through the crossroads again. They raised a
pile of dust – but no kangaroo.

Normally, this kind of story would have ended right there.

"Imagine, a kangaroo in Lanark County!" one outsider
laughed.

"The old guy's got too much sun," said another.

"Must have been nippin' the nectar," said yet another.

But some things never die. Like the Sasquatch and the Loch
Ness Monster, they capture the imagination and live on as
legends. Two years later, Herbie was in the press again. This
time, it was an interview with newspaper reporter Marina
Quattrocchi of the *Carleton Place Review*. Herbie had been
ridiculed mercilessly over this "sighting" business. So had his
children. Herbie's wife, Keitha, suddenly hated going to town.
Something had to be done. It was time for Herbie, like Custer, to
make one last stand. On June 19, 1975, a blazing headline
appeared on the front page of the *Review*: "WHAT I SEEN, I SEEN!"

Clearly, this kangaroo business was far from over.

Almost ten years after the initial sighting, I was bouncing along
in the back seat of a CBC truck on my way to Watson's Corners
with my production team.

It was now the summer of 1983, and Herbie Butts was long
dead. He had passed on into "Lanark County Heaven" at the ripe
old age of eighty, just a few short months after his last interview.

But the legend of the kangaroo refused to die with him. There had even been more sightings near Herbie's place. It was, in short, the kind of stuff that made for fun television. Once again, the story of the Watson's Corners kangaroo was about to be told, and I could almost hear Herbie chuckling in his grave.

My producer, Sheila Petzold, handed me a copy of Quattrocchi's story. It made a wonderful yarn:

"His ears were that long," he said, spreading his hands about two feet apart. "And it was grey in colour – the same as deer in the fall. Its body was four feet high and three feet across. When the dogs chased it, it jumped twenty feet in one leap! I'm tellin' you, it was a pretty sight to see."

Our cameraman, Maurice Chabot, an endearing, great-bearded Quebecer who loved to wear tuques cocked on the side of his head, was driving.

"You ever see a kangaroo, Maurice?" I asked.

"Not lately," he replied. We all laughed. Just the thought of finding a *Macropus canguru* in Lanark County was hilarious. "I know they're very fast though."

"Yes," I said. "I read up on them last night . They bound along at up to thirty miles an hour. They're great boxers, too. Amusement shows used to make them fight in a ring. They'd put boxing gloves on their front paws. They'd stand there and fight just like humans."

"I thought they only did that in cartoons."

"No, no. It really happened. They're *great* fighters. In the wild, they're damn dangerous! They've actually killed a lot of people!"

"G'wan!" said Maurice.

"True story," I continued. "A red kangaroo will fight to the death. It'll kill dogs, too, by going out into deep water, grabbing one with its front paws and holding it underwater till it drowns. Those cute little hands on a big red are powerful enough to disembowel a dog *or* a man. Herbie didn't see a red, though. It says here that it was grey."

"What are you reading?" Maurice asked.

"An old newspaper clipping. Sounds like the old boy really liked all the attention. Listen to this:

> "I was on television, you know," he says proudly. "A gang from Ottawa got me on TV, see. They took pictures of me and I don't know what all they did. . . . One or two days later, a whole carload of people come from Ottawa. They started the story that I was a liar and I never seen such a thing. . . . Well, it went on and on that I was a liar until one day some school kids were in the bush with their B-B guns and they saw the kangaroo too!"

The problem was, nobody ever managed to get a picture of the elusive 'roo. Nevertheless, Herbie's claim put Watson's Corners on the map. His story fired up the imagination of the entire county. In no time at all, a huge sign was erected on the side wall of the Hannahs' store. It read: "Watson's Corners – Kangaroo Capital of Canada."

It didn't matter any more whether there was proof or not; this was "theatre of the mind" stuff and people loved it! Travellers came from everywhere to visit and to imagine. Even the good-humoured Australian ambassador drove up from Ottawa to officially recognize the new title of the little hamlet. Yes, sir, things were really hoppin' in Watson's Corners!

It was near noon when we finally arrived at Hannahs' store. Actually, it wasn't really a store any more. Dan and Verna Hannah were in the process of closing up shop, retiring, and moving on to other things. Over the years they had had a heck of a lot of fun over all this kangaroo business, and they were thrilled to be in the limelight one last time.

"So, Verna, they tell me you even sold kangaroo T-shirts in the store," I said.

"Yes. Buttons, too. After we put the sign up, we started the T-shirts. We had to take six dozen to get the crest made. The shirts were real nice. There was a picture of a kangaroo on them, and 'Watson's Corners, Kangaroo Capital of Canada' written underneath it."

"At first, we said we'll never sell six dozen," Dan continued. "We got 'em on Thursday, and by Saturday we were phoning back for six dozen more!"

We all laughed.

"Even the Watson's Corners baseball team changed its name to the Kangaroos!" said Verna proudly.

They did a booming business in their store at the height of the kangaroo story. Not only did they sell T-shirts and buttons, they also sold kangaroo pins, mugs, and credit-card holders.

"Do you think Herbie really saw a kangaroo?" I asked.

"Well," said Dan, "that's what I always figured it had to be. Old Herbie just wouldn't lie about a thing like that. They say a circus came through here years ago and a kangaroo escaped into the woods. Maybe that's what he saw."

Even though Herbie wasn't around any more to answer our questions, we knew we could still put a story together. People in the community still had fun talking about the kangaroo sighting when we approached them. Some of them had vivid memories of an animal that at least *resembled* a kangaroo.

Kenwell Ferguson, who owned the farmhouse Herbie had rented, remembered the day his tenant first came to him with the tale. "Herb said he saw that animal a second time, in the barn. Scared the hell out of him. It tore past him, and he said it cleared a six-foot fence like nothing!"

At first, Kenwell was a little sceptical. Then one day *he* saw something, too. "Now, whatever Herbie seen doesn't matter. I was wide awake. I wasn't half asleep, and I wasn't drinkin' neither!

But, this thing wasn't normal in the country. Jumped right in front of my car! I nearly took to the ditch."

Another Lanark County native, Art Paul, was positive there was a kangaroo out there.

"A friend of mine was knocked off his snowmobile a couple of years ago. And it was definitely a kangaroo."

"Were you with him?" I asked.

"No, I don't drive snowmobiles."

"Why not?"

"Because I don't want to get hit by that kangaroo."

Well, if there was a kangaroo out there, we didn't get to see it. But then, we weren't really expecting to see one. Driving home in the truck that night, we all agreed that some things are better left as legends anyway. Besides, we didn't come to Watson's Corners to dig up any bones or to discredit Herbie Butts; Lord knows, his sighting put his family through hell. We came to *celebrate* him, to thank him for leaving us all a good chuckle and for giving people something to talk about other than the weather. It may not have been Bigfoot or Nessie, but Herbie Butts's elusive kangaroo made Watson's Corners a special place to visit.

Just as we were leaving the county, I yelled, "Stop the truck!"

Maurice's foot hit the brake. Sheila swung around.

"What? What's wrong?"

"I saw something . . . there . . . in the woods!" I pointed out the window.

"Where? What?"

There was a brief moment of silence, then everyone guffawed.

"G'wan! Get real!"

Oh, well, it had been worth a try.

Red-Wattle Lincoln

In the course of an "On the Road Again" season, we use a lot of rental vehicles to travel the country. The crew always rents a van. They have the rental company remove the rear seat to make room for the heavy road cases containing all our shooting and lighting gear – eight hundred pounds of it. I usually rent a car, in spite of the fact I drive a truck at home. I'd love to rent four-by-fours all the time, but they're expensive. And I don't rent big luxury cars, even when they're offered at no extra charge. After all, I work for the CBC, a Crown corporation, funded by the citizens of this country, and I don't imagine that people would take kindly to any of its employees roaming around the country in them.

But for one particular shoot week in Saskatchewan, I did rent a luxury machine. I don't think it will ever happen again.

It was the spring of 1988, and I landed in Prince Albert, Saskatchewan, en route to the town of Spiritwood, an hour and a half's drive due west, where I was to rendezvous with my crew. We had three stories to do that week within a hundred-kilometre radius of Spiritwood. It was the first week of April, and spring was busting out all over. It was also the first shoot week of another "On the Road Again" season. After grabbing a cart and picking up my luggage, I walked over to the car-rental booth.

"Hello, Mr. Rostad. We've been waiting for you," said the young lady behind the desk.

"Hello," I replied. "Nice to be in Saskatchewan. Looks like you've been having great weather."

"Yes, it's been just beautiful." The girl behind the counter beamed. "Mr. Rostad, your producer, Andy Little, asked us to change the car you requested to a bigger car."

Cameraman Claude Lajeunesse and audioman François Pagé, ready to put the Red Wattle Lincoln to work

Elsie and Adrian Denis, the Lady and Lord of Wattle Manor

"A bigger car? I thought you had a full-sized vehicle waiting for me."

"Well, Mr. Little needs you to take one of our luxury cars. We have a Lincoln Town Car reserved for you."

"Really. Whatever for? Did he say why?"

"Well, actually, it's a problem we kind of created. The van your crew ordered wasn't available. Mr. Little had to take two cars. They could hardly get all your television equipment in them. That's why he wants the Lincoln. He needs trunk space. He's worried about tearing the upholstery in the cars."

"Isn't there some other car with a big trunk?" I asked.

"Not as big as the Lincoln's. We have some cars you could almost put in *its* trunk," she laughed. "You're a big guy. I would think you'd love the Lincoln."

"Well, it's not that I wouldn't enjoy driving it, it's just that working for the CBC makes it awkward. I mean, Lincolns do cost a lot more to rent."

"But we're not charging you for our mistake. All you're paying is standard car rate. And because of the mix-up, you're getting unlimited mileage."

"I certainly appreciate all that," I replied. "But I can't stop and explain that fact to everyone that sees me driving around in it. What about the vehicles Andy and the crew took? Are they Lincolns, too?"

"No, this is the only one we had available this week. It was just returned by another customer this morning. Your crew has a couple of standard-sized rentals. Mr. Little said that, if the Lincoln was returned as scheduled, I was to ask you to take it."

"Well, I guess I'd better do it, then," I replied.

"I'm sure you'll enjoy it," she said reassuringly. "All the paperwork has been processed for you. Here's your copy of the contract and your car keys."

"What colour is it?" I asked as I left the counter.

"It's white. You can't miss it."

"Thank you very much."

"Have a nice trip, Mr. Rostad. By the way, I enjoy your show."

"I'm glad you're watching. Thanks again."

There's something about a big white Lincoln that stands out – even in a sea of vehicles at an airport parking lot. First of all, it's white. Second, it's big. And third, it's expensive. People who own Lincolns and Cadillacs have money. I had to remind myself that this was not costing us any more money than a standard car.

I felt a little spoiled, at first, settling into the soft glove-leather seats, but the feeling quickly passed. In fact, I adjusted rather quickly to the automotive opulence the Lincoln offered. Tinted glass all around afforded a sense of privacy. The tilt wheel, power windows, and speakers-everywhere sound system were kind of nice. The heating and cooling system was fully automatic – set the desired temperature and the on-board computers did the rest. And the six-way power seat was a lot of fun – up, down, forward, and back, with a full-tilt seat back. Set the seat, set the power mirrors, set the temp, and set your brain for launch.

No doubt about it, the big Lincoln was smooth. It was brand spanking new and had next to zero mileage on it. Cruising west along Highway 3, I could understand why some people liked this kind of machine. My father would have loved it. All his life he drove big cars. While he *admired* Lincolns, his personal car of choice, the one he always left in gleaming condition out in front of the house for all to see, was a Cadillac. He was a big man, six-foot-five, and didn't like climbing into vehicles that didn't afford him leg room.

"Lot's of leg room in a Cadillac," he used to say. "Best riding car on the road. I like that long wheel-base and big engine."

Well, the Lincoln I was driving to Spiritwood that day was also his kind of car. It had the same qualities – wheel-base, engine, and *oodles* of leg room.

About an hour after leaving Prince Albert, I pulled over at a Husky service station to pick up a coffee. I drew the big Lincoln up along the restaurant, got out, and walked in. There were about six tables for four, and, since it was near suppertime, the place was nearly full.

"Nice car," said the lady behind the cash.

"Oh, yes. Yes, it is. It's a rental," I replied, trying to brush off the image of someone who likes to drive big Lincolns. "Could I have a medium coffee to go, please?"

"You're certainly travelling in style," she said as she began pouring my coffee into a Styrofoam cup. "You're that 'On the Road Again' guy, aren't you?"

"Yes, Wayne Rostad. Nice to meet you. Uh, normally I travel in a much smaller car. They had mix-up at the airport and I had to take this one. It's all they had."

"Is that one cream or two?" she asked.

"Uh, two, please. You see, we were supposed to get a van, but there was a mix-up and we had to take three cars."

"Any sugar?" she asked again.

"No sugar, thanks."

"Are the other cars the same?"

"No, no," I replied. "They're just little things. That's the only big one. We needed trunk room."

"Uh-huh."

As I left the restaurant – call it imagination or paranoia – I felt all taxpaying eyes at the tables were on the Lincoln-driving host of "On the Road Again." That is precisely why we don't rent luxury touring cars in the field.

That Saskatchewan shoot was the very first "On the Road Again" shoot for producer, Andy Little. He had just joined our closely knit team, coming from CBC Montreal, where he had produced, as well as hosted, shows. I liked Andy a lot. Claude Lajeunesse, our cameraman, was a neighbour of mine, who lived just twenty kilometres from my farm. François Pagé, our dashing French-Canadian crew member (who always turns female heads in restaurants), was handling audio, and Dan "The Man" Botsford, another neighbour who lived in my neck of the woods, was our lighting man. In those days we could still afford a lighting man in spite of the government cutbacks of the late '80s which hit the CBC so hard. (But the cutbacks kept coming and, by the early '90s, Dan's position was cut from our show. Ever since, we've travelled as four-member road crews, with producer, camera, audio, and host.)

Around six o'clock that evening I arrived on the outskirts of Spiritwood, which sits on the prairie about a hundred kilometres south of the tree line. The community is a small one; less than a thousand people live there, but the population doubles during the tourist season because of all the lakes in the vicinity. However, since our visit was in April, the tourists weren't on the road yet and things were pretty quiet when I drove into town. When it's quiet like that, people in small communities don't miss a trick. They notice everything that moves. If you so much as speak in whispers, they will hear you. So I knew my arrival in Spiritwood wouldn't go unnoticed. I couldn't hide the Lincoln. It was, quite simply, too big and just a little too bright.

I checked into the Spiritwood Carlton Inn, a cinder-block motel alongside the highway, and asked for a room on the quiet side.

"That's where we booked you," the lady at the counter said. "The other gentlemen are right next to you. Nice car."

"Thank you. It's a rental."

As I drove my white chariot around back to my home-away-from-home for another week, I saw Andy and the gang, cars loaded to the gunwales, pulling in from the other direction. They had just finished shooting for the day.

"Hi, guys!" I hollered, pulling into my parking spot.

"Hey, Wayne!" Andy called back. "You made it."

"You bet. How are you, guys?"

"Nice truck, Wayne," François Pagé chortled.

"Yeah!" I said, stepping out elegantly. "Kinda ritzy, huh? The only thing missing is a dump box."

"I thought you'd like it," Andy said.

"Good to see you, Andy. Welcome aboard the show."

"Thanks, Wayne. I'm very excited. Hey, guys, let's load some of our stuff in Wayne's . . . uh, truck."

"Andy, about this Lincoln . . ."

"I told him you'd have a problem with it," Claude Lajeunesse said.

"Maybe we can convince the Corp to rent Lincolns for you from now on, Wayne," Dan Botsford chuckled.

"Who'd like to switch cars with me?" I asked. "François?"

"No! The beast is yours," he replied.

"Andy, how am I going to drive around Saskatchewan in this? I've already been through a couple of head trips already."

"What happened?" he asked, holding back a smile.

"Oh, it was just the looks I got when I stopped for coffee on the highway, and just now, the lady in the motel office had this look on her face, too . . . You know what I mean?"

"Well, if it helps at all, our shoots are all out in the country this week, on farms," Andy said. "Spiritwood is about the busiest place we're going to be."

"Wayne, why don't you let Andy drive, and you sit in the back?" François said, kiddingly. "That way no one will recognize you!"

"Yeah, right," I replied. "How to make a bad situation even worse . . . the *chauffeured* look. No thanks. I'll drive."

The next morning, Andy and the boys headed out early to set up some of our equipment at the first farm on our list that week. I followed an hour behind with the rest of the gear in the Lincoln. Our location was a cattle farm owned by Fred Pepper. Fred was not only raising beef, he was gaining recognition as a pretty good maker of drum kits, which he called Canwood drums because they were handcrafted from Canadian maple. A lot of rock musicians in Canada, including the drummer for rocker Kim Mitchell, were starting to use them.

It took me a little over an hour to drive to Fred's place, and I drove it non-stop – no coffee break. Fred's lane was about half a mile long and a little muddy in places due to the spring thaw, but I took care not to hurt the Lincoln, avoiding the mud as best I could. A man was standing outside by the driveway when I pulled up in front of his house.

"Nice car," he said with a chuckle in his voice.

"Yes," I replied. "It's a rental. It's not what I normally . . ."

"I know. They didn't have a van. The boys told me you're a bit sensitive about driving around in it. I'm Fred Pepper. Welcome to Saskatchewan."

"Thanks, Fred. Nice to be here. Pretty good melt, huh?"

"Yes. It's gonna be mucky for a few weeks, I figure."

Just then, Claude came out of the front door of Fred's house and hustled over to the Lincoln.

"Hi, Wayne. Could you pop the trunk, please? We need the rest of the gear inside."

"You bet. Rostad's Moving and Storage at your service."

"Hey, Wayne!" Dan called from the verandah. "You've got a little dirt on the car! What do you think you're driving . . . a *truck*?"

"Cute, Dan. It's spring, remember?"

The car was a little dirty, all right. But it was nothing serious. It would wash off. Besides, the dirt helped take away some of that new-car shine. By the time we returned to our motel in Spiritwood for the night, the Lincoln was beginning to have that lived-in look.

After a late dinner, we all turned in and I reviewed my research notes for the next day's story. I was really looking forward to meeting our guests. They were hogs – red-wattle hogs, imported from Texas, where they were once common in the wild. We were going to visit the wattles of Elsie and Adrian Denis, two Saskatchewan farmers who had a breeding operation just a few kilometres north of Spiritwood, near Witchekan Lake.

As the name implies, these pigs have a reddish hue to them, but what really makes them different from regular pink oinkers are these interesting little appendages of soft cartilage about five centimetres long, hanging down one on each side of their jaws, which look a lot like fingers. They're called wattles; hence the name of the breed. Other than that, red-wattles look, act, and smell like pigs.

I knew a little bit about pigs. Back home, I spent a whole day with my neighbour Jack Semler's big pet pig. And my son, Josh, raised a pig named Mommar when we first moved to our farm in 1985. He and I fed it every day for months on end. I was fascinated at how quickly the little piglet grew . . . and grew . . . and grew. God, how that thing grew! Apparently, a wattle's growth rate is even more amazing. A local veterinarian in the Spiritwood area said he never saw *anything* grow quite so fast. A fully mature wattle can tip the scales at over a thousand pounds, or four hundred and fifty kilograms, about the size of Jack's big pig.

The next morning, a procession of vehicles wound its way along Highway 24 north: two large four-door sedans and a big white Lincoln, travelling in close formation, only a few metres apart, gliding silently across the prairies, en route to Adrian and Elsie's place. To neighbours accustomed mainly to the odd car or truck passing by, it must have looked like a scene from a gangster movie – either that, or like someone with a very small family had died and was being taken to a patch of prairie soil for burial.

When we turned onto the Witchekan Lake Reserve Road, we were reminded once again that spring had indeed sprung. The road was like mush. I could feel the muck from the wheels smacking up inside the wheel wells. My windshield suddenly grew dark with mud. Obviously, I was travelling far too close to Andy's vehicle, considering the sudden change in road conditions. Our tightly knit procession quickly stretched by a few car lengths. What a way to treat a Lincoln, I thought.

Adrian and Elsie were walking from the barn towards their house when our procession turned in their laneway. There was

very little dry ground in the yard, and we could see we were in
for a messy shoot. Adrian and Elsie stood waiting in well-worn,
knee-high gumboots as bodies unfolded from the three vehicles.

"Boy, you fellas really travel in style!" Adrian said, extending a
handshake. "You'd be better off with a truck out here. Especially
this time of year."

"I know," said Andy. "We normally travel with a truck."

"And," I added, "I normally don't travel in a Lincoln."

"Heck of a nice car, if you ask me," Elsie said.

"It's not my speed," I replied.

"Well, then," Elsie said, "when you go, you can just leave it
right there . . . right in front of Wattle Manor."

"Wattle Manor?" I queried.

"Yes. Our kids named our house Wattle Manor."

"Because of your hogs, no doubt."

"Yes. When the money started rolling in from all the sales of
our wattles, we were able to build this house, and the kids said,
'You've got to call it Wattle Manor.' So we did."

"This, then," I said, slapping the fender of the car, "would be
your Wattle Lincoln."

"Exactly!" Elsie replied.

"Nice-looking house," I commented. It was a new log house.
"I love logs."

"Come on in and have a look at the place. There's coffee on.
Watch the mud."

Elsie wasn't kidding about the mud. There was Saskatchewan
spring mud everywhere – good old gumboot-stickin' mud. Pools
of water concealed vats of the gooey stuff. And we were going to
be shooting a lot outside.

After a quick coffee, our first order of the day was to meet the
wattles. The lane from the yard to the pigpen looked formidable.

"Maybe we *should* get a truck," Andy mused.

"Hold it, Andy," I said. "Let's see what this Lincoln can do in
the mud. With its trunk loaded the way it is, we may be pleas-
antly surprised."

I was right. The Lincoln was like a Sherman tank; that thing just ploughed its way through the muck. And this was no ordinary Lincoln. This was a Red-Wattle Lincoln. It would have made Mr. Ford proud.

We spent a couple of hours watching the wattles grunt their way through life. They were huge, all right, and they loved the mud. They were in mud up to their pork hocks, having a pig-lovin', mud-sloppin' time! Claude and François were in it up to the ankles, too. Of course, Andy decided I had to be in the pen in order to interact with the wattles for the camera, and it wasn't long before pig slop was all over me, as well. Pig slop kind of does that. It gets over everything. I think it's like fungus. It grows.

By high noon, we had the shots we needed, and, after we put the equipment back in the trunk of the Lincoln, I put it in low gear and slithered my way back to the house. The Denises' pet pig followed us down. It had done that all morning, just like a dog.

"We'll break for lunch now," Andy finally announced. "And we'll be back to set up for the interview, say about . . ."

"Watch the pig!" Elsie exclaimed. When Andy had climbed out of the car to tell Adrian and Elsie we were breaking for lunch, he had come around to my side and left the passenger door open. The pet pig, just like a dog, was thinking of climbing inside the Lincoln! And he was loaded with mud.

"Oh, God! Stop him, quick!" I cried, as his muddy carcass slithered against the interior upholstery of the door's panel.

"Pig! Get out of there!" Elsie yelled. And, just like a dog, he did.

"I guess the little wattle just formally christened the Lincoln," I said.

"Shouldn't we change our boots before we get back in?" Andy asked.

"What for?" I replied. "It's hardly worth it now. Look at all the mud in there already. I'm going to have to get the car cleaned before I return it on Friday anyway. Leave the boots on."

"We'll be back by two," Andy said as he pulled his mud-wattled door closed.

"What a mess," I muttered. "And to think this is a new car."

We drove fourteen kilometres down the great bog road to the Robin's Nest Restaurant in the town of Leoville, following the same mud-filled ruts that had led us to Witchekan Lake the first time. By the time we returned to Wattle Manor, the Lincoln's exterior was definitely a different colour. There was wattle slop on the carpets from our boots, on the front seats from our hands, and of course wattle slop on the passenger-door panel. The trunk interior had a fair share of the goop, too. The car's exterior was covered from the rocker panels to the windowsills in mud, mixed in with just enough wattle slop to exude a hint of pig odour. I felt terrible. I couldn't believe we had done this to a brand-spanking-new luxury Lincoln. At the same time, it was awfully funny. Not many brand-new Lincolns have spent the day working in the barnyard of a pig farm with a gang of wattle hogs, serving as an equipment carrier/Sherman tank during the first thousand kilometres of its life. Without a doubt, few Lincolns have ever seen a wattle. And very few wattles have ever seen a Lincoln.

The vehicle that pulled into the Spiritwood motel that night, dripping in wattle goop and road mud, was not the same vehicle that had arrived in Spiritwood two days earlier. I'm sure everyone in town wondered where the shiny white Lincoln had gone.

Sometimes, I wonder about that Lincoln. As far as I know, the rental companies sell, or auction off, their cars every year or two, and they usually end up on car-dealership lots, for sale as used vehicles. So, if you bought a used white Lincoln around 1990, and you notice a slight, odoriferous whiff of pig on a damp day . . . you're driving my Red-Wattle Lincoln.

Clarence the Caribou

Clarence the caribou was really only passing through
The tundra land of Newfoundland when the town got in her way.
The Buchans mine was all shut down, everybody was leaving town.
They were out of luck, they were out of ore,
And she knew she had to stay.

– from the song "Clarence the Caribou"

In the spring of 1984, the American Smelting and Refining Company – Asarco – closed its mining operation in the town of Buchans, Newfoundland. The mine was the town's principal employer. The people of Buchans had hoped the mine would hang on and continue to operate for at least a few more years, but Asarco was losing too much money and had no choice but to stop production. The townspeople had known it was coming. The mining giant had told the community as far back as the early 1970s that it would be streamlining operations at the local mine. It was running out of copper, lead, *and* zinc – and there was hardly any gold left, either. Still, when the first layoffs came in 1978, the town's three thousand residents were devastated. By 1981, the population of Buchans had fallen to seventeen hundred. Further layoffs at the mine in 1981 reduced the town's population even further. People just kept leaving; there simply wasn't any work. When Asarco finally closed operations completely in 1984, only twelve hundred people remained. Buchans was in deep trouble.

Buchans is located in central Newfoundland, just north of Red Indian Lake, at the very end of Highway 370, a hundred kilometres southwest of Grand Falls. There is nowhere to go from

Clarence the Caribou, wandering the streets of Buchans with our cameraman Claude Lajeunesse, audioman Mike Champagne, and a few friends

Clarence, posing proudly with her team

Buchans but back along the same road that leads into town. A few of the laid-off mine workers were lucky. They managed to get on at the big pulp mill in Grand Falls and commute to work every day from Buchans. Others had to travel a lot farther to new jobs.

Jim Harnum, had worked at Asarco for thirty-eight years. After the mine shut down, he had found a job in Ontario fixing motors for another mining company. His wife, Jean, in her late fifties, was looking after things in Buchans until Jim retired and returned home. Their children were still living in town, as were several grandchildren. So, Jean and Jim felt it was worth living apart for a couple of years rather than giving up everything they had in Buchans.

Jean's trailer home was at the very edge of town, high on the hill by the graveyard. From her front window, she could see all of Buchans, including the abandoned Asarco plant, which sat at the edge of town like a great grey monolith, reminding everyone of a time that once was. The biggest building, the one that housed the entrance to the mine shaft, looked a little bit like a prairie grain elevator.

Some residents survived on seasonal work "away" and on pogey cheques. By the spring of 1987, spirits had dwindled considerably. In fact, they were at an all-time low. There was no real future for Buchans to look forward to. Then one day, from out of the tundra, a caribou came to town.

At first, Jean Harnum didn't know what to think when she saw the caribou. The little guy had obviously become separated from his mother and the herd, because he was no more than a year old, she figured. He was pretty scrawny, with a scruffy coat, light fawn in colour, with a white nose and rings of white around his big brown eyes. His entire underbelly was white, as was the underside of his deer-like tail. She could tell he was weak and would die unless he got some nourishment, and, kind soul that she was, Jean immediately went inside to fetch some food for him.

"Bread and molasses! That's what it needs," she said. "Bread and molasses."

As Jean stepped off the verandah with the food she had fetched from the kitchen, the caribou paid little attention to her. Even as she approached, he barely lifted his head.

"There, there, wee one." she said. "Here, this will give you strength."

The bread and molasses caught his attention. He ate everything she held.

"Maybe we can give you a little more of something else," Jean said, and went back across the clearing to the trailer.

Inside the cupboard, she took a container of Karo Pancake Syrup and filled one of her grandchildren's baby bottles with it. As she approached her little patient this time, he paid a lot more attention to her. He immediately took to the bottle. As he suckled, his brown eyes gazed gratefully into Jean's. He'd made his first friend in Buchans.

By autumn, Jean's buddy was a much healthier caribou. In six months, her love and care had brought a shine back to his fawn-coloured coat. He followed Jean everywhere she went. He would stand outside the post office and wait while she picked up the latest letter from Jim in Ontario, and then pad along behind her to the grocery store. That was one of his favourite stops. Jean always had an apple in her hand when she came out. By then, the caribou had picked up the name Clarence, and it stuck.

Back at Jean's trailer home, Clarence would sleep on the verandah and wait for the kitchen window to slide open in the morning.

"Breakfast, Clarence!" Jean would call, and his head would pop in the open window to a bowl of food waiting on the counter. As a matter of fact, everyone in town was feeding Clarence by now. People were dropping by with more apples, carrots, and bananas. Every child in town adored him, and he seemed to love them, too.

Something wonderful was happening to the people of Buchans. Clarence had given the whole town something to smile about. Instead of sitting around talking about another family leaving town, conversation turned to the latest *arrival* in town.

"Hi, Clarence!" children would call out, rolling up on their bikes, stopping to pet the caribou's back.

"Mornin', Clarence," Howard White would say on his way to work at the municipal office. "My, aren't you looking grand these days!"

"Cute-looking, isn't he?" another town resident would say.

"Did you see him playin' with the kids down at the schoolyard this morning?" said another. "I nearly split a gut!"

Clarence was on everyone's lips and in everyone's heart – everyone, that is, except for Leon Pritchard. Clarence was getting on his nerves. The healthy caribou had quite an appetite by now, and he simply couldn't resist the tasty nasturtiums and succulent chrysanthemums that grew in Pritchard's flower garden. Mr. Pritchard, a bespectacled man in his late sixties, was not very happy at all about having a caribou wandering freely about town.

"I'm after getting my second lot of flowers planted now. I had to go up to Mr. Hiscock's store and buy some more. I mean, imagine having a caribou as a town pet! It's foolishness. What about my garden?"

Clarence was eating everything in town. It was the most manicured community in the country. Lawns, ditches, and yards were trimmed to perfection. That's why Clarence couldn't understand why Mr. Pritchard was ready to blow a gasket every time he hopped the picket fence. No one else seemed to mind if he nibbled their grass or trimmed the hedges around their homes. Heck, they often *rewarded* him with an apple just for cutting their grass!

With the imminent onset of winter, the whole town, except for Mr. Pritchard, of course, agreed to help Jean arrange winter lodging for Clarence. At its October meeting, council unanimously

agreed that, once its fences were wrapped in canvas, the town
tennis court would be the perfect place to protect him from the
elements.

"I'll bring him some carrots from my store," said Mark
Hiscock.

Even Sergeant Dave Daley from the local RCMP detachment
agreed to help. "I'll make sure he gets lots of apples," he said.

Clarence spent the first winter of his life in utter splendour –
especially when you consider what his caribou brethren had to
contend with on the tundra. While they were forced to turn their
backsides to the frigid north wind, Clarence stood protected by
the canvas-covered fence of the tennis court. While they scraped
through the frozen ground, fighting for every little piece of
lichen, Clarence was eating warm carrots out of people's hands!
But the real jewel in Clarence's crown came at Christmas. While
several of his distant cousins were pulling a big, jolly fat man all
around the world in a sleigh, Clarence was lounging at the tennis
court, opening a big stocking full of food that the townspeople
gave him on Christmas Eve! This was the life! All this, just for
teaching a town how to laugh again.

By spring, the story of the caribou that had befriended
an entire town – and vice versa – had spread throughout
Newfoundland. The spring melt had only just begun when the
next part of the Clarence "miracle" happened. The staff at Ruby's
Restaurant noticed it first one weekend in May.

"Seemed awfully busy this morning," waitress Lily Rowsell
said. "Dinnertime too. I was nearly run off my feet!"

Lily had not seen a Saturday like that since the days of Asarco.
"And so many people from away!" Ruby added.

Down at Penny's Irving gas station, the bell out at the pumps
kept Gary Penny hopping all day. "I can't believe all these
strangers coming to see that caribou!" he said.

Now that winter was over, Clarence was back wandering the
streets again. One minute he was up at Jean's getting bread and
molasses, a few minutes later he was watching the kids play ball

hockey on one of the side streets. All Gary could tell people was to drive around until they saw him.

Store owners Mark and Patsy Hiscock were wondering what was going on, too. "Had somebody visiting ask if we had any souvenirs for sale," Mark said to his wife. "*Clarence* souvenirs."

"Well," replied Patsy, "maybe we have a celebrity on our hands!" Patsy didn't know it then, but she had hit it right on the button. Clarence the Caribou was indeed becoming a celebrity and would soon be on national television.

In August of 1988 "On the Road Again" arrived in Buchans to find out more about this enchanting tale of a town and its caribou – and we weren't the only ones in town filled with curiosity. Tourists from all over the island, as well as people "from away," had travelled to Buchans to see the caribou that had won the hearts of an entire town. By then, local businesses were selling all kinds of Clarence souvenirs, Ruby's Restaurant was packed solid on the weekends, and shop-owners were fattening up their bank accounts courtesy of the tourist dollars provided by Clarence.

When we arrived, it didn't take us long to find him. He was wandering the streets with a bunch of ten- and twelve-year-old kids. The Buchans Miners peewee hockey team had adopted him as their mascot, and a local photographer was taking a picture of the team in their jerseys standing beside Clarence.

The caribou was a lot smaller than I had imagined he would be. His back was little more than a metre off the ground. His neck extended straight ahead, level with his back, supporting what was rather a large head in proportion to his body. Each foot was made up of two huge shiny black toes pointing forward with a heel at the back that spread wide when he walked, ideal for getting across snowy tundra.

But what struck me the most about Clarence was how incredibly calm his disposition was. Our camera didn't bother him at all. He moved quite slowly, and his eyes were exactly as Jean Harnum said they would be: "Big, soft, brown eyes. The kind that could break your heart."

There had been one startling development over the winter, however. Someone had discovered that Clarence was not really what everyone thought he was. In fact, he wasn't a "he" at all; Clarence was a "she." Apparently, no one had ever thought to look! But when Clarence turned two and no horns were starting to sprout from his head, somebody had to take a peek.

For two days, we wandered around Buchans with Clarence, and I could see why Clarence had decided to make this place home. If I were a caribou I could happily have lived here, too. The streets were all nicely paved and, except for a few boarded-up Asarco buildings, the town was quite pretty. It looked much like many small company towns, with rows of small bungalows and split-level homes radiating from the mine site – in this case a lot of them yellow or white. Most had brown-painted roofs. Who knows, maybe they had a big sale on brown Tremclad roof paint? In back yards everywhere, people had their laundry hanging on outdoor lines. A few residents were busy painting their sheds. It was hot. Everyone was walking around in shorts and T-shirts; some even sported Clarence T-shirts.

Clarence had developed the most amazing routine. After her morning feed of apples, carrots, and molasses bread, she would go for a stroll right down the middle of the main street. Sergeant Daley, who drove the RCMP blue Suburban truck around town, was quite impressed with Clarence's road skills.

"She travels right down the centre of all the streets," he said. "Very rarely will she go from one side to the other. And traffic, believe it or not, travels freely on both sides of her."

Well, I saw it with my own eyes. It was true. She walked dead centre in the middle of the traffic. Drivers of cars and trucks would actually stop to give her a pat and a nibble of carrot or whatever they had handy and then would motor on. I even saw her stop at the stop sign and look both ways before crossing the intersection! I know, I know . . . as I said, it was hot.

Keith Courage, who ran a clothing and gift store in Buchans, was making a small fortune selling Clarence souvenirs. He was a hefty mustachioed man in his late thirties, who smiled at the very mention of Clarence. "Sales are great!" he told me. "As a matter of fact, we sold out of the large decal again."

"What do you mean, again?" I asked. "Didn't you just start selling them?"

"Yes. We ran out the first week of July. This is the second order, and I didn't order enough by the look of it. I've never seen so many visitors."

"Sounds like Clarence is pretty good for business."

"Tremendous."

I spoke with Leon Pritchard about Clarence, too. Unlike Keith Courage, he was not very happy. The second lot of flowers he planted to replace the first bunch that Clarence had eaten was gone now, too. Clarence had paid another midnight visit to her favourite snacking ground.

"It's madness," he lamented to me. "I can't keep a shoot in the ground. That Clarence should be fenced or kept on a line. It shouldn't be allowed to wander around freely like that."

I understood Mr. Pritchard's frustration. But other than him, and maybe Barry Pritchard, whose young birch trees were fast losing their leaves due to Clarence's midnight marauding, everyone else simply loved having Clarence at large.

"Most people are real happy with Clarence," Allan Lear told me. Allan, a stout man in his sixties, was a former foreman at Asarco. He was standing beside Clarence, talking to me while brushing her soft coat with a hairbrush. "You see, this is something that's never happened before, and probably never will again. For an animal to come out of the wild like that and settle down, you know, among the people. He's just like one of the family."

"You mean 'she,' don't you?" I said, correcting Clarence's gender.

"Right," Allan laughed. "She. We all kinda got off on the wrong foot, I guess."

That fall, Clarence was introduced to nearly a million viewers on the CBC television network when "On the Road Again" went to air. The following summer, after Clarence enjoyed a second winter of leisure in the tennis court, the town of Buchans was flooded once again with tourists from all over, and we were told that many of those people had decided to visit Buchans after we aired the story. For another season, Clarence continued to work her magic. Every store, shop, and restaurant in town was making money hand over fist. There were thousands of visitors to Buchans.

But, in the fall of 1989, Clarence left Buchans. Jean Harnum had known it was coming, because Clarence was three years old by then and the call of the wild was becoming too strong for him, er, her to resist. Oh, I'm sure Clarence took one last walk around before she left. I'm sure that in her own way she said goodbye to the kids. And I'm positive she had one last snack of Mr. Pritchard's chrysanthemums.

But Jean was really the only one who said goodbye to her. It was late in the fall, out on Red Indian Lake Road. Clarence had been wandering farther and farther from the town; sometimes, she was gone for hours at a time. On this particular night, Jean saw Clarence standing at the edge of town, and somehow she sensed the animal's time had come. Clarence gave Jean one last look, then walked off towards the distant tundra.

Jean's husband, Jim, is now back from Ontario. They have retired and are living happily in Buchans. The tourists don't come the way they did when Clarence was around – only the odd Clarence postcard or hat is sold at Keith's store. The town's population is now down to around eleven hundred. But there are no unhappy faces in Buchans. You see, Clarence gave them a great gift. She instilled in everyone an air of eternal optimism. In fact, many people in town believe that, some springtime in the near future, Clarence is going to come back to Buchans – with the whole blessed herd. Imagine *those* tourist dollars. Somebody had better warn Mr. Pritchard.

The Yellowknife Caper

When I was fourteen years old, I was held in custody at the local jail. My best friend, Ricky Patenaude, and I had "borrowed" his father's car late one night to take a little drive through Ottawa's Rockcliffe Park. It didn't seem like such a big deal at the time. After all, his older brother, Andy, had "borrowed" the car in the wee hours of the morning many, many times, and nobody ever caught him, including Mr. Patenaude. Mind you, Andy did have a licence. Whenever he was pulled over for questioning, he was legitimate. All he had to do was convince the boys in blue that he had his father's permission to use the car. Well, the night they pulled over two wild-eyed fourteen-year-olds with Mr. Patenaude's car, the police seemed to know instinctively that Dad had not given us permission.

Rick's father and mine showed up at precisely 4:13 a.m. I know, because I had been counting every minute on the big clock on the wall.

"Who was driving when you hit the mailbox?" asked the night constable.

I raised my hand timidly. I didn't dare raise my eyes. I knew my father was glaring down at me, expecting instant and *honest* answers.

"Gentlemen, if both of you sign these papers, we can release them in your care." Neither father spoke a word to either of us. It is amazing how powerful a weapon silence is.

A few weeks later, Ricky and I were in court. His father had pressed charges to teach us both a lesson we would never forget. My mother stood at my side, her face deathly pale. The juvenile-court judge turned to address her.

"Total" and Johnny Nault, standing out on Great Slave Lake

My Yellowknife "On the Road Again" team – Gilles, Andy, and François

"And what do you have to say about your son, Mrs. Rostad?"

"Nothing, Your Honour," she replied, with a trembling French accent.

"Nothing, Mrs. Rostad?" said the judge, a little surprised.

"Nothing, Your Honour." Mother's eyes were rivetted to the floor.

There was silence in the hall, save for the pounding of my heart. Mother had never been in a court of law before, and was in such a state of shock that she didn't know where to begin. She was convinced they were going to send her son "up the river."

"Mrs. Rostad, I'm going to release your son from all charges and send him home with no record, so that he will have a clean slate as a teenager." For a moment I thought Mother was going to faint. Rick was shown the same kindness by the judge. We left the courthouse that day eternally grateful that God, and judges, were merciful.

Looking back, I see that laying charges was probably the best thing Mr. Patenaude could have done. It taught his son and me a valuable lesson. For the rest of our lives, we would both think twice before knowingly doing anything illegal. But in 1989, something happened while I was on a shoot in the Northwest Territories, something that could have put me in jail again.

It was mid-January, and that particular week the weather was changing every hour on the hour in Yellowknife. I arrived on one of Canadian North's 737 jets in clear skies. Just a few hours earlier, my producer, Andy Little, and the crew had landed in near-blizzard conditions. My trip had been easy compared to theirs. I had flown from Ottawa to Edmonton and stayed overnight before travelling on to the Territories, so I was relatively fresh on arrival. My crew, by contrast, had been shooting in Pond Inlet on Baffin Island and, in order to get to Yellowknife, they had to take the high northern route, "the milk run," eleven hours and five stops! It was quite an initiation for our new

cameraman, Gilles Guttadauria. He had been one of our program's chief editors, before "On the Road Again," back when we
were called "Country Report." He had just turned forty when he
decided to shoot pictures rather than edit them. This was our
first season as "On the Road Again" and Gilles's first shoot as a
cameraman.

"And I used to think from all the pictures I saw in the editing
suite that doing this show was more fun than it was work," he
joked. "This is a big country!"

We were in Yellowknife to meet Jane Mayo. Everybody called
her "Total," because she was so totally committed to her way of
life in the north. She was a very pretty woman, who looked right
at home in blue jeans and Sorels. She had long sandy-brown hair
that fell over her shoulders, a great smile, and vibrant green eyes.
She had left Minnesota back in the 1960s and came to Canada to
escape the rat race. Total figured that Great Slave Lake was about
as far north as you could go, and that here she would find peace.
She also found a husband: Johnny Nault, a Métis fisherman.
Total had been living alone in a remote cabin by the lake when
Johnny paddled by and dropped in.

"I fell in love with his smile," she told me.

Since that fateful day, they had operated a fishing business
together on Great Slave Lake. At first they lived alone on a point
of land jutting into the lake. Here they could fish from their boat
in the summer and through the ice in the winter and for the most
part live in a world of their own making. Their house was very
simple. It was built into the frozen tundra and stood only a metre
or so above the ground, which afforded protection from the
frigid northern cold. Their needs were simple enough, too.
Several kilometres from civilization, they fished by day and,
when night came, the lovers would sit under crystal-clear Arctic
skies and listen to the wolves serenading them. But, in 1987, with
the birth of their child, Britta, Total and Johnny decided to move
closer to Yellowknife. They became squatters on Joliffe Island,

and it was there that we met them, a short drive from Yellowknife across the frozen ice.

"I miss the isolation," she told me. "We loved the incredible peace and quiet, but this is something we had to do for Britta. Our business is doing very well. We just spend a little more time travelling to and from work now, that's all."

By southern standards, they were still living in splendid isolation. Their cabin on Joliffe had very few amenities. Their freezer was the great outdoors; they kept everything buried under the snow until they needed it – whitefish, Arctic char, caribou, you name it. And there were only a few families living year-round on Joliffe Island. They, too, were squatters. Some lived in cabins and some in houseboats that were frozen in place for the winter. But as far as Total was concerned, this was nothing like the total isolation she had known on her little peninsula.

They made a fascinating item for the show. We had arranged to go out to the fishing camp by twin-track Bombardier. The big, steel-tracked machine arrived on the back of a flatbed truck on Wednesday morning, and we determined that it would carry all of us, including our gear, out to the camp where Johnny was already winter fishing. By mid-morning, we had everything loaded on board and were about to embark on our two-hour trek across Great Slave, when the ever-changing weather closed in again. The wind came up, big time, and visibility along the ground was next to zero. That cancelled the romantic six-on-board, smoke-belching, twin-track excursion on ice. Now what to do?

Fortunately, Andy Little had a back-up plan. He arranged for a helicopter to take us out to the camp in three separate lifts, one for equipment, and two for people. Enter our "On the Road Again" saviour, Bob O'Connor of Aero Arctic Helicopters. He was fine with the existing weather. In fact, the lousy visibility was only a few metres thick, and once we were airborne, we could easily see *terra firma* by looking straight down from the air on landing approach. Bob had us all on location at about the same time we were scheduled to arrive in the first place. Then the trick was to get everything done in three hours. Apparently there was another weather system – a much worse one – moving in later that afternoon. We had to start the first lift out of camp back to Yellowknife by three o'clock.

It may have been Gilles Guttadauria's first road shoot, but he had done his homework and came prepared. He had carefully researched the difficulties that come with shooting in the north – stuff like frozen camera gears, thickened oil in the motor mechanisms, and the condensation that forms on the lenses when a camera goes from minus-forty degrees Celsius outside to plus-twenty degrees inside. What, in fact, does every well-prepared cameraman bring in his travel kit to combat the northern elements? A hairdryer, of course! Gilles's thoughtfulness saved our shoot several times. Without the blower, a lens coated with condensation could take an hour or two to clear up, and mechanisms that would simply stop working after a marginal amount of time in minus-forty were able to continue functioning with periodic blow-drying, thanks to the power available from the diesel generator on site.

That afternoon we were able to move freely about the camp, in and out of different spells of weather, without difficulty. Total and Johnny harvested their catch for us, pulling long nets laden with whitefish up through small holes cut in the ice. This was nothing like the ice fishing I had seen back home in the Ottawa Valley! This was on a larger scale altogether, very large.

Bob O'Connor managed to get us back to Joliffe Island before dark. We had been successful in thwarting the weather again. We had the necessary fishing shots in the can and, more importantly, shots of Total and Johnny together at work and at play.

That evening, Total and I sat down in a friend's house and had a good chat while the camera rolled. I don't like the word "interview"; it sounds so formal. I always suggest we have a chat, a yarn, or just a darn good yak. Throw the word "interview" away – let's talk! Total was marvellous. Her "clock" ran so much slower than mine. The more we talked, the more I wound down to her speed. It started to evoke feelings I had not had for years. Feelings I had back in the 1970s when I lived in a little shack off the beaten path in the Gatineaus – when I was, simply and totally, a songwriter. In my own way, back then, I too lived in splendid isolation. It was good to take stock of those memories, those feelings, again.

Thursday morning, the crew and I went back to Joliffe Island to do the on-camera for Total's story. I was scheduled to leave that afternoon for Edmonton, where I'd take a connecting flight to Ottawa. The night before, during our chat, Total had promised that I would leave with some caribou and Arctic char.

"Wait a minute. I have to get something for you," she said, just as I was getting ready to depart. "A promise is a promise."

She grabbed a one-metre bucksaw hanging on the cabin wall and ran over to a cache in the frozen tundra. Moments later, she pulled an entire frozen hindquarter of caribou from the hole in the ground. Bracing her legs in the snow, she held the hind firmly with her mittened left hand and started to saw. A dozen strokes later, she had a sizable rump roast in hand.

"Here, hold this," she said. "Now, I'll just get you a bit of fish."

I felt like a kid being treated at a candy store. Caribou and char! I couldn't wait to get home. Leanne's mother, Mary, was visiting, and Mary just *loved* to cook. This will really make her day, I thought.

"How's this?" Total asked, holding up a magnificent portion of the greatest fish in the world.

"Beyond my wildest dreams," I replied. "But it's too much. I can't take all this back home. Besides spoiling me, how do I keep all this stuff from spoiling?"

"Put it in with your luggage," she said. "It's way below zero in the belly of the aircraft. It'll still be frozen when you get home. Here, let's wrap it in lots of plastic. Then, if it thaws, even a little bit, it won't get on your clothes."

Despite these assurances, I felt a bit uneasy putting a hunk of fish and a rather large rump roast in with my socks and underwear. What if there's a temperature inversion aloft on the way home and the stuff thaws? I wondered. I knew if it happened I would never be able to wear those shorts again. Raw fish is not one of my favourite lingering scents.

At the airport, I handed in my luggage, including one rather heavy flight bag, and got my boarding passes. My schedule showed I would have to wait about three hours in Edmonton before connecting to Ottawa. That's when an alarm went off in my mind. What if they bring the luggage inside the terminal in Edmonton and the stuff thaws, then freezes again airborne? I didn't like that idea. I was always taught never to refreeze anything other than Popsicles. I walked over to the Canadian North check-in counter.

"Excuse me, ma'am. Things that are frozen do stay frozen in the hold of the aircraft, don't they?" I asked.

"As long as you're not heading south, as in Caribbean south, at low altitude," she replied.

"Well, I have a three-hour wait in Edmonton, and I was wondering if my luggage is going to be brought inside a warm building or not."

"Well, it might be brought inside the holding bay before it gets loaded on your connecting flight. I don't know if it's warm inside or not. What are you concerned about?"

"Well, the meat and my fish," I said. "I don't want the meat to partially thaw and then freeze again."

"What kind of meat is it?" she asked.

"Caribou," I replied, sounding like a very lucky fellow.

"It says right on the permit to mark the box perishable," she replied.

"What permit?" I asked.

"The wild-game permit they gave you."

"I don't have a permit," I stated. "It was a gift."

"What was a gift?" she asked.

"The hunk of caribou that's in my luggage!"

"Shh-shh," she said, putting her finger to her lips. "Have you never seen this sign?" She pointed to a small placard stapled to the wall. There, in bold print, for all unsuspecting meat-smuggling travellers, was the following: "It is a FEDERAL OFFENCE to remove any wildlife or wildlife parts to a place outside the Northwest Territories without first obtaining a wildlife export permit."

Now, I have always understood a FEDERAL OFFENCE as something punishable by either a bloody stiff fine or an appreciable amount of time in jail. This was no local by-law. No, sir! I was committing a FEDERAL OFFENCE! That was real meat in that luggage of mine – *wild* meat. And it was filling my mind with *wild* images – like a federal-court judge with a huge caribou rump roast sitting on his federal-court bench. Talk about *déjà vu* . . .

"Well, Mrs. Rostad, what have you got to say for your husband?"

"Nothing, Your Honour. Nothing." . . .

"Mr. Rostad. Excuse me, Mr. Rostad." It was the voice of the airline agent.

"Yes, yes," I said, snapping back to reality. "You mean I could be charged with a federal offence for taking that caribou home?" I asked, incredulously. "What about the char?"

"Shh!" she hissed again. "The char is okay. That's legal. But everything's already in the hold of the plane. So don't say another word. I don't think this once is going to be a problem. Mind you, I didn't tell you that."

"Are you sure it will be okay?" I whispered.

"It's a heck of a lot better than unloading all the luggage," she assured me.

In the end, everything worked out beautifully. When I arrived in Ottawa, I sighed with relief as my bags came down the luggage carousel. They had not been confiscated. There were no federal agents waiting for me. No one seemed to notice or care when I tossed my heavy meat-laden bag onto my little luggage carrier. Happily, the meat and fish were still frozen solid. That night at the farm, Leanne, her mother, Mary, and I, had some great laughs over the whole business.

The following day, there was a feast at Indian Creek Farm. We invited our neighbours, John and Jonina, and their cousin, Colleen, over for brunch. Mary had prepared two incredible dishes: broiled Arctic char and a sumptuous caribou pot roast. Needless to say, neither dish was poached.

The Ruins of British Harbour

❧

Once, there were fishing boats moored in the harbour,
Men at work on the stages by the water,
There were kids playing "duck" on Little Brook Hill by the harbour.

And once upon a time the church was filled with people,
Gathered every Sunday by the bell in the steeple,
But all that remains are the souls of the dearly departed.

– from the song "Ruins of British Harbour"

There is a beautiful painting that hangs in the hallway of our home at Indian Creek Farm. It is a scene depicting the ruins of a community called British Harbour that once existed in a sheltered cove on the Bonavista Peninsula along the western shore of Trinity Bay, Newfoundland. It's a view from a grassy knoll above the harbour, overlooking the calm waters below. There are spring daisies in the foreground. Green fields slope upwards from the water's edge several hundred metres to the tree line at the base of the mountains that ring the cove on three sides. Straight ahead, in the distance, between two great craggy rocks, an opening leads out to Trinity Bay, and ultimately, the open sea.

Around the bay, several windowless houses are depicted, still standing, surprisingly, after years of abandonment – but some, just barely. Two or three lean precariously from their perches on the hillside. It's a beautiful painting, done by Newfoundland artist and photographer Ed Roche, a man who knows British Harbour very well, and loves the place. I love that haunting little cove, too. I've been there twice. Often, when I pass that painting

Some of the ruins of British Harbour

Ed Roche and I in front of the fallen Anglican church steeple

Whelan at the helm, en route to British Harbour

in the hall, I think back to the first time I ever laid eyes on British Harbour.

It was early August, in the summer of 1989. Summer or not, August can be cool in Newfoundland, as it certainly was the morning "On the Road Again" set sail for British Harbour. Ed Roche was travelling with my producer, Andy Little, and my audio man, François Pagé, aboard one of two vessels chartered for our trip that day. I was on the other boat with Keith Whelan, our cameraman, and a friend of his by the name of Wayne Tilley, whom everyone called simply "Tilley."

We were lucky. We almost didn't have a story to do that day. We had been scheduled to shoot a story in central Newfoundland, but it fell through at the last moment. Andy had to find another one fast. The question was, who could we get on a day's notice?

He remembered something he had seen on his desk a few months earlier that described Ed Roche as a Newfoundland artist and photographer whose mission in life was to capture, on film and on canvas, the old ways of life in Newfoundland. It was a lifestyle that Ed, now in his late forties, still remembered; he had grown up in a small Newfoundland outport himself, in a place called Middle Cove. But what caught Andy's attention was a place Ed researched, photographed, and painted more extensively than any other outport – British Harbour. That abandoned site had become the central focus of a planned exhibition featuring Ed's paintings of the outports. Andy had liked what he read, and at the time felt that Ed and his exhibition would make a great "On the Road Again" story. The question now was how to find Ed Roche on a day's notice.

Andy remembered that Ed lived in St. John's and, after looking up his number, placed an eleventh-hour phone call to his home. It was a long shot, but worth a try. There was no answer, however, and since Andy didn't know where to begin to track him down, it looked as if we were going to have the day off – not a good thing when every day on the road doing a television show counts. But

Keith, a Newfoundlander, had an idea. His wife was in St. John's, visiting her family.

"Debbie might be able to find him," he said. "She knows a few people who just might know where Ed is. I'll call her and ask her to do some checking around. In the meantime, I'll phone some people I know up in Trinity to see if I can line up a boat to take us to British Harbour."

The town of Trinity was just to the north of British Harbour, and was as good a place as any to set sail from.

"Keith, can you get two boats?" Andy asked. "I'd like you to shoot footage of Ed and Wayne entering British Harbour. We'll need another boat to do that from."

"I imagine we can find two boats in Trinity," Keith replied.

"Seems like awful short notice," François mused, shaking his head.

Well, before the day was over, we discovered how small an island – even a big island like Newfoundland – really is. Debbie Whelan found Ed, who, in spite of the short notice, agreed to take us out to British Harbour the next day. And, much to Andy's delight, Keith had lined up not just one, but two boats for our trip. Keith's buddies, Art and Louise Andrews, who ran a boat-charter operation and a bed-and-breakfast operation in the town of Trinity, cleared their day to help us out, agreeing to take part of our crew in their boat. And Ches Drodge, another friend of Keith's, who just happened to be in Trinity at his summer home with his family, agreed to take the rest of our crew in *his* boat. Talk about the luck of the Irish! We had a story to do. And we were going to British Harbour.

By mid-morning the next day, we were two hours out of Trinity, in the open water of Trinity Bay, amid wonderful, lazy swells. On our right, the cliffs of the island towered a hundred and twenty to a hundred and fifty metres above us, with the morning sun dancing off the vertical rockfaces which rose up from the sea. Art Andrews, at the helm of his boat, *The Marysol*, was off our starboard bow, less than half a kilometre away. I watched as he tacked his vessel from our starboard side over to our port and back again. He was obviously enjoying challenging the winds.

Our skipper, Ches Drodge, who had motored up till now, couldn't stand watching Art having fun any longer, and stopped the engine of *The Vigilante*.

"Keith," he called out, "lend a hand now. Let's set sail and play a bit."

I remember Keith's eagerness to help. He had a lot of experience with sailboats. In fact, he had owned one or two when he lived in Newfoundland. Keith had only recently moved from St. John's to Ottawa to join our television show, and he and Debbie had already become very close friends of my wife, Leanne, and me. For Keith, this trip to Newfoundland was a bit of a homecoming.

Once Keith unfurled the sails, Ches offered him the helm, and I remember watching Keith's face as he placed his two hands on the wheel. It was as if there were nothing else on earth he would rather be doing at that moment than sailing off the shores of Newfoundland. Keith had often told me nothing could beat a good boat, a good wind, and the sound of the sea. I was getting the picture. What a day, I thought. What a marvellous way to go to work.

British Harbour was one of hundreds of small outports without road access that once existed all over Newfoundland. Communities were tucked into coves all around the main island and on many of the smaller islands dotting the coastline. After Newfoundland joined Confederation in 1949, Joey Smallwood's government decided the outports were far too expensive for the government to maintain, citing costs of mail, food, and medical services, all of which had to come by boat. The solution, as the Smallwood government saw it, was to resettle all the people in these small fishing communities in the main centres, or at least in places with road access. The program was called Centralization. The notion was, since Newfoundland was now firmly entrenched as a part of Canada, that long-awaited jobs would come as soon as the workforce centralized.

So people were encouraged to leave their homes. Whole communities were moved, lock, stock, and barrel. Pressure was exerted on those who didn't want to move, and if they didn't, they were ultimately cut off from all services.

One of the ploys to move people away from places where families had lived for generations was to offer them a five-hundred-dollar cash settlement. Not only that, where it was feasible the government would move their existing home to its new location. To many, the offer was tempting. In those days many of the smaller outport communities never knew what it meant to have cash. Fish was their main trading commodity, and fishing schooners from big companies would come in the spring with sugar, corn, and molasses, as well as clothing and equipment supplies, leave the goods, and come back in the fall to collect payment when the fish harvest was finished.

Some people accepted the government's cash offer. Their houses were literally loaded on barges from the shore and towed to new foundations. But other people left their houses behind, determined to return faithfully every summer to maintain them and not let the place die. However, as the years went by, visitations became fewer and farther between, and the outports fell into ruin. Ed Roche was one of the lucky ones who didn't have to move as a child because the outport he grew up in had road access to St. John's.

"Middle Cove only had a hundred people," Ed told me. "What was great about it was everybody knew everybody else, who your grandfather was and who your great-grandfather was. They knew everything from the colour of your drawers to what you did last night and with whom. It was fun."

Ed was deeply saddened, though, by the stories he heard of others who had to move.

"You see, they didn't just move a community. That makes it sound too simple. That would suggest twenty-five families moved twenty miles down the coast. They didn't. They all didn't go to one place. They went all over. For many people, when they left their community, it was the last they saw of their neighbours and friends. I've talked to a lot of people who were forced to move after the government cut them off. They'd just as well be dead as go on living the way they are now. Their loved ones are buried back home, and they can't go back. That's the tragedy of resettlement."

For years, Ed Roche had been haunted by this tragedy. In 1985, determined to do something about keeping the memory of the outports alive, Ed began extensively researching abandoned outports all over Newfoundland, interviewing scores of former residents. For several summers he photographed, sketched, and painted what was left of them, hoping to capture what remained before it was too late. One of the outports he was particularly drawn to was British Harbour.

"Initially, I went there to see a community that had not been affected by modern amenities – cars, hydro, and the like."

On one of his visits to British Harbour, he came upon the fallen headstone of a young woman who had died in 1938, at the age of twenty-nine. The name inscribed on the stone was Caroline Leonard. Beside her was her daughter, Theresa. They had died just weeks apart. Ed sat there for the longest time, imagining what Caroline had been like, wondering if she and her daughter had died of something like tuberculosis, a thing not uncommon in those days, considering medical help was not always readily available.

It was there, kneeling in the graveyard, that a light came on in his mind. The answer to keeping the outports alive was not to paint the ruins of the communities but to paint them the way they were in their heyday, vital and alive, bustling with activity.

"Right then and there, I thought, if I'm going to do an exhibition like this, why not build it around a person? So I took this person, Caroline Leonard, and am now in the process of building a whole show around her life. The exhibition will be about life as it was before resettlement, up to and including resettlement."

This was the story that intrigued Andy when he read about Ed Roche back in Ottawa several months earlier, and, by now, I was quite intrigued, too.

"Just around that point we'll be seeing British Harbour," Ches announced. "We'll be there in a couple of minutes."

Ches had taken the helm back from Keith, who needed to prepare his camera to shoot footage. Ahead was a peninsula, a rocky, craggy point. High above the towering cliff to our right, an eagle soared, then another. There was still a bit of life here. As we came around the peninsula, there was an inlet of water off to our right, a long channel of water with great rock walls on both sides, beckoning us in. Sun gave way to shadow as we steered between them for the cove. British Harbour began unfolding. In moments, we entered a sun-filled basin, where green fields rose from the sea and climbed up the hillsides. Then the first ghostly house came into view. It had been yellow once. It stood all by itself on one of the bluffs, most of the yellow long since faded to grey. Then, two more houses, and a third, close to collapsing, leaning dangerously from years of being battered by the wind. Another house appeared off to our left; its roof had collapsed inward, leaving a framed house filled with rubble in its centre.

The houses on the hillsides seemed like sentinels, with ghostly eyes keeping watch over the harbour. The inlet walls closed in behind us as we sailed into the cove, our boats, gliding slowly, silently, into the heart of British Harbour. It felt as if we were entering a sacred place. What a beautiful spot. Straight ahead were the remains of a dock that had once had many boats tied to it. The pylons rising out of the water, and the planking on the walkway of the dock were still in place, though, I imagined, somewhat shaky. The fact they survived so many years of neglect was a credit to the community who built her.

We landed our boats at the dock, tying up to a couple of timbers, and sat quietly, absorbing the spirit of the place. No one said a word for the longest time. Ed was the first to speak.

"Look at this place," he said, fingers stroking his beard. "Who'd want to leave a place as beautiful as this?"

"It really is beautiful," I replied. "It's a little piece of heaven."

I got up on the dock and started walking along the planks, ensuring that I kept on the boards directly over the support beams. Ed Roche was right behind me, and the crew quickly followed. There was lots to do. Andy put on his producer's hat, directing Ed and me to walk around and chat about whatever came to us naturally. Keith would capture our moments on tape, François would capture our voices, the wind, and the sea.

As we walked off the dock, I noticed a carefully laid rock wall to the left. It was a retaining wall built to protect the road or pathway we were walking on.

"This was the main road. The school was up there," Ed said, pointing to the top of the hill. "There were two churches."

"Two churches?" I asked. "How many people lived here?"

"One hundred and twenty. But they needed two churches. One was Catholic and the other Anglican."

"But, those two denominations are real close. You'd think one church would have sufficed for such a small community."

"No. There was no way. They both had to have their own church."

Ed pointed out that there was a day when this entire harbour had been surrounded by footpaths that were actually mini-roadways for horsedrawn carts. British Harbour never saw a car, nor did it ever see a truck. There was no electricity. How charming this place must have been with only carts drawn by horses on pathways all around the cove. How beautiful this whole harbour must have been with its gaily painted houses and people bustling about on foot. It was easy to imagine with Ed's vivid description painting scenes for me.

"You know," Ed said, "if this had been some godforsaken spot, you could understand the idea of people moving out. But look at this place!"

Ahead of us was a fast-flowing stream of fresh water, from a lake up in the hills somewhere, which tumbled past us, down to the sea. It was cold and crystal-clear. How fortunate this community had been to have such wonderfully clean water in such good supply. After taking a drink, we continued along the main road to the first house that was still standing. It was the yellow one I had noticed first when we entered the harbour.

"That house," Ed said, "belonged to Arthur Gardner. Arthur was the last to leave British Harbour. Even after all the others had resettled, Arthur stayed for more than two long years, alone. He was in his eighties when he finally left."

"So, finally, he just gave up?"

"Well, he was here by himself, there was no medical attention, nobody delivered groceries. He was foraging on his own, and I guess two years was enough."

I tried to imagine living in that house after everyone else had gone, looking out at empty houses and empty foundations in the community, without a single "good morning" or "goodnight." To be completely alone – with no road in and no road out. Little wonder Arthur finally gave up and resettled.

Further up the hill, we came upon the remains of one of the churches. "This was the Anglican church," Ed explained. "It blew over a few years ago."

The once-proud steeple was on its side on the ground, its bell long gone. White clapboards lay in heaps around the church's crumbling foundation. The main door still clung tenaciously to one hinge.

Ed and I walked around the steeple and stood on the bluff overlooking the community below, imagining the bell calling its faithful up the hill to worship, to give thanks for life and all its blessings. People were christened here, married and buried here.

"You can bet when they were forced to move, there were lots of tears cried in this church."

One of the boat-crew members who came with us on our trip, Lance Short, was a friend of Ed's. Lance had grown up in British

Harbour. While my television crew did some taping with Ed, I sat with Lance on the bluff overlooking the bay. He vividly remembered the two churches, the Anglican church on one side of the bay and the Catholic church on the other. He remembered the sound of the bell in the Anglican steeple summoning its people and how his family wept their last day in church before leaving British Harbour.

"Many of the people had never left British Harbour until then, except for a trip over to Island's Eye, Black Duck Cove, or Deer Harbour, to find and bring home a 'good wife.' Life may have been isolated, but we were happy."

Lance spoke of children playing a game called "duck" on Little Brook Hill; it was played with a small wooden peg, sharpened on both ends, which was struck with a stick. The object of the game was to smack the peg on its tapered tip, making it fly through the air to land in your opponent's circle.

"It never cost us a cent, and it kept us occupied for hours," he said.

Lance also spoke of the one-room schoolhouse that he and his friends went to. But mostly, we just sat and listened to the sound of the wind. It was an exceptional place.

When my crew finished shooting Ed's scene, he came over to where Lance and I were sitting and said he wanted to show me something. He took me along a path up a small rise behind the old Anglican church, to a place overgrown with small saplings and tall grass. There were several headstones marking the resting places of those who never left British Harbour. Ed walked over to one corner of the graveyard and bent down. I knew he was visiting Caroline Leonard.

"I almost feel I know her," he said. "I'm painting a picture of her now, knitting with her mother. In those days, most goods were knitted – stockings, socks, gloves – or, as we call them in Newfoundland, 'cuffs.' Her daughter, Theresa, is helping her. I feel I owe Caroline a lot for showing me what to paint here."

I couldn't help but think how powerful this woman, Caroline

Leonard, was. She brought Ed to this place again and again. And now she had drawn a national television crew to tell the story of British Harbour. It was almost as if Caroline were directing us from her grave.

By day's end, we had a pretty clear picture of the way life had once been in British Harbour, and shared Ed's sadness for a way of life that will never be again.

We were a quiet group leaving British Harbour. The sun had fallen behind the hills, and old Arthur Gardner's house was very grey now as our boats slipped silently from the cove between the rockfaces of the inlet and out into the bay back to the docks at Trinity.

Two years later, in 1991, I returned to British Harbour on a holiday with Leanne. Keith had arranged for Art Andrews to take Lee and me, Keith's wife, Debbie, and Ed Roche for a day trip to the old outport. Ed's painting, hanging in the hall, which I had commissioned him to do for our home, had captured Leanne's heart. I guess the fact I talked a lot about British Harbour must have helped, too – not to mention that I had also written a song about British Harbour and released it on my *Storyteller* CD.

We anchored in the cove this time – since the dock had finally succumbed to the elements and was virtually gone – and Keith took us ashore in a little rubber dinghy, one at a time. We sat for a long time among the wild flowers on the bank of the shore, drinking in the scene. Lee and Debbie knew the moment we sailed into the cove why we had been so captivated on our earlier visit to British Harbour. They thought the place was beautiful, too.

I had a cassette of the song I wrote about British Harbour in my pocket. In the song, the refrain mentions Caroline's name and, for some reason, I wanted to leave it with her. We wrapped it in plastic to seal it from the elements and went to Caroline's grave in behind the old Anglican church and placed the cassette in a crevice under her headstone. I'm not sure why I did that. Maybe someday, someone will find it and fill in the blanks. Who knows? I just wanted to leave her something. After all, she left so much with me.

In spite of all the change, images remain,
And sometimes Caroline calls my name
In the wind that blows
through the ruins of British Harbour.

Among the Missing

❧

I've been a pretty lucky traveller over the years. I haven't lost too many things on the road. One time, travelling to location in Old Montreal, I left my favourite pair of black leather gloves on the back seat of a taxi and never saw them again. Not so unusual. You probably have a "lost gloves" story in your life.

Two years ago, I lost my beautiful Nova Scotia tartan scarf somewhere on the Avalon Peninsula in Newfoundland. I wandered around the country for the rest of that winter feeling quite undressed without it. But losing a scarf is not so unusual, either. I'm sure you too have a "lost scarf" story to tell.

So maybe I should skip the story about losing my purple shirt – one my wife bought and made me wear for the taping of a country-music show in Sudbury, Ontario, in 1991 – because that wasn't really a major loss either, except perhaps in my wife's mind. Let me get on to some of the more significant items I have lost on the road and which are still among the missing.

For example, my camera kit. It was a beautiful thirty-five-millimetre Canon kit, complete with telephoto, wide-angle, and portrait lenses, filters, bounce flash, and tripod. The entire kit was "babied" in a gleaming aluminum case that looked like serious business. "On the Road Again" was in its first year, and I was determined to capture, on film, every living thing that crossed my path. I was going to see Canada in a way I never dreamed of seeing it – hosting a television show that would take me to every nook and cranny of our country. It was an amateur photographer's dream!

Well, my gleaming silver baby went everywhere I went, except that last time, when I went to Regina while my luggage went to Saskatoon. I managed to get everything back except for my camera kit. Now *that* loss was a little more significant.

I've also lost two Ovation guitars in my travels. Ovation is the brand name of a particular guitar I used to use as a work guitar – a songwriting guitar – on the road. One had its top crushed by sloppy baggage-handling at Vancouver International Airport and was lost forever; the other Ovation was also damaged in airline transit, but was repairable. So I brought it home, intending to get it fixed, but I got busy and put it aside for the longest time. The joke is that, to this day, I can't remember where I put it. I actually *lost* it! Either that, or I gave it away. If I did, I can't remember to whom. That's called loss of memory. What worries me is that there's something significant about *that* kind of loss, too!

Some losses are more easily accepted than others. Like the ones in which a solution is completely beyond your power. It's cut and dried. What you valued is gone, and there is nothing you can do to bring it back. End of story, however sad. But some losses are not easily accepted because you *could* have prevented them; you just stood by and let them happen. These are the ones that tend to linger in the mind and haunt you forever. Take the loss I suffered in 1989, while travelling at seventeen thousand feet on board an Air Atlantic Dash-8 commuter, inbound for Saint John, New Brunswick, from Montreal.

I was on my way to meet eighty-two-year-old Mick Mickleburgh near Grove Hill, New Brunswick, about thirty kilometres east of Saint John. He was known across the province as "The Beaver Man" because of a wildlife sanctuary he and his wife, Nancy, had created for a beaver family more than thirty years before.

In the early 1960s, shortly after Mick and Nancy built a little house in the country, a family of beavers arrived on their property and started to build a dam. The Mickleburghs loved their little neighbours and allowed them to continue to build. What started out as a little watershed grew rapidly, and before long the beaver pond began to flood the Mickleburgh house. Something had to be done about it.

So Mick and Nancy *moved* their house, lock, stock, and foundation, to higher ground! It didn't take long for word to spread, and soon the Mickleburghs were celebrated far and wide as friends and protectors of the little critters that are our national emblem. At the time of our visit, Nancy had recently passed away, but Mick continued to help the beavers maintain their dam, naming the lake it created Nancy's Lake in her honour. Mick had arthritis and failing eyesight, but he wasn't about to stop helping his adopted family. "Nancy wouldn't want me to stop. Not yet," he said. (And he didn't stop until he died, three years after our "On the Road Again" visit.)

I finished reading my research notes on the Mickleburgh story just as the captain came on the intercom system informing us of possible turbulence along our route and asking that we remain seated with our seatbelts fastened. Bad timing! For several minutes, I had been feeling the need to visit the "little boys' room," but was so enchanted with Mick's story I had chosen to hold off and exercise bladder control to get me through the read. It's really tough, though, when your notes are describing water "passing by the door" and the "flooding of the dam." Now the captain expected me to sit for another half-hour, holding back a lake of my own!

I've learned that, sometimes, if you occupy your mind with other things, the urge to "go" often disappears for minutes, even hours, at a time. Well, I desperately needed a diversion now. Enough of reading research notes. It was time to turn back the surging waters!

I reached into my bag under the seat in front of me and pulled out my shiny new Ray-Bans. I was so proud of them. They were my very first pair of aviator sunglasses. Every pilot wore them, and I had just obtained my pilot's licence earlier that spring. Holding a pair of Ray-Bans in your hand was announcing to the world you had mastered the art of flight and were licensed to defy nature and slip "the surly bonds of earth," just like the big boys flying the Dash-8.

I cleaned my glasses with the special polishing cloth one of my cameramen, André Villeneuve, had given me and slipped them on. We were flying high above the clouds in brilliant sunshine. As I looked out the window, my Ray-Bans did their job, filtering out the UV rays and turning the brightness into cool, grey hues. I fancied the boys up front were enjoying the same hues with their Ray-Bans.

Minutes later, it was back – the undeniable need to "go." Turbulence or not, I was running out of options. The "Whoops, I spilled my drink" excuse wouldn't work if I had an accident, because they hadn't *served* any drinks yet. I reached down and pulled the clasp on the metal portion of my seatbelt. I hoped loosening it might relieve the pressure, but to no avail. It was time for action.

The washroom was a short dash away. I left my seat, explaining to the flight attendant on the way by that, despite the captain's warning, I had something very important to settle. I knew she had seen that look before. She didn't try to turn me back.

"Be quick," she said, sympathetically. "The captain has switched on the seatbelt signs." I fancied she noticed my sunglasses, which were pushed up from my eyes and sitting on top of my head. I figured she knew in an instant that I was a pilot and turbulence was nothing new to me! Ray-Bans tend to do that to people.

If you've never been on a Dash-8 commuter, let me explain the scene unfolding. I am now a six-foot-four, two-hundred-and-forty-five pounder. For metric fans, that's roughly two metres tall and one hundred and eleven kilograms in weight. When I walk the aisle of this medium-sized commuter, my walk is akin to that of a strolling Sasquatch. The knees are slightly bent, the head is forward and well down, especially if the Sasquatch is wearing Ray-Bans on top of its head. The washroom is *immediately* adjacent to the door that leads to the flight deck up front. All that separates it from the flight deck is one wall. One thin wall. As an experienced traveller, I must tell you this: don't go making any noises in that little washroom that you wouldn't want the pilots to hear. You may startle them, and that wouldn't be good, especially if they are hand-flying the airplane.

The washroom itself is an engineering marvel, designed to accommodate the *average* male or female traveller quite adequately. There is no sink on board the Dash-8, but then some conveniences must suffer in a small commuter plane. Let's face it, just being able to go at seventeen thousand feet, in relative privacy, is a bit of a modern-day miracle. Nevertheless, I wish the Dash-8 washroom had had just a little more room that particular day.

My height being what it is, when I stand in a Dash-8 "convenience centre," my head is at a forty-five-degree angle where it meets the sloping roof of the aircraft. On this memorable day, I stood, as I usually do on a Dash-8, head canted sideways against the roof – grateful, nevertheless, to be able to "go" at all. I didn't have a lot of room to move, but I really didn't need it. Gravity still works at seventeen thousand feet and, as long as one's aim is true, nature directs the flow of events. Everything was right on the money that morning – until, that is, the turbulence hit.

At first I managed quite well. Nothing major to report, and my mission was just about accomplished. Then we hit a really good bump, and my Ray-Bans started to slip from the top of my head just as my hand hit the flusher. I felt the glasses slide down the bridge of my nose, over my moustache, linger on my lower lip, then tumble down my chest. Good God! My one-hundred-and-twenty-dollar Ray-Bans were heading straight for that swirling, chemical, airborne depository!

It's been said that, when an accident happens, events seem to occur in slow motion. I remember my left hand rising to catch my aviator glasses, but the glasses bounced over my outstretched fingers and slapped against the wall before continuing their descent. Gravity really *was* doing its job. I pulled my right hand away from the flusher and grabbed for them as they plummeted past my waist. No luck! Down, down, down, they continued, past the lip of the bowl, and into the swirling pit. They floated there for a moment, seemingly screaming, "Grab us, quick! We're going down!"

My hand started down instinctively. These weren't just any old sunglasses. These were my first-ever Ray-Ban *pilot* glasses and they were going where no pilot would ever wear them again. For a moment, I thought I had them. One of the arms of the glasses had not submerged and was right at my fingertips. If I was lucky, I'd be able to pick them up without touching anything other than the glasses. The slow-motion panic continued. The big silver door at the bottom of the bowl started to drop down, exposing the pit below. It was in its final stage of operation. My glasses started descending. The one dry arm went under. If I was going to save them, I would have to follow them down – *now* – and pull them from the depths of that churning cesspool.

Well, I didn't do it. I couldn't. Ray-Bans or not, some actions are beneath a person's dignity; some things are better left among the missing. Quite frankly, I don't imagine you would have done it either. Still, it was a difficult loss to accept, because I could have prevented the loss, but I just stood there and let it happen! Oh well, it could have been a lot worse. Imagine how I would have felt if I had false teeth and lost those like I lost my Ray-Bans. Imagine seeing your television smile going down the toilet. Would *that* ever ruin your dinner!

When we landed in Saint John, I left the Dash-8 rather downcast. I didn't tell the flight attendant about the incident because there was nothing she could have done about it anyway. I wasn't about to ask the pilots to have the holding tank drained, either. I'd never be able to look a fellow pilot in the eye if that story ever got out. Besides, it was raining in Saint John. I didn't need Ray-Bans anyway.

Bruce Rees, undisputed Pepsi King, and Gerry Luzny, the Coke Lady

The Coke Lady and the Pepsi King

~

It's early morning in the north end of Winnipeg, Manitoba. In a little house on Magnus Street, sixty-nine-year-old Gerry Luzny is chugging back a can of Coke Classic. She is dressed in a red Coca-Cola sweatshirt, and is wearing Coca-Cola earrings, red Coca-Cola hightop sneakers, and Coca-Cola socks. Removing her lips from the can, she pauses, savouring the taste of her Coca-Cola.

"Nectar of the gods!" she exclaims. "Nectar of the gods!"

At that very same moment (actually two and a half hours later) three thousand kilometres away in Harbour Grace, Newfoundland, Bruce Rees is getting ready for work. He is wearing a Pepsi T-shirt, a Pepsi ball cap, and a Pepsi cooking apron. There's a plate of bacon and eggs waiting on his table as he sucks back a can of Pepsi.

"It's the only thing I know that cuts the grease. The only thing."

Bruce has been part of "The New Generation" for going on thirty years now.

"You *know* this is the right one, baby . . . uh-huh!" he says.

Gerry Luzny, for her part, has been downing "The Real Thing" for well over fifty years.

"I'm a Coca-holic," she told me. "I know I am, because when there's no Coca-Cola here, I can tell you truthfully, I get the shakes."

Bruce is also a self-confessed soft-drink addict, and proud of it. I asked him how many Pepsis a day he drank.

"Umm, on a normal day, I drink twelve tins, this size here," he said, gesturing to the typical ten-ounce Pepsi tin he held in his hand.

"Twelve tins, *a day*?"

"More in the summertime. I go through a case of twenty-four, no trouble. I've been doing that for twenty-eight years."

Now, I'm not a mathematician, but I'm pretty good with a calculator. That means Bruce drinks 360 tins a month in the winter and 720 tins in the summer. Now a *liberal* figure for the length of a Newfoundland summer – I mean a hot "gimme another Pepsi" kind of summer – is three months, June through August. That being the case, Bruce annually drinks 3-times-720 tins, plus 9-times-360 tins, for a total of 5,400 tins. Multiply that by 10 (ounces), divide by 40 to convert to gallons, and multiply by 28 (years), and you find that, in his lifetime, Bruce has consumed 9,450, close to 10,000, *gallons* of Pepsi. That's more than 40,000 litres! Little wonder that Bruce Rees is the undisputed Canadian Pepsi King.

Gerry Luzny knew she was addicted to Coca-Cola when she realized she was drinking eight sixteen-ounce bottles a day. Again, with my little calculator, and the help of my "On the Road Again" crew, we figured that, in her lifetime, she had consumed over *fifteen* thousand gallons of Coke, or 68,000 litres, making her the undisputed Coke Queen of Canada.

When I asked Gerry if she was surprised by her lifetime consumption, she just rolled her eyes and said, sweetly: "Well, it don't seem like it when you just drink them one by one."

Lately, she's cut that consumption in half as part of her new weight-loss program.

"Not that Coke adds pounds," she said quickly, defending her beloved Coca-Cola. "There are less calories in a can of Coke than in a glass of orange juice!"

She was right. I did a little research on Coke and Pepsi and was surprised by what I found. Coke and Pepsi have about 108 calories per 250 ml – as opposed to 120 for a 250-ml serving of orange juice. Milk, by the way, has approximately 145 calories per 250 ml, and hot chocolate has 190 calories per 250-ml serving. Colas are actually 85 to 90 per cent sparkling water, with edible phosphoric acids and colouring added. They contain between 10 and 15 per cent sugar.

When I called Coca-Cola's office in Downsview, Ontario, and Pepsi's operations department in Ottawa, requesting information on their products, I was faxed a bundle of stuff within minutes of my call, in spite of the fact I placed those calls on a Friday – at day's end. Talk about competitive marketing.

The material they sent me was filled with facts and figures. Coke, as it turns out, was officially here first. It was registered at the U.S. patent office in 1893, and registered in Canada a few years later. Pepsi was registered in 1902 in the United States and in 1903 in Canada. Pepsi claims its brand is the number-one-selling product of any type of cola in supermarkets.

Coke, invented by pharmacist Dr. John Pemberton of Atlanta, Georgia, back in 1886, started off slowly. Mr. Pemberton's con-coction of the fragrant, caramel-coloured syrup, mixed with car-bonated water, sold for five cents a glass at his pharmacy. That first year, more than a hundred years ago, Pemberton sold only eight or nine glasses a day. In the second year, it started to take off. Today, Coke boasts that more than 775 million servings of their product are consumed each day worldwide. They even go so far as to say that, if all the Coca-Cola ever produced were placed in regular-sized bottles and laid side by side and end to end to form a four-lane highway, it would wrap around the earth more than eighty-one times!

"So, Gerry, tell me," I asked, watching her guzzle back another can of Coke, "are you not concerned about your habit?"

"No. I mean, I've tapered off from what I was, right? You know, I went from eight sixteen-ounce bottles a day down to four or five cans. I've got *control*, now!" she said, throwing her head back and letting out a great belly laugh.

"Do you still start your day with Coca-Cola?"

"Well, sure. That's a good way to start the day."

"And what's the last thing you do at night?"

"Always Coca-Cola."

Bruce was the same way. The morning he downed two tins of Pepsi while eating his bacon and eggs, I asked him if he ended his day with "The Choice of a New Generation."

"Yes. Absolutely. You know what they say: 'Be Young. Have Fun. Drink Pepsi.'"

Bruce is in his fifties, clean-cut, slightly greying at the temples, and, like most Newfoundlanders, laughs easily. I asked him where he buys his Pepsi.

"I usually buy it at the corner store. But I keep my eyes out for sales on Pepsi. The biggest load I ever picked up was at the Dominion Store in Carbonear. They had a Christmas sale on. Four tins for a dollar. I had the trunk of the car full, the back seat full, the front seat full, with just enough room to get in and drive home. I left the wife and the two daughters down at the mall in Carbonear, and I came home here and unloaded and I went back again to pick them up and, if the wife hadn't stopped me, I would have filled the car again."

The Coke Lady and Pepsi King are also both heavy collectors of memorabilia. Gerry houses over two thousand Coca-Cola items in a specially built addition to her home. In her Coca-Cola room, her windows are draped with Coca-Cola curtains, and there are Coke mirrors and furniture covered in Coke fabric. She has Coke jewellery – watches and earrings – as well as Coke cups and dispensing machines, little ornamental Coke cans and big Coke garbage cans. There is a Coke barbecue and a whack of Coke lighters to light it with. And let's not forget the Coke key-chains, Coke toys, Coke hairbrushes, Coke telephones, and on, and on, and on! Amazingly, Gerry doesn't collect all this stuff to barter or sell. It's a labour of love.

"I don't know what all my treasures would be worth if I sold them," she said. "I don't have a clue; but they're worth a million dollars to me!"

The addition built onto the house is, in short, Gerry Luzny's personal "shrine" to Coke. She calls it her fun room.

When our show was visiting her sacred domain, I made one

foolish mistake. "Do you ever have even a little taste of Pepsi?" I asked.

"You're lucky I like your show. *Nobody* uses the P-word in here!"

I was relieved she said it with a smile.

Gerry spends the entire summer in her shrine, arranging and rearranging her collection. It's her favourite pastime. She couldn't care less about going to the cottage or travelling to Europe. She'd rather put money into enlarging her room. But recently, Stan, her husband of more than forty years, had to lay down the law. "We've already had two expansions to our house on account of this Coke business," he said. "I told Gerry if there is going to be another expansion, it will have to be an upstairs floor. We're out of room on the property."

Back in Harbour Grace, Bruce Rees doesn't have a special room dedicated to his passion. His Pepsi items are scattered all over the house. Luckily for him, his wife, Vina, doesn't mind. She rather enjoys them. And just how many does he have? Well, Bruce isn't quite sure.

"I know I don't have thousands and thousands of Pepsi things," he said. "A few hundred maybe. Pepsi things are rare. Like clocks, for example. You can find a hundred Coke clocks, but you're a real king if you find a Pepsi clock."

"Do you have one, Bruce?" I asked.

"They don't call me the Pepsi King for nothing," he grinned.

Over in the corner, I noticed a shiny, clean Pepsi garbage can. I knew better than to ask if he actually used it for garbage.

Another one of his jewels is the Pepsi licence-plate holder that adorns the bumper of his pickup truck. Inside the cab, he has a CB radio. And, yes, his "handle" is "Pepsi King."

Bruce works for the RCMP in Harbour Grace as a guard at the local jail. He helps watch over five cells and a drunk tank. Recently, the other guards started pushing for a Coke machine to replace the Pepsi dispenser.

"For a while, there was a heck of a row! Imagine me at work

for a day without my Pepsi! I never let up. Not for one minute, sir!"

Well, you guessed it . . . Harbour Grace prison still has a Pepsi machine.

There is a postscript to the story of the Coke Lady and the Pepsi King. When we got wind that Gerry had to visit St. John's, Newfoundland, Andy Little, who had produced both stories for "On the Road Again" was very excited at the prospect of having Gerry and Bruce meet for a Coke–Pepsi showdown. Once we knew when Gerry was going to be in town, we arranged for Bruce to meet her at the old Radisson Hotel on Water Street. It was High Noon at the Cola Corral when they met face to face for the first time – and we were waiting for them with our cameras.

Bruce was sitting at the bar when Gerry slid her leg over the barstool next to him.

"What'll it be, folks?" the bartender asked.

"Coke," said Gerry. "Things go better with Coke."

"Pepsi!" said Bruce, turning to his cola nemesis. "This is Pepsi country here, my dear."

"If you ever come to my place, you'll never get a Pepsi," Gerry retorted. "Have you ever even *tried* Coke?"

"Yes. But it didn't go down very good."

"Well, I've tried your stuff, and it doesn't do anything for me, either."

And that is pretty well how their visit went. For the most part, the Coke Lady and the Pepsi King agreed to disagree, both insisting their cola was the real thing.

But there was one test we couldn't resist asking Gerry and Bruce to take. The Pepsi Challenge. Was love blind, we wondered? Blindfolded, would they both be able to tell which was which? Well, they agreed to do it for us. We placed a can of Coke and a can of Pepsi in front of both of them to taste. So, how did the Coke Lady and the Pepsi King fare? Somehow, I don't imagine I need to tell you the outcome.

Gathering of the Gwich'in

❧

In the first week of July, 1990, the community of Fort McPherson, Northwest Territories, experienced a heat wave. It was high summer, and for several days the mercury sat at around thirty-two degrees Celsius. There was no relief. At night it only cooled to about thirty degrees. That's because it was the season of the midnight sun; it was daylight twenty-four hours a day. People were up and about at all hours, sleeping only when they felt like it. At one in the morning, with the sun high in the sky, people were out fishing in their boats, children were playing in the streets, and young boys were riding their bikes on the town's wooden sidewalks.

For several days "On the Road Again" had been shooting footage in the community, and we were tired. Twenty-four-hour daylight really messes up your internal clock. None of us really knew or cared any more whether it was morning or night. We only knew it was hot. I never imagined it could be so hot a hundred kilometres above the Arctic Circle. I mean, we were *up* there, a thousand kilometres northwest of Yellowknife, and five hundred kilometres northeast of Dawson City, Yukon. We were in the Mackenzie delta, at the headwaters of the Peel River, only two hundred kilometres from the Beaufort Sea. High Arctic or not, it was high summer, and it was like the Bahamas.

We were in the Northwest Territories to do a story on the indigenous people of the Mackenzie Delta, the Gwich'in, the northernmost Amerindians in North America. Gwich'in means "People," and there are six thousand of them, composed of fourteen different bands and tribes living in their traditional homeland of the Northwest Territories, Alaska, and the Yukon.

The Gwich'in begin pitching their tents at Midway Lake, N.W.T.

Elder Annie B. Roberts and I laughed till we cried

Charlie Furlong from Aklavik, one of the many entertainers who performed at the Midway Lake Festival

Two thousand of those live in the Mackenzie delta, primarily in four communities within two hundred kilometres of each other – Aklavik, Inuvik, Arctic Red River, and Fort McPherson. There was a big gathering of the Gwich'in taking place on the weekend, only the second such gathering in over a hundred years, and we wanted to be there.

"Gathering" is something the Gwich'in used to do every spring, for thousands of years. About a hundred years ago, the custom died out. But in 1988, the Gwich'in council, feeling their people had become too far out of touch with each other, revived the age-old custom and gathered at a place called Arctic Village in northeastern Alaska. Then they decided they would gather every other year from then on. Two years had passed since Arctic Village, and they were gathering again, this time at a place called Midway Lake, forty kilometres south of Fort McPherson.

The gatherings were always important to the Gwich'in, but never as important as they are now, in these modern times. The problems of abuse and alcoholism in the north, associated with the cultural invasion by southern ways, is well documented. Gathering not only gives the Gwich'in a chance to renew family ties, tell stories, and share a little gossip as in days of old, it gives them an opportunity to discuss how to protect their way of life, which is fast disappearing.

This year, the gathering was being held in conjunction with a music festival at Midway Lake. There was going to be some dancing at this one. Entertainers were coming from all over the north to entertain the Gwich'in, including one entertainer from the south – me.

Earlier that week, on Monday, I had landed at Inuvik, two hundred kilometres north of McPherson, a little tired due to the long journey from Ottawa via Edmonton and Yellowknife, but eager to get on the road to Fort McPherson where Karl Nerenberg, our show's executive producer at the time, was waiting for me with our crew. Karl had decided to produce this particular shoot, because he knew the Gwich'in well. He was also no stranger to Fort McPherson, having taught school there several years earlier.

Fort McPherson is a fair-sized community by northern standards. Nine hundred people live there, all native Gwich'in, except for a few resident workers from "away" – health and dental staff, a couple of RCMP officers, a few teachers, and several store and office workers. It is a town with a few problems. Karl described Fort McPherson as a community that was hurting and in need of healing. It is not a "dry" town, and there is great division and debate among its residents about whether to make it one. The gathering at Midway Lake on the weekend was going to be a good place to discuss that very kind of thing, especially since alcohol is forbidden at gatherings.

I was really looking forward to seeing the crew, since we were converging on Fort McPherson from different places. Karl had flown up from Ottawa two days ahead of me, landing in Inuvik on Saturday, to join up with Keith Whelan, our cameraman, and Alain Guay, our audio man, who had been working with our show in Tuktoyaktuk and Sachs Harbour on the shores of the Beaufort Sea. Keith and Alain had just finished taping three stories with Janet P. Smith, one of our talented "On the Road Again" producers, and at week's end they had left Janet and met up with Karl. Keith, a Newfoundlander and a first-rate cameraman – as all our camera people are – is always the principle source of mirth and humour on a shoot. Alain Guay, from Quebec (who would leave our show in 1993), also enjoyed a good laugh. In spite of having to work back-to-back weeks on the road, both men were thrilled to be on the northern tour.

Karl and the boys had gone ahead down to McPherson on Sunday, in a van rented for the shoot. Karl had arranged for me to follow in a hefty, three-quarter-ton Ford pickup, which a local construction company agreed to lease for the week. Ahead of me lay the notorious Dempster Highway, a massive roadway made of stone, covered in gravel, shale, and dust, which linked Inuvik with the rest of the world to the south. The big pickup looked like it had made the trip down the Dempster once or twice before – more like maybe a thousand times before. As I threw my gear in the cab of the four-by-four I noticed there were several tires in the back of the truck.

"Why so many spares?" I asked the man handing me the keys.

"Just to be safe," he replied. "Your man, Karl, said you were going to be running back and forth a lot between McPherson and Midway."

"But, there are *three* spares here," I pointed out.

"Sounds about right to me," he chuckled. "They don't call the Dempster the "Dumpster" for nothing. You may need one or two of 'em before you're through. Have a good trip."

Inuvik, for all those who travel there by air, is where the Dempster begins, and it is where the highway ends for all those who drive up from the south. It is as far north as you can go by road in Canada. Travel any farther north is done by boat, plane, and sled. There is pavement in the town, something people who fly in take for granted – until, that is, they turn their backs on Inuvik and head south on the Dempster. Several sections of the highway contain a lot of pieces of sharp shale – flat-tire makers. The Ford's suspension quickly spoke volumes about the drive ahead. It was going to be a long, dusty haul.

The Dempster is really quite impressive. It's the only public highway above the Arctic Circle that is open year-round. Prime Minister John Diefenbaker, who was my father's favourite prime minister of all time (probably because they were both from the same province, Saskatchewan), was the man who got the highway started back in 1959. It was a massive undertaking and, in its day, a costly one – one hundred million dollars for a seven-hundred-and-twenty-kilometre highway. To make it, countless truckloads of stone were dumped on top of the tundra in a long, snaking north-south line between Inuvik, in the Northwest Territories, and Dawson City, in the Yukon, to the south. It seemed to go on forever.

To say the trip was dusty would be an understatement, although it was not as rough as I thought it was going to be. I drove, non-stop, for a hundred and fifty kilometres, till I reached the ferry crossing at the Mackenzie River, sixty kilometres to the north of Fort McPherson. The ferry was a big diesel-powered rig, and it felt good to climb out of the hot cab of the truck into the outside air. The truck didn't have air conditioning, and you don't drive with your windows open on the dusty Dempster.

The ferry ride was quite short, about fifteen minutes or so. An hour later I turned off the Dempster Highway onto the main street leading into Fort McPherson, relieved that it had been a flat-free trip. It was nine-thirty at night, but the sun was still high in the sky, making it feel more like noon. I rambled in slowly, drinking in the scene. So this was the place Karl had once called home, a town of wooden houses, older log houses, wooden sidewalks, and gravel streets lined with tall hydro poles. There were power lines everywhere. There was a building that had a graffiti message, condemning the use of alcohol, on one of its walls, scrawled in faded red paint with a paintbrush. A few children were hard at play in front yards along the road. A few adults were walking about.

The crew loomed up ahead on the left. They had their gear out by the side of the road and were shooting visuals. Keith was bare-chested.

"Hey, Whelan!" I called out, rolling up in my pickup, "Where's your shirt? What do you think this is, the south?"

"Feels like the south," he replied. "It sure wasn't like this up in Tuk."

"Hi, Wayne!" Karl said. "Isn't this incredible? We're in the middle of a bloody heat wave! Welcome to McPherson." We shook hands on the street. "How did you find the drive?" he asked.

"Actually, I'm impressed with how well-kept the highway is. It wasn't that bad at all."

Alain approached, extending a handshake.

"Hey, Alain!" I said. "*Ça va, mon ami?*"

"*Mais oui. Ça va bien!*" he replied. "We're having fun."

"We're just going back to the Co-op," Karl said. "You must be tired. It's that beige building up there on the right. The one with the gas pumps out front."

"I'm right behind you," I replied.

We pulled up alongside the Tetlit Co-op, a combination hotel, restaurant, and gas station, owned by the Fort McPherson Gwich'in.

"The manager of the Co-op is a Newfoundlander," Keith said.

"You found a Newfoundlander in McPherson?" I replied.

"We're *everywhere*, sir!" he laughed. "There was one in Tuk, sure! I mean, we're everywhere!

"Where's this guy from?"

"Grand Bank. His name's Charlie. *Nice* fella. Watches our show."

The Co-op was a two-storey wooden building. A couple of people were at the gas pumps filling their thirsty vehicles, and kids were hanging around, checking out the activity. Inside the double glass doors of the building was a lobby, with a staircase leading upstairs and another set of glass doors to the right leading to a restaurant, which was filled with about thirty people. Two customers appeared to be arguing with a guy behind the cash register. It had to be Charlie.

"We're supposed to sleep in this building?" I said, quietly. "It looks like the whole town hangs out here."

"What do you mean, sleep?" said Keith. "You can't sleep till it's nighttime, and we ain't getting any of that this week." He laughed.

"It's been like this since we got here," Alain muttered. "So many people. I slept last night with my earplugs in."

"Other than that, it's a perfect place!" Keith exclaimed. "Just like home, sir. *Lots* goin' on."

"No kidding," I replied.

"Here, let me get the door," Keith offered. "After you, skipper."

"Hey, it's Mr. 'On the Road Again,'" said one of the patrons who had been arguing at the cash. "You come for Midway Lake?" he asked.

"Yes, sir. We're here for Midway and for your gathering. You must know *this* guy," I said, pointing to Karl. "He used to teach here in McPherson."

Indeed, he did know Karl. Just about everyone in the restaurant remembered Karl quite well. They were happy to see him and happy our show was in town to do a story on the Gwich'in. Karl introduced me to several people. They were a friendly lot. I shook a few hands and signed a few autographs.

It had been a long day and I was looking forward to a good night's sleep – but not very optimistic about getting one after being told the gas pumps would be staying open late and opening quite early because of all the people coming through town this week. My room was at the top of the stairs and down the hall a little, though not far enough down the hall to escape the din. The floor of the hallway was plywood covered with carpet, and it creaked when you walked on it. My room was quite small; it had two single beds, with a night table and lamp between them, and a closet. There was one small window in the room, covered with a Glad garbage bag, which had been taped firmly to the window frame. At first, I didn't get the connection. I thought the window was broken and the bag was there to keep bugs out, but I quickly realized that this was not the case. It was there to bring on the night! With the door closed and lights off, the room was pitch-black, and for that, I was "glad." But I was not very happy about the lack of air. It was very hot in that little room, which, like my truck, had no air conditioning. I had one of two choices to make: leave the bag on or take the bag off. Since I needed the dark of night to sleep, I chose to bake.

On Tuesday, I wandered around with the crew, spending the early morning in the hot sun, shooting visuals of the town. Around noon, a small army of town residents began picking up trash from its streets, ditches, and front yards. Men, women, and children were out in force, stuffing cans, bottles, and paper trash into, what else, Glad garbage bags. It was important that their town look good. After all, Gwich'in were coming to Midway from all over the north, and many of them would be dropping into McPherson. The upcoming gathering had started to work its magic, instilling a sense of pride amongst members of the community. They worked away at the town for several hours; by three o'clock they had every bit of litter gathered and bagged.

I travelled to Midway Lake for the first time late that afternoon. Keith travelled with me, and we followed Karl and Alain, keeping a lot of distance between us, because we didn't want to eat their dust.

"Here, you're gonna want to put some of this on when we get up to the lake," Keith said, throwing a plastic bottle of Musk Oil on the dash. "The mosquitoes are fierce."

"Musk Oil? This stuff reeks," I said.

"Well, it's that or they're having *you* for lunch," he laughed, poking his finger into my shoulder.

Each round trip to Midway Lake meant *another* eighty klicks of Dempster dust and gravel, and this was the first of many to be made that week.

"Wait till you see the ferry up ahead," Keith said. "It's *cable*-driven."

The ferry that crosses the Peel River is about ten kilometres south of Fort McPherson. It goes into the water after the Peel River breaks up around the end of May and operates until freeze-up in mid-October. For the five-minute crossing, the big rig literally pulls itself back and forth across the river with a big steel cable running through pulleys turned by a motor. The operator doesn't have to do much except push a lever one way or the other.

"Make you homesick, Keith?"

"Yeah. We used to have a really big one of these goin' between Port aux Basques and Sydney," he said, pulling my leg. "Worked fine till the cable snapped."

We had a good laugh, imagining a steel cable spanning the water between Nova Scotia and Newfoundland. I think the sun was getting to us.

A half-hour later, we arrived at Midway Lake, a very pretty spot nestled in the foothills of the Richardson Mountains. It is a large lake, over a kilometre wide and nearly two kilometres long and very clean, as northern lakes usually are. The gathering was well under way. There were already thirty or forty tents set up and more in progress. Many Gwich'in had come early to the lake because they wanted to be "on the land." It was a good place to be, simply because there were no alcohol or drugs around. The celebrants were in their ancestral element and enjoying every moment of it.

As Keith had warned, there were a lot of mosquitoes "gathering" out at the lake, too. The air was thick with them. We fought back as best we could, coating ourselves with Musk Oil and Deep Woods Off, but stink as hard as we might, they weren't deterred in the least. Keith was certainly not bare-chested out here. These Mackenzie delta "skitters" were vicious. Alain was looking a little pale, probably due to loss of blood.

In spite of the bugs, not to mention the heat, people continued to cut poles and fasten them together with rawhide to form a framework, over which folds of white canvas were hung. On this first visit, we stayed several hours. I interviewed a few people and Karl had Keith and Alain capture more sights and sounds of the people setting up at the lake. The Gwich'in were in a good mood. It was the way it was in olden times.

The next day, if you can call it that, since there was no real night to separate the days, we returned to the lake. Karl felt the Gwich'in festival and gathering would make a good "On the Road Again" special. I thought so too. Karl got increasingly excited as more and more Gwich'in set up tents, while Keith rolled tape constantly. He shot video as workers constructed the stage and shot more as they built the dance floor. The Gwich'in love to dance at their gatherings, and they were building a huge dance floor with bleachers along two sides, so that, even when people weren't dancing, they could sit and watch people who were.

We got back to Fort McPherson around midnight that day, and decided to cut the dust with a cold pint at RJ's, the one and only bar in town. We parked our vehicles at the Co-op and walked the block and a half back to the bar, getting there just in time for last call.

It was evident not everyone was "on the land." The bar was packed. And it was dark. The curtains were drawn and the lights were low, making us feel it was actually "nighttime." Of course, there was a rude awakening waiting for the patrons when closing time came around and everyone had to step out into the bright light of day. After all, it was one-thirty in the morning and some people had been inside for hours. It was comical. They stood outside the bar for a minute or two, squinting and blinking their eyes, getting used to the light. Then, in a long, slow procession, everyone walked down the middle of the street, homeward to bed. It was quite a sight.

Thursday was another long day down at Midway Lake. We got back to the Co-op at whatever hour it was – it really didn't matter any more. Our brains were in daytime mode, and we just kept working till somebody announced that maybe we should consider going to bed. Sleep was beginning to become a novel concept.

When I walked into the Co-op, Charlie, the manager, motioned for me to come over to the counter.

"Your friend arrived a few hours ago and he's upstairs."

The friend was Doug Nickerson, the man who operates sound and lights for me when my musical self is performing on a stage somewhere. Saturday, I was performing at Midway Lake, and Doug was here to do the set-up for me.

"Good, I'm glad he made it," I said.

"I had to put him in your room, though. We're full."

"What happened?" I asked. "I booked his room in advance."

"I don't know. Something got mixed up. I'm sorry."

"Will we be able to get an extra room for Doug tomorrow?"

"I doubt it. We won't have anything until the festival's over."

"Well," I said, "at least there are two beds."

I wasn't very happy. Not because I had to share my room with someone, but because I had to share my room with Doug. You see, Doug snores. *I* snore, sometimes. But Doug *really* snores, and he's a big guy like me, around two hundred and fifty pounds. So, not only were two two-hundred-and-fifty-pounders about to share a tiny room that had no air conditioning, they were going to snore together in a room that had no air! My sleep quotient was about to get a lot worse.

Doug, who's worked with me for twelve years, was, not surprisingly, sawing logs when I entered the room – four-foot-thick logs. He had ripped the garbage bag off the window and the screened slider was open. The room was flooded with light. To bag or not to bag the midnight sun, *that* was the question. Since Doug was out for the count, I had to make the decision. I opted for air. For the next three days, Doug and I would sleep with black socks draped over our eyes, while filling the second floor of the Co-op with a cacophony unlike anything heard before north of the Arctic Circle.

Friday morning, Karl, the crew, and I, were standing by the pumps in front of the Co-op interviewing people on their way to the lake. It was a good place to conduct interviews. People were descending on McPherson from all over, gassing up and getting supplies to take to Midway. They arrived in vans, cars, and pickup trucks filled with family and friends.

"People are coming from miles around," one enthused Gwich'in told me. "They drive in and they boat in, hitch a ride in – whatever. They come from Inuvik, Aklavik, Arctic Red River – from all over. Some may even fly in from Old Crow."

Old Crow is in the Yukon. Four hundred Gwich'in live there on the banks of the Porcupine River. They are called the Vuntut Gwich'in, the "People of the Lakes." Old Crow is due west of Fort McPherson, not far as the "crow" flies, but a long haul if you follow the airways of the airline companies. Air North, for example, will fly you from Old Crow to Dawson City, but from there it's north to McPherson via the Dempster, a good long haul.

I wondered if I would see Edith Josie, an Old Crow elder in her late sixties, at the Midway gathering. Edith is a long-time writer for the *Whitehorse Star* newspaper, who, through her column, "Here Are the News," has given people in the south, even some readers of an Edmonton newspaper, a sense of the way of life in Old Crow. The Gwich'in revered her because of her strong commitment to her people and appreciated her constant efforts to promote the Gwich'in language and way of life. Wouldn't meeting Edith Josie be a treat, I thought.

People were indeed coming from all over. The music festival was drawing a crowd of its own. Not only Gwich'in were coming to Midway. A young blonde girl and her boyfriend had driven all the way up from northern British Columbia.

"You must intend to do a lot of dancing," I said.

"Yeah!" she said enthusiastically. "Until at least six in the morning."

A taxi driver from Inuvik, who stopped to gas up at the Co-op, told me this was his second run down to Midway.

"People actually pay taxi fare to come here?" I asked incredulously. "That's a two-hundred-kilometre fare!"

"Nobody wants to miss an event like this," he said. "I'm on my way back to Inuvik now. I have another gang waiting for me to bring them tonight."

I was just about to ask the driver how much it cost to come by cab, when Alain fainted on the spot. At the time, we were naturally quite concerned, but looking back, it was almost as if the thought of paying cab fare all the way from Inuvik to Midway Lake was too much for him to bear. He just sort of . . . folded . . . silently, in slow motion, like an accordion, right in front of us, with no warning and no sound, not even so much as a sigh. He went down, ever so slowly, into the dirt. His head was the last thing to touch down, gently coming to rest against the sidewall of the taxi's front wheel. He didn't even lose his glasses. Keith and Karl and I stood there for a moment, kind of wondering where Alain had gone – the heat does that to you; you even *think* in slow motion. When it hit me what had happened, I quickly bent down, gathered Alain in my arms, and carried him up the Co-op stairs to his room. I laid him on the bed, while Karl fetched a cold, wet facecloth. Within a few moments, Alain came to.

"What happened?" he asked.

"You fainted," I told him.

"Is it true?" he asked, looking up at Keith, as if seeking confirmation.

"No question of that," Keith said. "Down like a leaf in the wind, sir."

Alain was okay. He just needed rest and a little time out of the sun, so he stayed in McPherson that night, while the rest of us, including Doug Nickerson, went back to the lake. Doug checked out the staging and put musical equipment in place for the performance I was going to give on Saturday, while Karl and the boys began shooting the first "night" of the music festival.

Neil Collin, a Gwich'in in his mid-fifties, who had a show on Fort McPherson radio, was hosting the stage show. He began the night by dedicating the concert to the Gwich'in elders – the wise ones – gathered at Midway. The young chief of the Fort McPherson Gwich'in, James Ross, spoke too. He said: "We want the white people who have come to join us for our gathering to come up to our people and say hello to any one of our families and have a cup of tea, here, away from the town and all its problems, and experience the real native people gathered in these tents – the real Gwich'in."

That is very much what we did. Besides taping the music festival, we went amongst the tents and shared tea, food, and conversation with the Gwich'in. They were very warm and kind. There was a good spirit at work at Midway. There were no sad faces. People were smiling a lot, happy to be on the land. Yukon

Jack, a four-piece band from Whitehorse, entertained on stage. On Saturday, Charlie Panagoniuk and his family, who came from his Inuit village in the eastern Arctic, sang and joked on stage for the Gwich'in. Saturday night, bathed in Musk Oil, I entertained for an hour, singing songs to an appreciative audience.

When I was finished, around eleven-thirty, Karl suggested we hustle to catch the last ferry to McPherson. If we missed it, we'd be staying at the lake for the night.

"With all these mosquitoes?" I said. "I don't think so. Karl, maybe you and the boys should go ahead. Doug has a few things to tear down. That way, if we're late, maybe you could hold the ferry for us. We should be right behind you."

Keith decided to stay and lend a hand.

It sounded logical enough. After all, we knew it took exactly thirty minutes to get to the ferry. Therefore, if we left by eleven-forty-five, we'd be at the ferry by twelve-fifteen, in plenty of time for the final twelve-thirty crossing. That's the law of logic. But there's another law one should always consider when catching the last ferry of the day. It's called Murphy's Law, and it is often far more powerful than laws of logic.

After we put our road cases in the back of the truck and covered them with a tarp, Keith and Doug and I jumped in the cab and left for McPherson. It was just about eleven-forty-five. About a half-hour later, two kilometres from the ferry crossing, we saw the cable ferry, way off in the distance, pulling into the dock on our side of the river.

"Piece of cake," I said.

Now, article 446 of Murphy's Law states: "Never say 'piece of cake' unless you are asking for one. If you ignore that law, and say 'piece of cake' with a cocky we've-got-'er-made-now attitude, things happen.

Bang!

"What was that?" Doug said.

The noise sounded like a gunshot. The truck started to vibrate and the steering wheel shook in my hands.

"Blowout!" I said, keeping the truck on the gravel and out of the three-metre-deep ditches.

It was the right rear tire. There was a ripped sidewall and a hunk of tire tread missing. A full week on the Dempster, and we had had not so much as a slow leak – till now. It was twelve-fifteen. How were we ever going to change a tire and get to the ferry in fifteen minutes? We knew one thing for sure. We didn't want to have to sleep three abreast in the cab of a pickup truck, with windows closed to keep mosquitoes out, in broad daylight, until the ferry came to get us in the morning. We had to fix that tire and we had to fix it now!

Murphy's Law continued to run its course.

"Where's the jack?" Keith asked.

"How would I know?" I replied. "It must be in the back of the truck somewhere."

We pulled the tarp back. No jack.

"Here, Keith, grab this tire and put it down there. Where the heck is the jack?"

"Under the hood!" Doug suggested. "It must be under the hood. Keith, pull the hood release."

No jack.

"Here it is, boys!" Keith exclaimed. "It's behind the seat."

I figured by the time we jacked that vehicle we had about five minutes to switch tires and make it to the ferry.

"Quick! hand me that tire iron so I can get these nuts off," I said.

"Piece of cake," Keith muttered.

"Don't say, 'piece of cake'!" I sputtered, hauling on the first of eight big nuts holding the wheel to the hub. "You never say 'piece of cake' till it's a done deal."

It was too late. Murphy had heard him and decided two of the nuts should not come off. I pulled with all my might on the four-way bar.

"Give me a go at it now," Keith said, taking the tire iron in his hands and hauling for all he was worth.

No joy. It was well after twelve-thirty by now.

"Doug," I said, "you grab one side of the iron and I'll grab the other. Ready – go!"

There was two hundred and fifty pounds on one side of the bar and two hundred and fifty pounds on the other, five hundred pounds of torque. The lug came loose. So did the other nut cursed by Murphy.

"Quick! Gimme the tire," I said. "Keith, flash the lights or something."

"What for? It's broad daylight."

"Right," I said, spinning the first nut on. "I forgot. Blow the horn, then. Actually, never mind," I said spinning a second nut on. "I'll just put one more nut on and we'll do the rest on the ferry. What time is it?"

"Twenty-five to one," said Doug.

"Is that enough to hold the wheel in place?" Doug asked. "That wheel will never stay on with only three nuts."

"G'wan," Keith said, throwing the blown tire in the back of the truck. "We do it all the time in Newfoundland."

I threw the jack back behind the seat.

It was twelve-forty.

"Do you think they're holding the ferry for us?" Doug asked.

"We'll know in a minute," I replied. "Let's go."

The ferry was, in fact, waiting, but it wouldn't have been for much longer. Karl kept telling the ferry operator we were coming, but, if we were, the operator answered, why couldn't he see road dust in the distance? They didn't know we had broken down. Well, once we fired the truck up and slammed it in gear, it took only a minute to convert that ferry guy into a believer. Suddenly, there was a tall rooster-tail of dust that started forming on the Dempster in the very place Karl and the operator were hoping to see it, and by the time we careened around the last curve and the waiting ferry came in view, that rooster-tail was a kilometre long. Luck of the Irish, the wheel stayed on. Murphy, be gone.

"Thanks for waiting, boys," I said as we drove onto the rig.

"What happened? Why did you leave so late?" Karl asked.

"We weren't late. We were right behind that rise up there all along with a flat tire. It took three of us to get it off."

We slapped the remaining nuts on the wheel before the ferry docked on the other side, and then drove on into McPherson.

Sunday, we returned for our final day at Midway with the Gwich'in before heading to Inuvik and home. We arrived around noon to the strains of "How Great Thou Art" coming from a throng of Gwich'in, song books in hand, gathered around the stage.

We asked Neil Collin how the night had gone after we left.

"It was wonderful. People dancing all night long. Still dancing at four in the morning. Everyone had a wonderful time."

Well, we had a wonderful time, too. The fun and adventure of being in the north always outweighs any difficulties or minor discomforts. Whether it's standing on the shores of Baffin Island trying to deliver an on-camera in minus-forty degrees, or dealing with heat waves, mosquitoes, and midnight sun, I never come home from a northern trip without having been filled with the wonders of the north and the warmth of its people. Every member of our show who travels to the north feels the same way.

I never got to meet Edith Josie from Old Crow, but something else really nice happened before I left Midway Lake. I spent half an hour sitting with a Gwich'in woman in her late eighties by the name of Annie B. Roberts. She wore on her head a little kerchief tied in a knot under her chin. Annie had lived out on the land for the first forty years of her life before moving into Fort McPherson in the 1950s. She was very sweet, bright as a box of birds, and loved to laugh. She had the most wonderful infectious laugh, especially when the camera pointed in her direction.

We had been walking around the tents taping a few final things for our program, asking a few last questions, when we came upon Annie's tent. She was sitting on a log near the cook fire with members of her family. Keith rolled camera as I sat down beside her to capture whatever conversation transpired between us. Well, as it turned out, she didn't understand a word of English, and I certainly didn't understand a word of Gwich'in, but that didn't matter. I'd ask a question, she'd look at the camera, and laugh that laugh. In no time at all, I was in stitches. We laughed for minutes on end. We laughed till we cried. People do that sometimes in the land of the midnight sun.

Jim Thompson, harvesting a few little critters for lunch

Bug-Eater

❧

In High River, Alberta, Jim Thompson eats bugs – all kinds of bugs. He eats big ones, little ones, cute ones, and ugly ones. He eats bugs with six legs, and bugs with sixty legs. He eats juicy bugs and skin-and-bone bugs. He's been doing it for over fifteen years now, making him a bit of a gourmet in the world of insect ingestion.

Now, I have a cast-iron stomach. Ten years of crisscrossing the nation, eating three meals a day in every kind of eatery imaginable, does that to you; in very short order you develop a bullet-proof intestinal lining. There are very few things I can't take in and hold down. One of them is bugs. So, when producer Lauren Sawatsky asked me to entertain the notion of doing a little "taste test" on an upcoming shoot in High River, I choked.

"Bugs? You want me to eat bugs?"

"Just little bitty ones," Lauren replied. She was speaking softly and persuasively – setting the table for me, so to speak. "Wayne, they'll be prepared in a very special way. They'll be served in batter and Rice Krispies and stuff."

"I don't care how they serve them up. I don't *like* bugs. I swallowed one once, when I was seven years old, and I nearly choked to death on it."

I told Lauren about how I had been playing at the edge of the forest with my six-year-old neighbourhood girlfriend, Lynn Adamson, running through the trilliums in great circles, laughing to beat the band, and I got the hiccups. The more I hiccupped, the more we laughed. Right on the intake stroke of one particular hiccup, I ingested this big, horrible, hairy fly. I remember choking, and panicking because I couldn't breathe. I choked and hacked till I found my breath again. But, I never spat that fly out. He went in and stayed there.

"Well, you're in luck," replied Lauren. "This guy doesn't eat flies."

"It doesn't matter. A bug is a bug. I don't think I could eat one. You mean to tell me you actually found someone who eats bugs?"

"Yep. He's a schoolteacher."

"Tell me, does he eat dead bugs or live bugs?"

"Both, I think. Mainly, he drops them in the pan and cooks them."

"What kind of bugs?"

"All kinds. Meal worms, ants, crickets . . ."

"And you want me to eat a few?"

"Well, yes. But not a lot of bugs, and certainly no live ones. I promise, yours will be cooked. And dead."

"Lauren, if I ever so much as saw a bug coming towards my mouth, I'd lose it. I could never get it down."

"Maybe we could get Jim to hide the bugs inside a marshmal-low square, so you couldn't see them. Or maybe it would be easier if you ate just *one* little bug, coated in chocolate or something."

She was serious! She wanted me to ingest a creepy-crawly! In all the years of hosting "On the Road Again," and seven preceding years with "Country Report," I had never, ever, said no to a taste-test challenge. But I was having a problem with this one.

"I'm really going to have to think about it. I don't believe I'll even be able to give you an answer until I actually see those things."

"That's fair. I think you'll be okay with it when you see the way Jim prepares them. Once they stop moving, they're not so bad. They're actually kind of cute. Try to think of them as little candy thingies."

"Will you stop it? Candy thingies! Lauren, I don't like bugs!"

Lauren was having fun. She had found my squirm button and

was leaning on it. "All we need, Wayne, is one shot, one bite. It's not like you have to eat a meal."

"I don't know. I just don't know."

"Okay. Just promise me you'll think about it. If you don't want to do a taste test on camera, we'll have to work around it. It's just that I was hoping to get your reaction for our viewers."

"Lauren, you'd get a reaction all right. I'm just not sure it's the kind our viewers would appreciate."

We were laughing, now.

"Jim actually goes around to schools and holds classes where kids get to eat bugs."

"Excuse me?"

"He goes around to schools dispelling the myths about bugs. Then he invites the children to taste them."

"Do the parents know this is going on in school?"

"Yes, of course. They are all advised. And most parents allow their children to take part in the taste test. There is tremendous nutrition in bugs. Jim's a promoter of that. He feels if people can bring themselves to eat bugs, at least once, that it will have an effect on the rest of their lives."

"No kidding," I said. "That fly I told you about had an effect on the rest of my life. Now I detest flies."

"You're actually a little concerned about all this, aren't you?"

"To be perfectly honest, Lauren, yes. Pardon the pun, but I just don't know if doing this particular item on our show is in good taste. Maybe I'm a little naive about this bug-eating thing. Like I said, I just don't know."

What I did know was that the military, in survival training, taught soldiers to eat bugs in order to stay alive, particularly a certain kind of ant which is very high in protein. Mind you, you'd have to eat hundreds and hundreds of the little critters before they'd begin to fill up your stomach. It would be like eating tiny grains of Uncle Ben's rice, one grain at a time – a pretty time-consuming way to eat supper, maybe, but better than dying. Still, people have chosen to die rather than eat ants. Survival studies have shown that many people starve to death because they are unable to bring themselves around to eating them when the time comes.

"Lauren, is this Jim's way of teaching a survival course?"

"Well, partly. I think he's more interested in enlightening people about other cultures for whom eating insects is a normal way of life. He wants to make us aware that insects could be used as a supplemental food source in our culture, too."

"What else motivates him?"

"Well, like I said, he really believes that overcoming the hangups most people seem to have about bugs will help make them better people. By doing something they've never done before, they'll achieve a victory over self."

Nice theory, I thought. But, why not use something more appealing than bugs to overcome oneself?

A couple of weeks later, in the plane en route to Alberta, I was still undecided whether I would eat bugs, and for most of the flight I played with the pros and cons of doing so. As I've mentioned, it's not as if I hadn't chewed on a few unusual things in my life. I have. In my role as a television host, I've savoured dozens of assorted offbeat culinary delights which were featured on my show over the years. Once, in Ontario, I sat crosslegged in an organic garden with a garlic guru, feasting on giant cloves of raw garlic, fresh from the soil, until my esophagus ignited. Another time, on Grand Manan Island off the coast of New Brunswick, I sat with Leroy Flagg, the greatest dulse picker that ever lived, and downed a couple of pounds of dulse, the edible purple seaweed for which Grand Manan is world-renowned. We had some shooting problems that day with the eating scene and Leroy and I had to do it over and over again until we got it right. Well, that little culinary adventure haunted my internal highways and byways for a week and resulted in several emergency dashes to the john that rivalled Donovan Bailey's best times ever.

Mind you, I have also treated my system quite kindly at times. I've sucked on rose petals, nibbled on tender nasturtiums, and feasted on edible weeds from forest floors and rolling meadows. I've savoured beefalo and buffalo and dined on pheasant under glass, set resplendently in the centre of a great oak table adorned with fine china and cutlery. I've sat with Inuit on a barren rock in the high Arctic eating seal from a pot boiling over a fire. My stomach has seen it all. Was eating one little bug such a big deal? Was I going to live forever with that hiccup-ingested memory or ultimately achieve victory over self? It certainly wasn't going to kill me. As the plane descended into Calgary, I was still undecided. I reasoned that I'd wait till I saw the little zingers firsthand, in a pot, and let my stomach make the decision for me.

The nice thing about Air Canada's 8:25 a.m. flight to Calgary is that it gets you there at 10:40 a.m. local time. Since High River is less than an hour's drive from the airport, you can be there shortly after twelve noon. That's the nice thing. There is, however, a down side to that scenario when you're doing a bug-eating story. It's also lunchtime. And when I arrived at Jim's modest yellow-and-brown house on 7th Street, "lunch" was in full swing. High River's "Galloping Gourmet" was hard at work in the kitchen, wearing a red plaid short-sleeved shirt and white cooking apron, busily stirring up some kind of concoction in a glass bowl.

"Hello, Jim. Wayne Rostad."

He was a tall, lean man, just shy of six feet, with short brown hair brushed forward on his forehead. I guessed he was in his late forties.

"Hi, Wayne," Jim replied, wiping his hand on a tea towel and extending it for a handshake. "You're just in time. Lunch is on its way. Lauren tells me you can't wait to see what's cooking."

"That's an understatement," I laughed. Obviously, Lauren had told Jim of my apprehension. "But I'll bite. What are you cooking, anyway?"

"Several of my favourite recipes. We're taking them to school tomorrow for a grade-two class to sample. There are one or two here with your name on them, though."

"Yeah, right. What does the chef recommend?"

"Well, for starters, you could try a couple of these," Jim replied, reaching for a Tupperware container on the counter.

"What are they?"

"Roasted crickets."

Jim peeled back the cover. Inside the container were dozens of the little guys, looking much like tiny dead soldiers, lying symmetrically, row upon row. Jim reached in with his fingers, picked one up, and gingerly popped it in his mouth.

"These are very good," he said.

"It sounds a lot like, uh, eating popcorn," I replied, mustering my best that-didn't-bother-me-much smile. "What's it like?"

"Kind of crunchy. A great starter snack. Here, look at these," Jim continued, reaching for a slightly larger container. "Marshmallow Rice Krispies squares."

"Oh, I *love* those!" I exclaimed.

"Then you'll *really* love these," Jim replied.

"Why, what's so special about those squares?" I asked.

"Ants. I put ants in them. They're 7½ per cent protein and 23 per cent fat. Want one?"

"Uh, no, thanks. I gave them up years ago."

"These are more nutritious in a lot of ways than our standard food."

"Marshmallow squares?"

"Actually, any of these dishes with insects in them."

"You seem to know the exact percentages of protein and fat these bugs have in them. Where did you get that kind of information?"

"There have been many studies on insects and their nutritional value," Jim replied. "One book called *Butterflies in My Stomach* is the first I ever read. It's a good one to get you started. There's also a great book, called *Bug Wise*, and another one, loaded with information, called *The Amazing World of Insects*."

"So what do marshmallow squares – with ants in them – taste like?" I asked.

"Like marshmallow squares," Jim responded. "I only put a few ants in this batch, so there isn't much ant taste.

"So why eat 'em if you can't taste them?"

"Protein. Protein."

"Oh, yes, I forgot."

"Now, had I loaded this mixture full of black ants, you'd taste them."

"And what kind of taste would that be?" I asked.

"It would taste like raspberries."

"You don't say!"

"Yes. Here, go ahead. Try one."

"Uh, maybe later. I just had a big snack on the plane."

The more we chatted, the more I learned about this bug-eating, cricket-loving connoisseur of things insectile. Jim was a program co-ordinator for continuing education in Calgary and, for more than a decade now, had successfully offered his insect-enlightenment courses both within the school system and to outside interests. He was a well-educated man, having studied anthropology and archaeology at university. His wife knew about his bug fetish long before they were married. Back when they were dating, Jim went so far as to offer her tacos filled with insects! Well, snuggling up on the couch with the one you love was one thing back then; snacking on tacos with *mucho insectos* was quite another. That was not her idea of a food treat. Still, she ended up marrying him. Their four children have all tried eating a few bugs over the years and never appeared squeamish about it.

"Do you eat spiders?" I asked.

"Sometimes."

"I couldn't imagine putting a spider in my mouth. What does a daddy-longlegs taste like?"

"Well, a daddy-longlegs, technically speaking, is not a spider. It's an arachnid. But, a lot of people eat them and claim that they taste like a lemon drop."

"I can't believe people could swallow one!"

"People do, all the time. If you were a bushman in Africa or an Aborigine in Australia, certain spiders, meal worms, and grasshoppers would look like very tasty morsels to you. They'd look like candy."

"Give me a couple of recipes."

"Well, you can melt two cups of marshmallows over low heat and add one cup of roasted meal worms for a nice snack. My favourite, though, is this one: again, first melt two cups of marshmallows, add half a cup of roasted grasshoppers, stir in six cups of organic popcorn, and *voilà*! It's great stuff to snack on if you rent a movie or something."

"Jim, I've got to ask you this. Do you ever pull these treats out at the dinner table when you have guests over?"

"I do, on occasion. Sometimes, when we have visitors, a drink or two tips their curiosity to the point where they want to try them."

"So, what do they try?"

"Well, all the marshmallow squares I just talked about are easier for a first-timer. We have a tendency in our society to judge a food based on its looks. You see that all the time in children. The squares are at least a little familiar, and therefore easier to stomach."

Jim reached over and placed another container in front of me.

"But these," he continued, "would be very hard for someone to eat first time out if you just served them in a bowl like this."

The bowl was half-filled with squiggling, inch-long, worm-like bodies.

"And what are these?" I asked.

"These are the meal worms I'm about to fry up and make into squares for the kids at the school tomorrow."

"They're alive."

"So is beef until we kill it."

"Would you actually eat one of these meal-wormy things while it was alive?"

"Oh, sure. They're quite good, actually."

"Would you eat one for me now?"

"Sure."

Jim reached down into the bowl without hesitation and pulled out one of the meal worms. Raising his hand to his mouth, he bit the little squiggly in half, taking two or three delicate bites before popping the rest of the worm in his mouth. It took only a few seconds. It felt like minutes. I sat, transfixed.

"That is wild! You ate it."

"Of course I ate it. You can try one, if you like."

Well, I didn't. Much to Lauren's disappointment – and probably Jim's as well – I just couldn't.

The next day, at Blackie Elementary School, just outside High River, the children of Mrs. Lowrie's grade-two class gathered together and sat on the floor as Jim began his one-hour bug presentation. Needless to say, he had their undivided attention. At first, there was a lot of moaning and groaning as he passed the roasted crickets and meal worms around. But by the end of his presentation, most of the children's apprehension had waned and several of them bravely downed their first, if not their last, bug. It was a far gentler introduction to bugs than my childhood fly-swallowing experience. Their experience was sugar-coated, with no forced ingestion or choking. Mine was black and dirty, and shoved down my throat. Maybe that's why I couldn't eat what was offered for lunch that day in High River. Maybe I don't have a cast-iron stomach after all. Who knows? The one thing I *do* know is this. I'm sure not going to let it bug me.

JONATHAN CRAVEN

Maman Louise with some of her twenty-four children

Maman Louise

~

One of the most remarkable women I have ever met in my "On the Road Again" travels lives on a thirty-five-acre farm near the village of St-Anselme, about twenty-five kilometres southeast of Quebec City. It is a picturesque setting. The farmhouse sits on a hillside, overlooking the St. Lawrence River valley, a large, well-kept place, made of fieldstone and wood, with a great tin roof, painted sky-blue. In many ways it looks like a lot of the farm-houses in that part of rural Quebec – but, this one is special. So is the woman who lives there.

Her name is Louise Brissette, and she is a small woman of incredibly strong character, fifty years of age, who lives in this pastoral setting with her children. She has not one, not two, but, *twenty-four* children, ranging in age from two to nineteen years. Now, my grandmother, Rose Seguin, lived in rural Quebec and had eleven children. Large families were not uncommon back then. However, to have twenty-four kids in this day and age is incredible.

What makes Louise's family scenario even more remarkable, though, is that she is a single parent. She has never even been married. And she has legally adopted each and every one of these children. If that isn't enough, consider this. All twenty-four are disabled – five, quite severely. Eight children suffer from Down syndrome, two are deaf, and two are completely blind. Of the twenty-four, five are unable to feed themselves, seven are in wheelchairs, and no fewer than eighteen are still in diapers; she changes her children *a hundred and twenty* times a day. Little wonder that, to many people, Louise Brissette is a living saint.

The magnitude of care required for a family of twenty-four

children with special needs is hard enough to imagine, let alone describe, unless witnessed first-hand. I had the opportunity to do just that when our show paid her a visit in the spring of 1991. Back then, Louise had fourteen disabled children.

It was April, and the snow had just left the land. It was morning when we arrived, and Louise was already out on the deck with several of her loved ones, soaking up the warm spring sunshine. The children were all dressed warmly in fresh, clean, gaily coloured clothing, and Louise wore a red sweatshirt and blue jeans. Her dark brown hair was cropped short and simply brushed forward over her forehead. She was busily talking up a storm with a beautiful little blond boy on the deck.

The cedar deck, attached to the south side – the sunny side – of the house, was quite large, obviously built to accommodate a large family. It was about four metres wide by ten metres long, with posts and railings that safely surrounded the children as they played. One child was in a wagon pulled by a tall, kindly looking woman in her fifties, with glasses and grey hair. She was one of Louise's helpers, one of two nuns who had recently taken up residence at the farmhouse to help her.

Two other children were in walkers, laughing and squealing joyously in the spring air, while another, on a tricycle, attempted to negotiate his way around the obstacle course presented by a big white patio table and scattered chairs. At the end of the deck, a small above-ground pool awaited summer, and, in the yard, beneath the towering poplar and oak trees, a swing set sat idle, waiting for the spring mud to dry. There was also a very large sandbox. It had to be four metres square; talk about a great place for your Tonka trucks!

Over by the garage entrance, there was more activity: two children, shooting basketball hoops. The hoop was fastened to the garage wall only a metre and a half above the asphalt driveway, to accommodate tosses from wheelchairs. Adjacent to the house, in a separate outbuilding, I could hear chickens. My producer, Jonathan Craven, had told me about them. The older kids were in charge of collecting eggs for the family, and Louise also kept rabbits and cats on the farm for the children's enjoyment. There was a lot of activity here. Everywhere, I could hear the sounds of conversation and laughter, the sounds of a happy family.

Louise did not speak much English, and she spoke haltingly at the best of times. However, we had no difficulty communicating; the love in her eyes said it all. She certainly wasn't looking for children that were easy to look after. For the most part, they all needed special care that went far beyond that afforded by hospitals or clinics.

"For me," Louise explained, "it's not important to see if they can walk. It's not important to see if they can see. The most important thing for me is to see the heart of the child."

Her face was beaming.

"My children . . . each one of them . . . it's like a gift, that is wrapped in paper that is not so good . . . they have no ribbon, maybe . . . but, inside it's so nice! You just have to take off the paper to see that it's nice inside!"

I felt my heart well up. What beautiful description! What incredible devotion! How many people, I wondered, would be able to give their entire lives to such a calling?

For Louise, it all began back in the 1960s. She trained as a physiotherapist and went to work abroad with CUSO in Ecuador. In the 1970s, she went to work with Cardinal Léger in Africa. It was there that Louise found her calling.

"In Africa, the children were . . . all alone in life. For me it was a . . . *grande crime?*"

"Yes," I said, helping her along. "It was a crime. Go on."

"The children . . . I saw . . . they don't have parents. And . . . I was so sad for them. You need to say, 'Mama, I love you' . . . or, 'Papa, I love you' . . . no?"

Louise came home to Canada and, in 1979, adopted her first child, an eight-month-old boy named Jean Benoit. Because she was a single mother, that first adoption was difficult; in many ways, she was breaking new ground. It took six years of bureaucratic wrangling before, in 1985, the papers came through. The second child was easier. The third, easier still. By 1990, Louise's family had grown to fourteen.

The lesson learned in Africa had stayed with her. Louise had ensured each child was legally adopted, giving each and every one of them the kind of security that comes only with having a parent – with being able to say, "Mama, I love you." She had not only seen their special needs through the eyes of a physiotherapist, she had removed the wrapping paper that was "not so good" and had bonded with them, heart to heart. I could sense that security as I watched them at play on the deck.

The little boy in the wagon, dressed in blue coveralls, who was being pulled around by the nun, was introduced to me as Emmanuel. He was gorgeous, with curly brown hair, big brown eyes, and a smile that instantly stole your heart. To me, he looked as fit as rain.

"He breaks easily," Louise said. "You know?"

"How do you mean, breaks?" I asked.

"His bones are . . . how do you say that . . . brittle?"

"Yes. Brittle. His bones break?"

"Yes. Generally, he broke his legs . . . just turning in the bed. He was put in a . . . I think you call it a cast . . . and after four weeks in the cast, he broke again – *in* the cast. You see, he's very fragile."

He was such a beautiful little boy. I wondered how anyone could possibly have given him up for adoption. In the hours to come, I would learn a lot about each of Louise's children.

Several of them came to her directly from parents who just couldn't handle them. I thought that was very sad. Louise certainly knew how to handle them. Why, she could handle *fourteen* at a time!

Some came to her from institutions – like Cathy, a pretty blonde girl who was confined to a wheelchair.

"Cathy is nine years old," Louise told me. "And she is blind. She spent one whole year at a very good hospital in Quebec . . . and . . . uh . . . they never did see in that year, she was blind."

"That's incredible!" I said. "You mean, they missed it?"

"Yes. She has cerebral . . . uh . . . palsy, I think you call that . . . and they only see that. They don't see she's blind."

I was grateful Cathy was in Louise's care. Cathy was lucky.

By noontime, I had learned a lot about Maman Louise. I knew before setting foot in her world that I was going to meet a woman of faith. However, I was surprised to discover how great her faith really was. When she found the farm she now lives on, back in 1988, there was no way she could afford it. All she knew was that this was where she wanted to raise her loved ones. So, she prayed, for her children's sake, that she would find a way to live here, and one day, several months after she began praying, a friend, out of the blue, gave her enough for a down payment to buy the place.

"Now, is this place paid for yet?" I asked.

"Oh, no. No, not yet," she said with a smile. "It costs a lot of money."

"So you have a mortgage every month?"

"Yes."

"Do you have a regular income to pay for this house? I mean, do you have a way to make sure you can pay the mortgage each month?"

"No," she replied, with a slight shrug of the shoulders.

"Is this one month to the next?"

"Yes, yes," she said, nodding her head.

"You say that so calmly," I exclaimed.

Louise simply smiled and laughed gently. Faith would see to the mortgage, just as it had in all the years since the down payment. Money has always found its way to her door – money enough to pay the mortgage and money enough to care for the children. Donations have come to her from everywhere, from the natural parents of the children to people who simply learned of Louise's sacrifice and were moved to help. One of the biggest

gifts she ever received was a thirty-foot, or nine-metre, bus, complete with dual wheels, big rectangular viewing windows, and
a hydraulic wheelchair lift. It was donated, free of charge, by a
Montreal charity organization. They had heard about this wonderful woman from St-Anselme, and, when they were informed
she'd parted with her old van and was in dire need of a means to
take her children on outings away from the farm, they delivered,
and how! In less than three days, Louise went from praying for a
way, to driving away in a brand-new sixty-thousand-dollar
machine! Little wonder she has faith.

Since then, Louise and her children have travelled to Prince
Edward Island in the east and and as far west as Alberta. They
often go for day trips; sometimes, they camp out overnight. Put
yourself in her shoes for a moment, and think of the energy that
would take.

Inside the farmhouse, cameraman André Villeneuve began
shooting as lunch was served to the Brissette children. There were
actually three people assisting Louise around the house now: the
two resident nuns and a lay person who came daily from the
village to help out.

The house was even larger inside than it looked from the
outside. Louise had converted the garage into a large playroom,
with several playpens, a common television area, and lots of
carpet for all to play on.

The dining area, off the kitchen, was also quite spacious. On
the wall were paintings of hearts and loving salutations to
"Maman." There were two big tables set apart from one another,
where the children gathered round, some in wheelchairs, some
strapped in high chairs. A couple of the more able children were
helping a brother or sister to eat. Seven-year-old Véronique
helped feed one of the two-year-old Down-syndrome kids that
Louise had adopted by that time, all the while chatting away to
beat the band. Another child hugged his sister. Louise spoon-fed

one of the youngest, at the same time talking to all around the table, cooing at one, praising another. Several of the children were singing "Frère Jacques."

"*Chante pour moi, Tania,* sing for me, Tania," she would say. And when Tania, unable to sing, yelled out her version of the song, Louise would applaud her effort with a hearty, "Bravo, Tania! Bravo!"

The activity in the room reminded me of the large gatherings my wife and I hold at Christmas in our home – only, in this house, the large gatherings round the table happen three times daily, year-round! Providing for fourteen children with special needs meant putting in a very long day, every day. But no one complained.

"We can work twenty hours a day," Louise said. "And it's not difficult. It's just . . . fun. Whether it is to change a diaper, to give something to eat . . . or anything! It's interesting, because there is so much love."

Louise told me a typical day began at six in the morning. Three of the children were out of the house by eight and on their way by school bus to regular school in St-Anselme. Then, the remaining eleven children had breakfast and morning baths, followed by playtime and therapy. Lunch was followed with afternoon naps and more playtime. Because all of the children who stayed at home were in diapers, they received baths again in the afternoon. Twice a week, their daily routine also included school – not in St-Anselme, but on the property, in a building across from the farmhouse. Three teachers, trained to educate children with special needs, travelled out from Quebec City, and to Louise their visitations were a godsend. The teachers came the day we were there, and it didn't take long to see why she felt that way. They were wonderful with her kids.

We spent the latter part of the afternoon with Louise and her children at a special Mass for kids at the church in St-Anselme. Louise and members of the congregation gave thanks to God in song, holding hands with each other, and with the children who were lined up in their wheelchairs in the aisle. Louise, a deeply religious woman, stood with her eyes closed, swaying to and fro, lips in a tiny smile, completely free from stress, at peace with the world.

By the time supper concluded that evening, we were in complete awe of this tireless, petite woman, and the unending stream of love that poured from her heart. I have met many people over the years who are full of energy and boundless creativity, but precious few like Louise, who has an unlimited quantity of pure, selfless love. Watching her prepare her children for bed was one of the most heartwarming scenes I have ever been privy to. In the laundry room, on top of the washer and dryer, the little boy with the tousled blond hair, hands bent, and body wracked with spasms, had his diaper changed. All the while, Louise cuddled and kissed him, filling him with a feeling of well-being. Then she changed another little one on a comforter spread out on the carpet in the playroom – again with cooing affection and warm embraces.

In one bedroom, three white cribs, a metre apart, sat in a row. There were clean, fluffy comforters for all, and a gaily painted border of animals encircled the room. The little guy with the tousled hair was lifted over the rail of one crib and cuddled down between the pink and blue blankets. A kiss goodnight, a "*bonne nuit*," and Louise was off again, only to return moments later with another. Another kiss and hug, another "*bonne nuit*," two more kisses for good measure, before the child was placed in her crib for the night.

When Emmanuel entered the room in her arms, there was a little extra tenderness evident in Louise's movement – sweet Emmanuel, the one who "broke" so easily. En route to the crib, he received no fewer than three goodnight kisses. She gave him his bottle and set in motion the butterfly carousel that hung, suspended, above his head.

"*Bonne nuit, chérie. Je t'aime.*"

We caught it all on tape. It was so very touching.

I have thought of Louise often since our visit that spring day several years ago. She stands in my memory as a shining light, a beacon of kindness. I am filled with warmth when I think of her children and how fortunate they are, not only to have found Louise, but to have found one of the best "mamans" in the world to help them travel through life.

When I returned home to my farm in Ontario, I sat and composed a song for this wonderful woman and her children. Sometimes, I sing a portion of that song when they cross my mind.

It's time again to say, bonne nuit,
I love you and you love me.
It's time to lay you down to sleep,
Bonne nuit.
There are gifts that have no ribbon;
They may come in tattered paper;
But there's no greater gift to treasure
Than a child.

Tale of Two Charlies

Love is a powerful thing. It knows no bounds. We don't usually direct the course it follows; love directs us. When love enters our lives and beckons us to follow, we usually do. I guess that's how love stories are born.

Now, I just happen to really enjoy a good love story. Maybe it has something to do with the fact I'm six-foot-four and easy prey for the old "bigger they are, harder they fall" syndrome. My heartstrings are very easy to play. A few short weeks after first meeting my wife, Leanne, those little left ventricular strings (my harpsichord aorta) helped me compose "Song in My Heart," a five-verse outpouring of emotion that Leanne, happily, still enjoys hearing on occasion. I suspect the song played at least a minor role in bringing our hearts together. We were married a year after it was composed, and it was the song that filled the small Catholic church in Corkery, Ontario, for Leanne's wedding march.

But, over the years, many "On the Road Again" stories put songs in my heart as well. They didn't necessarily have to rival *Gone with the Wind* or *Love Story* – all they had to do was start a tune in my heart. Well, here are two love stories that did just that. They are, to say the least, different.

The first story is about a woman by the name of Phyllis Olson, who lives in Salmon Arm, British Columbia, a small community in the Shuswap region, just north of the Okanagan Valley, about a hundred and twenty kilometres east of Kamloops. Phyllis is a petite woman in her late forties. Up until fifteen years ago, her life was filled with pain and turmoil. She was an alcoholic, and unable to hold down any kind of regular job. She was in and out of jail. She spent most of her life looking for love in all the wrong places.

One day, love stepped in and beckoned her to follow. She met a tall, handsome fellow with a rather common name – Charlie. And, as if that wasn't common enough, his full name was Charlie Brown. Common or not, Charlie and the power of love were about to change Phyllis Olson's life forever.

The second love story takes us eight hundred kilometres further west, to the tiny Pacific community of Kyuquot, British Columbia, located in Kyuquot Sound on the northwest coastline of Vancouver Island. It's kind of an eternal-triangle story. It involves a stocky, bearded man by the name of Esko Kayra, his wife, Lucy, and a female boarder they took in who also had the common name – though unusual for a lady – of Charlie.

Actually, everyone called her *Miss* Charlie. And everyone in Esko and Lucy's family, including their three daughters, took an immediate liking to her. Charlie took an immediate liking to them, too, *especially* to Esko. It wasn't long before that liking turned into love, and the relationship between Lucy and Charlie quickly went downhill. Suddenly, they didn't get along any more. Everyone in the community was aware of it. They noticed Esko and Charlie starting to spend a lot of time "chatting" down by the water's edge. They even saw them going for the odd moonlight swim together! But, almost as quickly as the love triangle started, it suddenly appeared to be over. Charlie slipped quietly out of town one night, and everyone figured it was the end of the affair between her and Esko.

But love is a powerful thing. A few months later, Miss Charlie returned to the quiet little harbour village of Kyuquot and her beloved Esko. A few of the locals saw her arrive at the dock and watched as she made her way slowly up the ramp leading to the Kayra household. The moment she pushed open the garden gate at the base of the verandah stairs, they knew Esko and Charlie's love story was far from over. It was just beginning.

Phyllis Olson and her beloved
Charlie Brown / Shagra

JANET P. SMITH

JANET P. SMITH

Now, you may wonder, why do these two particular tales stand out in my mind and live in my heart? After all, there are *millions* of love stories out there. Well, it's because the tale of two Charlies is about love with a difference. The guy Phyllis Olson met, Charlie Brown, isn't just *any* old tall, handsome kind of guy. He's a horse. And Miss Charlie? Well, she's a lot more than just the other woman in Esko Kayra's life. She's a seal – a harbour seal. Esko and Miss Charlie and Phyllis and Charlie Brown all discovered an important thing about love. It has no bounds.

When Phyllis Olson was released from British Columbia's Twin Maples Correction Centre in 1980 after serving time for impaired driving, she swore it was the last time she would spend behind bars. The pretty Alberta native was determined to turn over a new leaf. She had lived on the edge long enough, and she wanted out.

The only reason Phyllis was in British Columbia to begin with was because of her boyfriend, Andy. What a life they had led! In the late 1970s, Andy was on the run from the Alberta authorities. He was classified as an habitual criminal and had served about ten years of a "life indefinite" term in Alberta when he was let out on a day pass. Well, he hadn't gone back that night for lock-up. He and Phyllis had high-tailed it out of town, and he was free as a bird until the law caught up with him near the coast and slapped him back behind bars.

For a while, Phyllis hung around the town of Agassiz, not far from Vancouver and close to the new penitentiary that Andy now called home. But, as you may well imagine, boyfriends, girl-friends, and penitentiaries do not always make for storybook endings, especially when the partner on the outside throws alcohol into the mix. Phyllis was not a happy woman. At night, when she watched the sun sink into the Pacific, her hopes and dreams for a future with Andy *on the outside* sank with it. The only glow on the horizon was the setting sun. It wasn't long before Phyllis would find herself back in jail, usually for impaired driving.

During that last stint behind bars in 1980, Phyllis was let out on a Christmas pass and went to a party in Vancouver. There she met a cowboy who told her about an Arabian stallion that was for sale up near Chilliwack. Phyllis had been carrying a dream around for most of her life of one day owning a horse, and the more she heard about this particular stallion, the more she wanted him.

"He's not been very well looked after, and I imagine two or three hundred would take him," the cowboy told her. "Hell of a horse, though. Hell of a horse."

"What's the horse's name?" she asked the cowboy.

"Charlie Brown," he replied.

Now what kind of name is that to give an Arabian stallion? she thought.

Two weeks later, Phyllis was set free with three hundred dollars in her pocket, earned while doing time, and a heart full of yearning for this horse with the rather unusual name. So, she said goodbye forever to boyfriend Andy and travelled to Chilliwack in search of Charlie Brown.

It's a good thing she did. As it turned out, Phyllis actually rescued the stallion from going to the glue factory by a few lucky hours.

"Oh, he was a mess!" Phyllis recounted. "I walked in and there he was, in this little box stall – this skinny little horse with the big, sad brown eyes. I just fell in love with him right there. I couldn't have walked away and left him."

When Phyllis left that day, she had no money; it had taken everything she had to buy that horse. But it didn't matter. She had just realized the dream of a lifetime.

The horse we met in 1991 when our "On the Road Again" team showed up at Phyllis's house in Salmon Arm was a far cry from the sickly stallion Phyllis bought back in 1980. The horse she introduced us to in her back yard was magnificent – a big, healthy horse, a gorgeous, bay-coloured Arabian, who strode through his paces like he was performing for cameras on the set of *Lawrence of Arabia*. He had a beautiful black mane that flowed gracefully from his muscular, arched neck, and a majestic black tail he carried high in the wind, as all Arabian horses do. He was the picture of health, spinning left, then right, nostrils flaring and snorting, declaring to one and all what a pretty boy he was. Phyllis looked great, too. She hadn't had a drink in over ten years.

"Wow! He's a lot of horse!" I exclaimed.

"Isn't he gorgeous?" she replied, beaming proudly. "He's such a ham."

Phyllis and Charlie Brown's story is a little like the fairy tale "The Frog Prince," in that Charlie Brown emerged as Phyllis's Prince Charming – and a very talented prince, I might add. In fact, it was his talent that brought my crew and me to Salmon Arm in the first place. A few months earlier, in our office in Ottawa, we studied a tape which was sent to us of Phyllis and her remarkable horse appearing on "America's Funniest Home Videos." Charlie was a singing horse! Move over, Francis the Talking Mule! He lip-synced his way through "Old MacDonald Had a Farm" and won ten thousand dollars in the process! Then we watched him mock-croon a ballad on the David Letterman show. The audience loved that performance, too.

When my producer, Janet P. Smith, first returned from Salmon Arm, having completed her survey of the story, she was bubbling over with excitement.

"Wayne, the singing-horse aspect of the story is really just one small part of the overall story. This is a story of looking for love and finding it in a horse!"

"Sounds like you were rather moved by your meeting."

"You're going to love her. What a story! What a life she's lived! And wait till you meet this horse! I've never seen anything like it!"

Well, the horse in the paddock certainly had my attention. I stood there, mesmerized. He was poetry in motion. Phyllis stood looking, too, her eyes filled with loving tears.

"You really *love* this horse, don't you?"

"Oh I do! I owe him my life."

The tears started running down her cheeks. She didn't turn away, though. Instead, she looked straight at me with a big glowing smile.

"These are happy tears, okay?"

"Yes, that certainly is okay," I replied. I, too, had filled up with tears.

"He's part of me," Phyllis continued. "A really big part. Before I met him, nothing went right. It was all alcohol – ever since I can remember, since I was a kid! I ran away from home, and everything that could possibly happen to a person happened to me – I married, divorced, lost my kids, was on the street, spent time in jail. I just seemed to be wandering through life looking for love – until I found my Charlie Brown."

"He had that big an impact on you?"

"Yes," she said, nodding her head while wiping another tear from her cheek. "He's my best friend."

Phyllis led me around to the side of her little bungalow to show me the stable she built.

"See the sign I had made for him?" she said, pointing to the top of the door leading to his stall. "I don't call him Charlie Brown any more. I call him Shagra. I had a man carve that. See? 'Shagra.' That's the name I gave him."

"Well, it's certainly a much nicer name than Charlie Brown," I said, looking up.

"Shagra's way too *beautiful* to be a Charlie Brown," she replied, proudly.

The sign was made of pine. "Shagra" was carved in relief and stained chocolate-brown to stand out against the natural golden hue of the nameplate. It adorned the entranceway to one of the finest-kept stalls I have ever seen. In fact, it looked as clean, if not cleaner, than some of the hotel accommodations I remember suffering through during my early days on the road as a musician.

"You keep treating him like this and he'll forget he's a horse," I quipped.

"He doesn't even think like a horse," Phyllis replied. "He's beyond that. If you treat him like one, he's insulted."

"Did you move here when you bought Charlie . . . I mean, Shagra?"

"Actually, I didn't come to Salmon Arm until 1985. See, after I bought Shagra, I stayed in Chilliwack for a while, because I had no money. I got a job outside Chilliwack and managed to board Shagra at the same time. One day, my Aunt Eileen called me – she lives here – and said she wanted me to come live near her in Salmon Arm. Well, we came, and I lived in a rented trailer for about a year while I boarded Shagra down the road. Then I heard about this place being for sale and bought it in '86."

"I gather you had some money by then."

"Heck, no! I wasn't making very much money. I was only a long-term-care aide for the elderly at Pioneer Lodge. My Aunt Eileen, God love her, gave me most of the down payment to buy this place. I never had enough saved on my own."

"Sounds like a great lady."

"Besides Shagra, she's the best friend I ever had."

"I noticed another sign at the head of the lane as I drove in here this morning. What does it say again?"

"God's Little Acre. That's what I call this spot . . . God's Little Acre."

It was a cute place – actually slightly less than an acre – situated on the outskirts of Salmon Arm. The house was a tiny, white-sided bungalow, with a black-shingled roof. The small barn adjacent to the house and the wood-fenced corral out back were Shagra's domain.

"C'mon in and have a coffee. There's something I want you to see."

Phyllis led me into the kitchen and over to the counter, where she reached up and opened the sliding window above the sink.

"Shagra," she called out. "Come and get your teeth brushed. Come on, Shagra."

Phyllis closed the window and said, "Watch this."

Shagra came trotting over to the window from the far side of the yard. It was exactly horse-head high. Placing his mouth at the edge of the glass pane, Shagra quickly swung his head from left to right, deftly sliding the window over in its track, an action that much resembled someone throwing the carriage of a manual typewriter over to begin a new line of script. Then, Shagra popped his head into the kitchen through the opening and began rapidly raising and lowering his head a few inches, which caused his lips, for lack of a better word, to flap. Phyllis reached in a drawer under the counter by the window and pulled out a white-handled brush, about a foot long, as well as a tube of toothpaste. The brush was actually one of those giant toothbrushes you buy at joke shops. It was the perfect size to use on a horse. Spreading a goodly portion of paste on the well-worn bristles, she raised the brush up to Shagra's mouth and began brushing, first his upper teeth, then the lower.

"That is the darndest thing!" I exclaimed. "He actually lets you do that?"

"He loves it," Phyllis replied. "We do this at least once a day. Don't we, Shagra?"

That being said, Phyllis leaned over the counter and kissed Shagra on his Colgate-smeared lips.

"Good boy, Shagra," she said. "You're a good boy."

But there was something else Shagra did for our television camera that was even more amazing than getting his teeth brushed. Shagra answered the telephone! There was a big ringer on the outside wall of the house and, whenever the phone rang at God's Little Acre, Shagra heard it too, resulting in a race between Phyllis and Shagra to see who would get to answer it first. If the two them were in the corral together, it was Shagra who got to the phone first, because, in order for Phyllis to answer the phone, she had to open and close the corral gate, enter the back door of the house and walk down the hall, and cross the kitchen to get to the phone. All Shagra had to do was trot over to the window, open it, and pick up the phone. And I mean that literally. Shagra's old horse lips were quite talented. He would just reach down and pick the headset off its cradle and place it on the counter like a dog putting a bone down. Then he'd stand and entertain whoever was on the phone by flapping his lips until Phyllis came, an action which, I should add, was quite audible. Pity the poor caller who didn't know of Shagra's penchant for answering telephones and had to figure out what all the "smacking" on the line was about.

Back in Kyuquot Sound, telephones would start ringing off the wall when Miss Charlie showed up in town. It was an annual ritual that residents looked forward to every spring: Charlie coming in from the sea, returning to her summer home in Kyuquot, rejoining her beloved Esko.

"Miss Charlie's back! Saw her in the harbour this morning!" one neighbour exclaimed.

"First thing she did was find the kids down by the wharf," said another. "She was jumping in and out of the water, and the kids were yelling, 'Charlie! Charlie!'"

"Somebody call Esko! Tell him Charlie's back."

Yes, sir! When Miss Charlie returned to Kyuquot in the spring, it was exciting!

The story of Miss Charlie begins over thirty years ago, in 1964, when Charlie's mother was shot by a hunter. As he was cutting open the carcass, out popped Charlie! A few hours later, the orphan pup was placed in the loving hands of the Kayra family, and Esko and Lucy added another member to their clan. Miss Charlie became daughter number four. Lucy immediately started bottle-feeding her and supplemented her diet with big, healthy, daily doses of cod-liver oil. Yummy!

Esko and Charlie exchange loving glances

Esko and Lucy – the "other" woman in Esko's life

"Miss Charlie"

"You really did accept her as a daughter, didn't you, Lucy?" I said, as we pulled up a few chairs to chat.

"Yes, I did. She wasn't one of my smaller babies though. She was *big!* Twenty-one pounds," she chuckled.

One of Lucy and Esko's daughters, Sandy, had joined us on the wharf and remembered what it was like having someone in the house getting more than her fair share of attention.

"Dad spent a lot of time with Charlie, especially during our early years – the formative years!" Sandy recalled with a playful twinkle in her eye. "He sure ignored us," she sighed. "But, we managed to get through it all," she concluded, with a hearty laugh.

In reality, the entire family spent a tremendous amount of time with their new baby. Charlie and the girls took their baths together, played in the front yard together, and swam in the waters of Kyuquot Sound together – after Esko introduced Charlie to the sea. Her first salt-water dip was actually in an enclosed basket, fashioned especially for her and lowered into the water on the end of a rope. She made several "deep-sea dives" before Esko felt comfortable enough to set her free. After all, Charlie didn't *know* she was a seal. She had imprinted with the Kayras, and had bonded deeply with Esko! Going out to sea and making like a seal was the last thing on her mind . . . pass the cod-liver oil, if you please!

"Lucy, what happened between you and Charlie? You helped raise her from a baby, even bottle-fed her, yet she barks at you whenever you go near her now."

"She just doesn't like me any more. She's jealous of me, I guess."

"Yeah," Esko interrupted. "Charlie's jealous of Lucy. She's got that human imprint where she figures she's a human and I'm her mate."

"Where is she now?" I asked. "I'd really like to meet her."

"Well, she was here yesterday," Esko replied. "Let's go down to the dock and see if she's around."

The community of Kyuquot is little more than a cluster of houses ringing the southern shore of the sound. Besides the fish-processing plant with its giant, humming diesel generators, there really isn't much going on. Lucy runs the only guest accommodation in town: a bed-and-breakfast that Malcolm Hamilton, François Pagé, Paul Morisset, and I stayed in during the three days we spent shooting the story of Miss Charlie. There's a general store beneath the bed-and-breakfast, also run by the Kayras, that supplies the community at large with just about everything needed to live in Kyuquot Sound; there is a restaurant, located at the opposite end of the community, which, I must say, serves *mighty* fine food; and there are no fewer than three wharves servicing its seafaring population. One of the wharves doubles as a float-plane base, and several single-engine planes are usually anchored at that one; then there's a huge government wharf sitting on giant nine-metre cedar pylons and extending sixty metres out over the water, with a helicopter pad at the very end, in case a resident needs to get to a hospital in a hurry; and finally there's a small private dock supplying Esko's combination storehouse and workshop – as well as providing a berth for his boats. This is Miss Charlie's favourite hangout.

Esko escorted me down to his wharf, hoping Charlie would be around. She had been back in the community for only several days and was possibly off visiting some of the children around the community.

"Charlie! Charlie!" he called.

"Charlie actually comes when you call her?"

"If she's anywhere within earshot, she usually does, yes. Mind you, she's getting older now, and not quite as predictable as she used to be."

Esko called her name again and stamped his foot lightly on the dock.

"There she is," he said, almost matter-of-factly. "Look . . .

right over there, coming towards us. C'mon, Charlie, come gimme a kiss."

Esko got down on his belly, flat out on the broad cedar planking, with his head extended out over the edge of the dock, gently coaxing Charlie to the surface. I could see her quite clearly in the clean water of the sound, slowly making her way towards us, a picture of effortless motion, reminding me more of a graceful bird gliding through air than a large mass of blubber moving through water.

"Wow! Look at how smoothly she moves," I said.

"C'mon, Charlie," Esko continued. "Come and see me."

Miss Charlie was dark grey to grey-black, with mottled white streaks all over her body.

"Neat colour!" I said. I'd never seen a seal up this close before.

"She's a lot lighter-coloured after she's out of the water for a while. When she dries out, she's almost white. That's the nature of sealskin."

Her front flippers were like little arms, with five long finger-like endings where your elbows would be. Her rear flippers were about the size of the flippers I wear snorkelling, with five flowing toes propelling her along.

Charlie's head broke the surface of the water without so much as a ripple. She eyed the stranger standing beside Esko on the dock for a moment, popped back under the surface, and continued towards us again. I noticed a cute little physical reflex – she would close her eyes, momentarily, during the transition between her watery world and the surface, before popping them open again.

"God, she looks like a cat without ears!" I exclaimed. "Look at those whiskers. Just like a big cat."

Charlie was only a metre away now.

"Gimme a kiss," Esko said, again. Charlie raised her upper torso effortlessly out of the water, and their lips met.

"That's wild! Does Charlie do this often?"

"Oh, yeah. She's very loving. Now, give Wayne a kiss."

"What? Kiss me? She doesn't bite or anything, does she?"

"No, no. She won't bite you. Bring your head down here over the edge of the dock."

Not being one to offend a lady, I recited a very quick Hail Mary quietly to myself, dropped to my belly, gave the sexiest come-on-I-want-you look I was capable of giving without being unfaithful to my wife, and pursed my lips.

"C'mon, Charlie," I whispered, huskily. "Gimme a kiss."

Well, Charlie didn't even *think* about it, not for a single moment. She ignored my voice, my lips, *and* my "look." Esko had set me up for a fall! There I was, not just on my knees to a lady, but on my belly! I was flat out on a dock, head hanging out over the Pacific, grovelling for one little kiss – not from Miss Beautiful, Lisgar Collegiate, 1964, but from Miss Charlie, harbour seal! And without so much as an ounce of concern for my feelings, Charlie closed her lids, dropped beneath the surface, and, with a haughty spin of her plump little body, disappeared beneath the dock. How I *hate* rejection!

"She's gone," I said, somewhat deflated. "Where'd she go?"

"Hard to tell," Esko replied. "She'll be back. She sort of comes and goes now. It's not like the old days."

In the *old* days, when Charlie was a baby, she was inseparable from Esko. She followed him everywhere – up and down the path between the verandah of the house and the dock where Esko kept his boat, along the trail that led to the general store – wherever Esko went, Charlie went. She was just like a dog, heeling behind Esko as he walked, and barking at Lucy whenever she got too close to them. Having no legs didn't impede her progress what-soever. She just "rolly-pollied" along with a tireless, rhythmic, undulating motion. She quickly became part of everyone's life in Kyuquot, the darling of the community.

It wasn't long before Charlie was weaned from the bottle and eating orange sockeye salmon right from Esko's hand. After he introduced her to the sea, she had a ball, swimming along with the fishing boats and playing with the children in the water. Signs were quickly posted throughout the community warning people not to harm their town pet. That first year, Esko even painted Charlie's head white so hunters could distinguish her from any other seals that might wander into the neighbourhood.

But Charlie kept coming home every night for supper. No one had taught her that there was an ocean full of food out there, and that it was time for her to fetch it herself.

"She had to learn that those silver things she saw swimming in the water were fish," Esko recounted. "We had to attach herring to a string and drag them through the water until she caught on. Eventually, she started getting her own supper. But what she enjoyed doing even more was stealing it from the fishermen when their boats came in at night."

"Did the fishermen mind?"

"Hell, no! They loved it when she came around. They'd stand at the stern and hold a big juicy sockeye up for Charlie and swing it above her head, around and around so Charlie would put on a show for them. She'd be half out of the water, going round and round, following that fish like a dog following a bone in your hand."

"Any close calls with hunters or anything, over the years? Did she ever get shot at?"

"No. Not in this harbour, anyway. One time, though, she came into the harbour like a bat out of hell. There was a pod of killer whales on her tail. She may not have known how to eat on her own, but she sure knew when something wanted to eat *her*!"

"How did you feel the first time she left you and went out to sea? Did you know she was going to return?"

"Well, actually, we left her first. Lucy and I were leaving Kyuquot to go winter in Victoria, and Charlie hopped onto the pontoon of the float plane, barking at Lucy and wanting to get in with me. Well, she couldn't come, naturally, and she sure wasn't too happy when we pushed her away. But when we came home in the spring, there was Charlie on the dock waiting for us. After that, I think Charlie started going out on her own. But she's never stopped coming home about this time every year."

That afternoon, I watched Esko and two of his grandchildren play in the water with Charlie – a grandpa, two kids, and a seal, tirelessly chasing each other around in Kyuquot Sound, hugging, laughing, and carrying on. It was quite a sight.

Love tends to make us stand up and pay attention. It reaches out to us in many ways and in many guises. But whatever form it takes, one thing is certain. Love is powerful. Phyllis Olson probably would never have pulled her life out of the spin it was in had she not found love in a horse by the name of Charlie Brown. The power of love turned Charlie into Phyllis Olson's Prince Charming, Shagra. And the people of Kyuquot would certainly have missed a lot had they not witnessed the story of Esko and Miss Charlie – love, in the guise of a common harbour seal. Their community is far richer for having had the opportunity to share in it.

And there you have it. Two love stories I carry around in my heart. A tale of two Charlies. Charlie "Shagra" Brown and Phyllis are still sharing their love with everyone in Salmon Arm. Shagra is now the star of an educational video for children called *Sing and Learn with Shagra*. *Miss* Charlie is now in her fourth decade of annual visits to Kyuquot. She and Esko still meet every spring on that little wharf down by the sea. And, yes, she still barks at Lucy.

Iceberg Ice

~

My first real job, at thirteen, was delivering the *Globe and Mail* in Ottawa's ritzy Rockcliffe Park neighbourhood. I used to get up at five in the morning, fetch the bundle of papers that the route truck had dropped off in front of the Rexall store on Creighton Avenue, do my deliveries, and make it to school by nine. I lived with my parents in a rented row house on McKay Street in New Edinburgh, right next door to Rockcliffe Park and directly across the street from the Governor General's estate, and I had some pretty neat customers: Governor General Georges Vanier, the French Embassy on Sussex Drive, where they always gave me morning salutations *en français*, and Prime Minister John Diefenbaker, who personally gave me a five-dollar tip at Christmas. I recall Mr. Diefenbaker inviting me into the main hall of 24 Sussex, patting me on the head, and telling me always to remember Canada was a great country and I shouldn't be afraid to go out and become whatever I wanted to be. I was really excited about that meeting. It was a special kick-start for a kid who was living in a rented row house.

Often when I made my morning rounds, I would cross paths with a man named Frank, who delivered milk in Rockcliffe Park for Clark Dairy. I'd have the odd word with him if our deliveries coincided, or wave at him from my bike as we passed on the road. One morning, we met up on the verandah of a mutual customer and Frank asked if I had ever considered changing jobs. Would I be interested, he wondered, in working with him as his helper on Saturdays during the school year and full-time during the summer? I accepted the offer – partly because it paid more than my paper route did, and partly because Mr. Diefenbaker had more

Haddon and I, flirting with one of the berg "brothers" in Conception Bay

Haddon Strong with a few "bits and bergs"

or less told me that, if I wanted to try my hand at something in this country of ours, I should simply go for it. Who was I to question the advice of our prime minister?

So, I gave notice to the paper and, starting two weeks later, at five in the morning, instead of going around the corner to the Rexall store, I would bicycle halfway across town to the Clark Dairy plant, just off Somerset Street, and help Frank load the truck with our day's deliveries – three hundred glass bottles of cold, refreshing milk and several cases of butter and eggs. There was also a special duty I had to perform all on my own, something Frank said every "milkman-in-training" did during his apprenticeship. I was put in charge of loading the ice.

After I finished heaving the crates to Frank in the truck, he would have his morning cigar while I went to the ice house in the middle of the loading dock to begin hauling a dozen or more big blocks over to our truck. The ice house held hundreds of blocks, covered in sawdust to keep them from melting, and all the helpers, including me, would be running back and forth to our respective vehicles, hauling one block at a time. After I hosed off the sawdust, I would break the large blocks into smaller pieces with a pick and hammer and place the ice on top of the milk crates to help keep the bottles cool for the day. It was a morning ritual I actually looked forward to. By the time I was done cleaning and chopping, that ice *glistened* on top of our crates. Frank was always very pleased, and often reminded me how important the ice job was; clean ice meant clean bottles left at the doorstep. More importantly though, lots of ice meant cold milk for breakfast and cold milk kept customers happy.

Well, whether this was a con job or not, I took pride in my role of morning iceman, and I always gave Frank the best ice an ambitious teenager could possibly deliver. It was nothing like the stuff we buy today in bags from outdoor freezers at the corner Petro-Can or the whitish cubes our home freezers dispense. The stuff I loaded on board was so clean and tasty you wanted to eat it! And eat it I did.

By summer's end, I had savoured more cool chunks of ice than
most people put in their mouths in a lifetime. When I returned
to school in September, I was not only educated in the work
world, I was a connoisseur of good ice! But, I would not enjoy ice
as much again for another thirty years – not until I met a
Newfoundlander by the name of Haddon Strong. He too was a
connoisseur of good ice, and he wanted to introduce me to what
he claimed was the finest ice in the world – "iceberg" ice!

We first heard about Haddon in a letter sent to our "On the Road
Again" office, suggesting him as a story idea for our show.
Attached to the letter was a copy of an advertisement that had run
in the *St. John's Evening Telegram*: "Genuine Iceberg Ice for sale.
$5 per 16-pound bag. Great for punch-bowls, screech-ins, etc.
Call Haddon Strong. 834-4964. Chamberlains."

The ad certainly got *my* attention. I knew all about ice.

"This is really neat," I exclaimed. "*Iceberg* ice! He actually sells
the stuff?"

"According to this, yes."

"That would be awfully *salty*, wouldn't it?" I queried.

"No. Icebergs are made of *fresh* water," said Ruth Zowdu, one
of our researchers.

"Of course," I replied. "It's the water they're floating in that's
salty."

"Exactly."

"So, how does he get all this ice? Does he just go out in the
ocean with a rope and haul 'em in, or what?"

"Don't know yet," Ruth replied. "We just got the letter. I think
he uses a small boat and just picks up the stuff that breaks off the
iceberg as it travels."

What a great idea! I thought. Imagine, genuine *iceberg* ice in
iced tea, in a nightcap, or in a tall glass of tomato juice. And what
a bargain! Five dollars got you sixteen pounds of the stuff.

"So, are we doing the story?" I asked.

"Well," Ruth said, "if we are, it has to be soon. Apparently, the icebergs in the bay only have a few weeks left before they melt down completely."

"What bay are they in?"

"Conception Bay. The icebergs just floated in this week. I'm waiting for a call to see if this Haddon fellow can tell us when we need to be there to shoot the story."

Less than two weeks later, Haddon Strong and I were speeding away from the community of Chamberlains, Newfoundland, out into the wide expanse of Conception Bay, a magnificent bay on the northeast tip of the Avalon Peninsula. On one side of the bay, you can see the city of St. John's and the towering sea cliffs of Bell Island; on the other side are the communities of Carbonear and Harbour Grace. The bay is shaped like an open lobster claw – but it's a very *big* claw, twenty-five kilometres across and about fifty kilometres long. Every year, Conception Bay manages to entice a few icebergs to interrupt their journey towards the sunny south and come in from the open sea for a little visit, and the icebergs that had entered the bay several days earlier were, according to reports from residents further up the bay, magnificent!

There were two of them, travelling like brothers, heading our way at a pretty good clip; even Haddon was quite surprised at their progress. They were already just a few kilometres north of Bell Island, doing what Arctic icebergs and outlaw cowboys do best – drifting south. What the bergs didn't know, though, was they'd gone up a dead-end street. This was not the highway to the equator. This was a back alley leading to Haddon Strong's freezer!

Haddon's boat was quite small, no more than four metres from bow to stern, but it was fast! We were really barrelling along, and as we rounded the big steep cliffs of Bell Island, the bay opened up before us and I caught my first glimpse of the icebergs. I could just see them off in the distance, jutting a little above the horizon, several kilometres to the north of Bell Island.

"There they are!" Haddon exclaimed. "Looks like two of 'em, all right."

Haddon shoved the throttle to the wall. I felt my brain lobes move to the back of my cranium. He was like a man possessed! We weren't so much in the water as we were airborne! So, this is what iceberg ice does to people, I thought. It makes normal people go like stink in piddly little boats on the open sea! I probably would have felt safer if I'd contracted rabies.

Malcolm Hamilton, my producer, and our "On the Road Again" crew were following us, but in a much bigger boat, a much slower boat, and probably – in my mind at that very moment – a much safer boat. Oh well, I had always wondered what it would be like to run smack-dab into a towering iceberg at ram speed, anyway. And judging from the gleam in Haddon Strong's eyes, this was starting to look like the day I would find out.

A week earlier, I had read with great interest how our Arctic and the western coast of Greenland release around fifteen thousand icebergs from their icy grip every year. Of these, about one thousand "rogues" escape into the Labrador current and head out to open sea, causing great concern every spring for shipping in the Atlantic. It was one such rogue that sank the *Titanic* in 1912, claiming over fifteen hundred lives. Experts estimated that that particular iceberg had been slowly drifting southward from Greenland for two years or more. It was a massive berg. When it struck the *Titanic* it was going at a mere two knots, yet it still drove the big liner to her icy grave. Just two knots! You and I *walk* a lot faster than that.

The icebergs that were trapped in the bay ahead of us had almost made it past Newfoundland. They had resisted the beckoning arms of all the other bays as they travelled south; Notre Dame Bay, Bonavista, even Trinity Bay had failed to catch them.

On average, only about three hundred and seventy-five icebergs a year actually make it as far south as Newfoundland, and the majority of those end up in the bays, much to the delight of the local residents, who get to enjoy a little of the Arctic's bounty every spring. And let's face it, Newfoundland is a good place for a berg to finish its journey. After all, they get to die a half-hour later here than they would anywhere else!

Mind you, over the years the odd berg has managed to make it around the Avalon Peninsula into the Gulf Stream, where, depending on the combination of wind and currents at work, they were able to travel as far south as Bermuda or as far east as Ireland! The Irish monk St. Brendan encountered one such berg in his travels. He referred to it in his journal as a "floating crystal castle on the high seas." Well, we were about to encounter two icebergs from the frigid north that decided to end their days as "crystal castles" in Conception Bay. They were pretty wise old bergs. Conception Bay was Haddon Strong's bay, and Haddon was about to help little bits and pieces of the brother bergs stay around even longer by filling a few neighbourhood freezers. Now, that's Newfoundland hospitality for you. They even make icebergs feel at home!

This annual ice harvest was nothing out of the ordinary for Haddon. The Strong family had collected iceberg ice for their own use for years, either to make ice cream or simply to give a glass of rum that extra-special zing. Conception Bay was their little "Iceberg Alley."

"This ice is nothing like that artificial stuff," he shouted, over the roar of motor, wind, and waves. "This stuff has fizz!"

"I still can't believe this is happening!" I replied, very excited about it all. "I've never seen a real iceberg up close – just pictures of them in magazines or movies. I've heard some of them are five thousand years old."

"Most of them are a lot older than that," Haddon replied. "Some are fifteen, even twenty thousand years old, absolutely pure and pollution-free!"

"Just how big are the ones we're going out to see?" I asked.

Haddon's gaze was fixed on the bergs in the distance. His jaw had a decidedly determined jut to it. His fingers clenched the steering wheel firmly, as if squeezing it hard would get us there faster. What bothered me most, though, were his glasses. Not that I don't like glasses. It's just that Haddon's spectacles were dripping with seawater from the spray coming off our hull. He couldn't see where he was going! On top of that, they were the type that darkened when exposed to bright light. Call it my imagination or fear of meeting my Maker in the depths of Conception Bay, but, as I looked at Haddon trying to *look out* for us, I swear his specs turned blacker than coal. Good Lord! I thought to myself. He's drivin' her stone-blind! I bet we were lucky to miss Bell Island!

"Well now," he finally responded, breaking into my panic-stricken imaginings. "Let me think a minute here . . . You want to know how big those bergs are?"

"Yes. I read that some icebergs can be almost as tall as the Peace Tower in Ottawa."

"You don't say."

Haddon's head was now cocked high into the wind. I guess it was an effort to clear his lenses. His eyes were peering through a little clear spot near the bottom.

"The Peace Tower, eh?"

His left hand was scratching his beard as if searching through his whiskers for the answer to my question. He turned, glasses black as black could be, dripping with sea spray, and gave me his best shot.

"Probably the size of a building, maybe a three-storey apartment. How high is the Peace Tower?"

"I think it's about three hundred and eighty feet."

"What's that in metric?"

"I haven't a clue."

"Well, I've seen 'em a lot *wider* than that, the size of a football field and bigger! You could land a plane on some of them. But most of the bergs that drift in here are starting to run out of steam. I usually get 'em just before they sweeten the bay."

"Well, Haddon, a three-storey apartment building still seems an awfully decent size to me. How far out are they, anyway? They look fairly close."

"They're out there a good piece. I would say . . . four, maybe six miles or more."

Haddon was *standing* in the boat now! One hand was on the wheel and one hand was manhandling his glasses, trying to rub the water off on the sleeve of his jacket. I was starting to do the Stations of the Cross. Here I was, out in the middle of the ocean in a four-metre skiff, my skipper, blind as a bat, glasses in hand, our little boat, pounding against the incoming swells, miraculously still going in a straight line.

"Six miles!" I exclaimed. "But they look so much closer than that."

"That's 'cause they're so big."

I wondered how much more pounding the little powerboat was capable of taking. Six miles! That's ten kilometres! We'd only just left the harbour.

In spite of my ride being a little on the wild side, I knew I was in capable hands. This wasn't Haddon's first iceberg expedition, and I was certainly not about to suggest it might be his last. Besides, once we got two kilometres or so out from the harbour, I settled down quite a bit. (Mind you, the fact the sea became a lot smoother may have had something to do with it. Or maybe it was because Haddon managed to clean his glasses and was able to see again.)

All kidding aside, if you ever decide to go out in a small boat to play with icebergs, it's best done with someone like Haddon, someone who has experience doing it. You have to keep a healthy distance from the really big bergs and always bear in mind that the ice mass under the water is a lot larger than what you see on the surface.

On the way out to our twin-brother bergs, Haddon told me how some of the real big babies can split in half and roll over right in front of you – or on top of you, if you foolishly get too close. Not too many people have actually seen hundreds of tons of ice go topsy-turvy, but those who have gain a healthy respect for icebergs.

"Did you ever see a berg split in half, Haddon?"

"Yes, I did once. It was a really big berg. I just had to have a chunk or two of that one. I was maybe a hundred yards away from it when, all of a sudden, I heard this crack, like a big explosion, and the whole thing split down the middle. It was like somebody had smacked it with a giant axe! There were chunks floating everywhere when that one settled down. I loaded my boat full that day. Filled my deep freeze at home, my neighbour's freezer, and seven or eight coolers my friends owned."

"What does iceberg ice taste like? Can you describe it?"

"Like no ice on the face of the earth! Can't stand that store-bought stuff. It's white, cloudy-like, nothing like what you're gonna see. Now, hopefully, we'll find a few growlers – that's a piece about the size of a floating grand piano, baby bergs, I call 'em. We can chop chunks off of them real easy."

"Baby bergs. Then what's a 'bergy bit'? I think I read about those last week before I came out here."

"A 'bit' is a berg about the size of a house," Haddon replied.

I started to laugh. It was getting confusing. Baby bergs and bergy bits, and piano-sized growlers – it was a whole new language!

"Are you making any money selling your ice?" I asked him.

"No, no. I don't do it for the money. It's just a great way to spend a day. As long as I make enough money to cover my expenses and put a little gas in my boat, I'm happy."

We'd been motoring along for a good twenty minutes by now, and the icebergs were really starting to take shape.

"Wayne, when we get out there, you can take the fishing net, there under the bow of the boat, and you'll be able to scoop up little pans of ice – 'pans' is what we call them. There should be lots of 'em bobbing in the water. Kinda hard to see at first, but once you get on to it, it's just like netting fish. I think I heard your producer, Malcolm, say he wants lots of pictures of that kind of thing while we're out here. Is that right?"

"Yes, sir. And if it's not too dangerous, he'd like us to circle the bergs when the camera's rolling. What do you think? Will we be able to do that?"

"I imagine. Yes, we can do that."

Seeing an iceberg up close for the first time in your life is quite an experience. As we approached our two bergs, Haddon slowed to a putter. The biggest berg was about a hundred metres in front of us. We continued slowly towards it. Then, about twenty-five metres away from the big guy, Haddon cut the motor completely, letting me sit there in silent awe for a couple of minutes.

"My God!" I said, almost in a whisper. "Look at these things! You call these small? They're huge!"

St. Brendan's description was a good one. They truly were "floating crystal castles." As we sat bobbing on the waves, time took on a different perspective. These towering monoliths of snow and ice didn't just happen overnight; they were thousands and thousands of years old! Where did they come from? I wondered. Greenland? Baffin Island? There is almost a sense of life here, I thought to myself. Nothing this beautiful is without soul.

By now we were pretty well right in the middle of Conception Bay. The waves out here were big and lazy, coming from the north. Swell after swell gently caressed our visitors, and the two bergs, spaced about two hundred metres apart, responded in graceful rhythm to the lapping of the waves by swaying majestically, ever so slowly, to and fro, to and fro. As they did so, their glacial-blue undersides lifted out of the water and danced in the sunlight.

"Haddon, did you know that, if you were able to find a way to haul five or six of these babies straight south to Miami, they could supply fresh water to the millions of people who live there for well over a month?"

"Now who's been feedin' you that?"

"I read it last week. And not just drinking water, either."

"Showers and everything?"

"Yep. Everything they could possibly need."

"They'd buy this stuff?"

"Maybe not right at this very moment. But, when you think a few years down the road . . ."

"Well, they're running out of trees pretty quickly, just like we're running out of fish. So someday you figure they might want our water?"

"Who knows? That's one thing we have lots of."

"I should look into that! We do have the bergs, don't we? All we need now is the technology! Hell, maybe someday this'll be Newfoundland's biggest resource, even bigger than all that oil they're promising to get outta the Hibernia oilfields," he said, referring to the giant project under development off the coast of Newfoundland.

"How's that deal moving along?" I asked.

"*Millions* over budget, and, so far, not a drop of oil, sir!"

"Well, you could certainly haul a few bergs south for a heck of a lot less than that," I said. "And very little overhead!"

"Why sure, our only expense would be rope, crew, and fuel. Imagine getting cold, hard cash for a berg. Wouldn't that just frost a few people!"

We had a good laugh at that thought.

When the boat carrying the crew arrived, I knew from the look on their faces that they, too, felt a sense of awe in the presence of our northern visitors. We sat a few oar lengths apart, gazing at the two icebergs, continuing to drink in the moment.

Keith Whelan, our Newfoundland cameraman, had witnessed many such iceberg scenes before.

"Hey, Keith," I called out, "it's like they've come here to die."

"Proper thing," Keith replied. "Couldn't think of a better place to die, myself, than Newfoundland."

"Do you hear them squeaking when they move?" I asked. "Listen. They squeak. This one even groans!"

"You would too if you were that old!" exclaimed Haddon with a great laugh.

Malcolm was champing at the bit to get started.

"Maybe we should start rolling," he said. "We have great light right now on those icebergs."

Well, the bergs weren't exactly getting bigger with each passing minute, so we fired up our engines and got to work.

We had a great day of shooting. Even the Newfoundland weather was on our side; we had lots of sunshine, which was a real treat, and very little wind, which was unusual. You just don't get a lot of still air in the middle of Conception Bay.

We played with the berg brothers for several hours, circling around them in our little boat and picking up the pans Haddon had referred to with the fishing net we had on board. It took a little getting used to. Because of all the bobbing on the water, I missed on my first two attempts to net a pan. My third pass was on the money. Haddon pulled our little skiff right up alongside a glistening chunk of ice about the size of a big lake trout. I hauled it aboard with all the zest and zeal of a fisherman landing a big trout, too.

"Wow! Look at this one. Must be thirty pounds or more. What a beauty!"

It *was* beautiful-looking ice! When Haddon pulled out the hammer to break a piece off for me to eat, my taste buds went into overdrive. After all, this wasn't *ordinary* ice I was about to put in my mouth. This was crystal-clear, pollution-free, *iceberg* ice! This was a very special experience. I had waited thirty years for this moment – the berg, twenty thousand! I closed my eyes and slipped the cold morsel of iceberg into my mouth.

Clark Dairy had nothing on this stuff. Their ice came from an ice house on Somerset Street; this ice came from the great ice house north of the sixtieth parallel. Clark Dairy's ice was made of city water; this was made from rain that fell eons and eons ago, long before there were was anyone on this continent. I felt that I was tasting time itself.

"Un-be-lievable! This is absolutely un-be-lievable!" I uttered.

Haddon sat there smiling, sucking on his own piece of ice, knowing full well how much I was enjoying that moment.

"Now, that's *ice!*" he said.

I didn't bother to answer. I simply nodded my head. The look on my face said it all.

We had a quiet run back to Chamberlains. The setting sun brought a very calm sea, and Haddon, having had his iceberg fix, seemed quietened down now as well. I watched the two brother bergs fading in the distance for the longest time. I knew I would never set eyes on them again, and that if I wanted an iceberg fix of my own I would have to raid Mr. Strong's freezer at a later date.

Turning my attention to Haddon, I noticed he was very deep in thought. I knew exactly what was going on in his mind. He was thinking about the conversation we had had earlier and was dreaming up another advertisement to place in the newspaper – a *Miami* paper.

I imagine it probably read something like this: "Haddon Strong, Newfoundland, Canada. International agent for genuine iceberg ice. Why not let us look after all your water needs? Call (709) 834-4964. Free delivery."

Well, maybe someday, Haddon. Maybe someday.

Mile-Long Hill

Probably the most important thing about travelling on the road is ensuring adequate overnight accommodations. Travel is inherently tiring, and a good night's sleep is essential. Getting it, however, is another thing. Since I live on a farm, I have become accustomed to a pretty silent sleep environment. We don't live on a busy road, and our dog, for the most part, guards the grounds quietly. Rottweilers are like that. If the house creaks or groans, as it is prone to do on a very cold night, I hear it. Should there be a loose piece of tin on the roof doing a Gene Kelly tap dance in the wind during the night, a ladder goes up the side of the house the next day and we nail Gene's shoes into retirement. If Leanne has a restless night, tossing and turning, I notice every twist and turn she makes, all night long. In a nutshell, I am a light sleeper.

More than once, away from home, I have faced a long day of shooting after having lain awake the entire night. One night, in northern Ontario, the man on whom we were doing a story decided it was time for he and his uncle to have a lengthy argument outside my motel-room window. It was the first year of our national show, and I was far too polite to open my door and say anything. I spent the night trying to use my pillows as ear plugs. It didn't work.

Another time, in Port aux Basques, Newfoundland, I was staying at the CN hotel. There was a heck of a mild spell that night, and a lot of snow was melting on the roof. I didn't hear it at first, but once I was all snuggled away for the night, I began to notice an incessant drip hitting a piece of metal outside my window. The more I noticed, the louder it got. By three in the morning I was convinced someone was out there with a hammer, hellbent on ruining my day. I changed rooms at about four-thirty. Later, when I was checking out, I commented to the clerk about room 448, explaining how unbearable the noise had been outside my window that night.

"Yes!" she said cheerfully. "We get a lot of complaints about that room. Especially when it rains!"

I'm sure you can appreciate that, with years of travel under my belt, I have developed a kind of sixth sense when it comes to assessing the merits of motels and hotels. I can sense trouble the minute I drive into the parking lot. For instance, if there is a lounge attached to the Weary Travellers Inn, with two hundred cars parked outside, you know you're not staying if they haven't any remaining rooms at the *other* end.

My standard check-in drill now goes something like this: "Hello. How are you? Rostad. R-o-s-t-a-d. Am-Ex guaranteed. Nonsmoking, please."

I think what *that* does is let them know this is not your first night away from home. In my mind, it's important that they *know* they're dealing with a seasoned traveller. If they haven't raised their head by now, this next statement makes them start thinking about it: "If you don't mind, no convention or party floors, please, away from the ice and Coke machines, down the hall from the elevator, and preferably an end room."

I love the silence after that volley is delivered. Usually, they stop looking at the "standard" check-in procedural list and turn to what I am sure is called the "problematic guest" list. Clients who end up on that list get bulletproof rooms – usually the ones at the very end of the hall, with double doors and televisions that work.

Most clerks don't seem to mind serving someone who knows exactly what they want, but there's always the odd one who doesn't appreciate being pushed to the limit. They usually hand you the key with a firm hand and frozen smile. "Here we are, Mr. Rostad. There's a convention on the ninth floor; you're on the fifteenth. It's a nonsmoking floor. You're in room 1536, well down the hall from the elevator, the ice and Coke machines, and planet earth. Have a nice night."

Some people just have no sense of humour.

I hate being such a picky check-in. It's just that I've learned you can't be careful enough. I guess that's why I knew something was wrong the night we started up the big hill just outside Baie St-Paul, Quebec. The motel was, to quote the man walking his dog in town that night, "Just at the top of the hill as you leave town. You can't miss it, all newly renovated, with lots of orange lights."

"Look at the size of this hill!" said our producer, Jonathan Craven. "That must be the motel, way up there on the right."

We were staying in Baie St-Paul overnight so we could catch the early-morning ferry to Ile-aux-Coudres, a small island less than a kilometre off the north shore of the St. Lawrence. We had just finished doing a story on Gertrude Madore, the first licensed fisherwoman in Quebec. She lives in Kamouraska, on the south shore, and makes her living fishing eels from the great river and shipping them to European markets. When we left Gertrude, with our stomachs full of crackers and smoked eel, we took the Rivière du Loup ferry across the mighty Fleuve St-Laurent to Tadoussac, on the opposite shore, and travelled down to the town of Baie St-Paul, halfway between Tadoussac and Montreal. In the morning I would meet Gilles Moisan, a resident of Ile-aux-Coudres who plays saxophone with the Montreal Symphony Orchestra. Gilles travels all over the world with the orchestra. Of equal interest to us, though, was Gilles's obsession with collecting bicycles. He had scores of them from around the globe in his collection, renting many of them out to visitors on the island. I would be riding several of them in the morning.

As we started up the hill leading out of Baie St-Paul, I noticed a highway sign printed in French. I know just enough French to be dangerous. Loosely translated, the sign read, "Trucks should prepare to use lower gears." That's when my sixth sense went into *high* gear. We had a problem here.

We hadn't gone even one-third of the way up the hill when I felt the transmission of our rental van automatically shift down out of overdrive.

"We're pretty heavily loaded," said our cameraman, Gilles Guttadauria. He was driving this leg of our trip. "Normally, Wayne, we don't have you with us. I hope we can make the hill."

"Cute, Gilles, cute!" As if two hundred and forty-five pounds, or one hundred and eleven kilos, and a little luggage made that big a difference. Actually, considering our mini-van was already carrying Gilles, Jonathan, and François Pagé, our audio man – *plus* all our equipment and luggage – I probably made a significant difference. Normally, one person rides with me in my rental vehicle to share the load when we travel, but the rental office in Baie St-Paul had closed by the time we arrived, and I wouldn't be picking a car up until morning.

"This is a truck route," I said apprehensively. "Jon, did anyone check this motel out before booking it? Do they have rooms at the back, facing away from the highway?"

"I don't know. I think our travel people checked everything out for us. Don't worry, I'm sure it'll be fine!"

"That's easy for you to say, Jonathan," said François. "You sleep like a log! I think we –"

"Jon," I interrupted, "I'll never be able to sleep in that motel. Never! We're talking major truck route here!"

The mini-van had now slipped down into second gear. We were only halfway up the hill.

"We can't do anything about it anyway," Jonathan explained. "Am-Ex guaranteed reservation on our cards. Even if we could get out of it, how do we know there's even a place with vacancies? We need four rooms, and it's eight o'clock. Our cancellation deadline was six o'clock. We're too late."

"I can't believe this hill," I said again. "A truck route! I'm gonna be a wreck in the morning."

The motel at the top of the mile-long hill really looked as if it didn't belong there. There wasn't a lot of room between the highway and the side of the mountain that rose seventy metres behind and above the motel. The two-storey building seemed to be attached with Velcro to the cliff face. It had twenty rooms, ten on the bottom and ten stacked on top, and they all faced the highway. Aargghh . . .

Our van was in a lather as we pulled into the small lot of the motel. When Gilles turned off the ignition, the little four-cylinder engine gratefully shuddered to a stop.

"It'll never start again," someone muttered.

Down below was a grand view of the bay. We were probably high enough to see Nova Scotia.

"I can't stay here," I said. I was starting to break out in a cold sweat. "Do you believe this? Every room faces the highway! Jon, there has to be somewhere else to stay."

"This place is supposed to have a good rating. We'll be fine."

"Let's go in and talk to the people at the desk," Gilles said. "Maybe they have super soundproofing in the rooms or something. Maybe we're making a mountain out of a molehill."

Another eternal optimist! My argument was quickly losing ground. No one was listening to me.

As we climbed out of the van, I noticed traffic way down below, rounding the curve out of Baie St-Paul. No fewer than two diesel-spewing eighteen-wheelers had started their assault on the mile-long hill.

"There's two of them starting up the hill there now! Not one – two! Is there no way out of this?"

"Tell you what we'll do," said Jonathan. "We'll start checking in, and if the noise is real bad when they go by, we'll address that question."

My sixth sense already knew the answer to that one. My father was a trucker. For seventeen years, he drove for Taggart Transport out of Ottawa. When I was a teenager, I went with him on many overnight trips to Toronto and back. I knew all about big rigs *and* big hills. I remember the heavy loads my dad hauled, twenty-five tons or more, and how frequently he had to downshift his big dual-range transmission as we climbed even moderate hills. In the dead of night, a heavy-pulling rig going up an incline could be heard for miles! This check-in, I knew, was pointless!

As we started to climb the stairs leading to the lobby office, I could hear one of the big rigs beginning to gear down. The resonating blat of its twin-exhaust stacks signalled the first of many eye-opening, lift-you-from-the-mattress downshifts. He was now in eleventh gear. One mile and ten gears to go . . . times two.

The man behind the counter was a young fellow, about twenty-five, who seemed very happy to see us. At the back of the room, there was another man installing drywall.

"Ah, yes. You have arrived then," said the man at the counter. "You must not mind the dust here. The *chambres* are very clean. *Nouveau!* Come, sign *ici*, please."

There were no other cars in the lot. We seemed to be the only customers checking in that night. As Jonathan reached for a pen on the counter, I heard another transmission shift – and this time, the trucks shifted in harmony. Dual shifts, four blatting exhaust stacks, and nine gears to go.

"Ah, Jonathan, listen to that sweet sound. Reminds me of the trips I used to take with my father on his big rig when I was a kid. Before you sign that, maybe we should ask how many trucks pass through here overnight. What do you think?"

"I didn't really hear anything."

"Then just listen for a moment," I suggested, a sweet smile crossing my face.

Another series of blats heralded another downshift of the two rigs. I guessed they were about one-third of the way up the hill by now.

"Oh, *that* noise!" Jonathan acknowledged.

"Yes, *that* noise," I replied, still maintaining my sugar-coated smile. "Tell me, *monsieur*," I said, shifting my attention to the man behind the counter, "is this the main highway that all the trucking companies use overnight?"

"*Pardon?*"

"*Les camions,*" I continued, "*et le grand chemin – l'autoroute –* do the trucks go all night . . . *toute la nuit?*"

"*Non, non.* Just a couple of times," he responded. Just as he did, both trucks punctuated his statement with twin blats. Half a mile, and seven!

"A couple of times?" I needed to be sure. "*Deux? Deux seulement?*"

"Well, maybe five or six times. But you get used to it very fast. Beside that, she is *très tranquil* – how you say? – quiet." Another blat, longer and louder than the others. Six to go.

By now, Gilles and François were paying a good deal of attention to the sound of the big rigs. They heard the same comment I heard: *You get used to it very fast.* What did he really mean by that? You get used to it over a period of a week? a month? twelve years? I noticed Gilles and François had filled everything out on their check-in cards, but had stopped short of signing them. They were too busy listening to the roar beginning to resonate in the lobby as the two trucks reached the quarter-mile pole and shifted down to fifth. Even Jonathan was paying attention.

"*Monsieur,*" I said again to the man behind the counter. "This noise will never allow us to sleep tonight. Would you be offended if we asked you to allow us to check out?"

"*Pardon?*" the clerk replied, raising his voice to compensate for the sound of the blatting exhaust stacks. The oak-plank flooring under the heel of my left cowboy boot began to vibrate. I had visions of furniture moving across floors in the little motel rooms!

Gilles and François could remain silent no longer. They were converts by now. The trucks were no more than a few trailer lengths from the front door, their engines roaring mightily to reach the crest of the hill. I didn't have to push my point any further. It didn't matter any more whether we were "Am-Ex guaranteed" or not. We would *not* be staying at this motel tonight, even if it meant buying our way out!

After we left the motel, we drove back down the hill and found a beautiful four-star inn, well off the beaten path, several kilometres from Baie St-Paul. Not only did they have four rooms available, they offered us an off-season rate that included a seven-course meal we could order until ten that evening.

The clerk reached for my card.

"Your name, please?"

"Rostad. R-o-s-t-a-d. I'll take any room, any floor. I even like conventions."

The Chignic Incident

❧

I have rather large feet. Size fourteen, with a fifteen-and-a-half-inch instep. On top of that, I wear cowboy boots. So, when I put my foot in my mouth, I do it big time.

I will never forget one particular incident that happened in 1991 in Newfoundland. "On the Road Again" was doing a profile of a wonderful lady who had grown up in the town of St. Alban's on the Bay d'Espoir. Her name was Minnie White. At seventy-five, she was acknowledged to be one of the finest players ever of the button accordion. To accommodate our shooting schedule, a Sunday concert starring Minnie White had been arranged at the only club left in the Codroy Valley, the Chignic, a well-kept two-storey building beside the Molly Chignic Brook, which boasted rooms and cabins "from $36 up, with a special rate for truckers."

Minnie had played in the region many times before. The valley, situated on the southwestern tip of Newfoundland, was her home base; she lived with her husband in Tompkins, a small community just down the road from the Chignic. She used to play regularly at another club in the Codroy called the Starlight Lodge, but, when it burned to the ground, Minnie started to concentrate on the road circuit, playing concerts and festivals throughout the Atlantic Provinces. When our show paid her a visit, Minnie had not appeared locally for some time, so her concert that night was rather special. Everybody in the Codroy had shown up for the event – people from Tompkins, Doyles, even a bunch who drove up from Port aux Basques, a good forty-five minutes away. The club was full well over two hours before show-time. All indications were that it would be a night to remember. Little did I know how memorable it would be.

The local house band was a five-piece group who had backed Minnie on many occasions. They wore matching shirts, and each member had his name embroidered on his left shirt pocket. The band leader, who for the sake of telling this story I will have to call "Frank," was also the master of ceremonies for the evening. He was about my age – in his mid-forties – with a moustache that reminded me a bit of the one my brother, Vince, had. Frank and his band had been at the Chignic for three years now – in fact, Frank lived at the lodge. He used to work for Terra Transport as an operations supervisor, responsible for the movement of CN cargo containers between trucks and railcars. When the railway pulled up its tracks in Newfoundland, he was given his travelling papers. He got as far as the Chignic, fifty kilometres from the CN yard in Port aux Basques.

"How's she now?" he asked, as we met by the side of the stage.

"Excellent, Frank. Looks like it's going to be a wonderful evening."

"What would you like us to do?" he asked. "Anything special?"

"No, no, Frank. Just do what you normally do and enjoy yourselves. I wouldn't mind saying a few words to the audience, though, if that's okay with you."

Frank turned on the sound system and handed me a microphone. I thanked everyone for being at the Chignic that evening and explained how delighted we were to be doing a profile of someone as talented and well-loved as Minnie White.

"Now, before the cameras start rolling," I said over the PA system, "make sure you're sitting with who you're supposed to be with. Remember, this is going on national television!" There were a few chuckles as people glanced around at their partners. "The important thing tonight is to have fun," I continued. "Try to ignore the lights and the camera when it points in your direction. We'll be asking Minnie to perform a couple of songs two or three times in a row because we have only one camera and we need to shoot her performance from two or three different angles. When we put it all together, it'll feel like the Chignic was full of cameras."

I turned the microphone off, handed it back to Frank, and thanked him for letting me use it. "Knock 'em dead, Frank!"

"Would you like to do a tune or two later on this evening?" he asked.

"Well, normally I would," I replied. "But, this is really Minnie's night. Let's see how it goes. Maybe later."

One of the band members was an accordion player. But, with Minnie about to grace their stage, he played rhythm guitar that night. Frank sang a couple of country songs to open the set, and then the band launched into more-traditional Newfoundland jigs and reels, *sans* button-box.

It was a great crowd. They had been waiting a while and were certainly ready to have a good time. They hit the dance floor before the band even hit their stride. By the time Frank barked out Minnie's name, the room was in a sweat. Minnie, quite tiny – only about five feet tall – dressed in a formal evening gown, made her way to the stage. She sat down on a stool, adjusted her eyeglasses on the bridge of her nose, slipped her arms through the straps of her accordion, and began to play. When the strains of Minnie's button accordion flew forth, the room went wild.

Keith Whelan, our Newfoundland-born cameraman, was right in his element. On the floor, camera rolling, he weaved his way between the dancers, and floated towards the stage to reveal Minnie perched on her stool, fingers flying. Then, lowering the camera to just inches above the floor, he circled the pounding feet and flashing shoes of a few more dancers and swung around to fill the frame of his lens with a close-up of Minnie's face, her eyes a-twinkling!

The night seemed to be going extremely well. By the end of Minnie's second performance we had enough footage to make our producer, Malcolm Hamilton, a happy man. Minnie did not disappoint us. She was everything we hoped she would be. But the thing that impressed me most was her musical history. Earlier that afternoon, in a sit-down interview, I had found out a lot about her. Throughout her entire marriage, her priority was always raising her six children. To do that and still make music, Minnie White and her husband used to throw a lot of house parties. The "White House" was renowned in the region for throwing a Friday-night bash that would "fill yer boots" with scores of foot-stompin', knee-slappin' jigs and reels. But not because of the accordion.

Back in those days, Minnie played a huge foot-pumping organ that sat in her living room, and she would accompany the fiddle players who dropped in for a "time" in the Codroy Valley. It wasn't until she was in her fifties that she took up the accordion. Once she did, though, it didn't take long for word to spread that the organ lady in Tompkins sure knew how to make the button-box sing. She actually had to turn down a few offers to play at festivals and shows across Newfoundland because of her priorities at home. Minnie was fifty-six by the time her last child left home. Then, and only then, did she begin the pursuit of her musical dream. Now here she was, twenty years and three successful albums later, about to appear on national television. I was delighted for her.

"Ladies and gentlemen . . ." Frank was back at the microphone. "Ladies and gentlemen, as you know, the big fella – Wayne over there – sings a lot of songs on his television show, "On the Road Again." Well, I think it would be kinda nice to have him come up and sing a couple of songs here tonight, don't you?" The audience made the decision easy for me. They were most enthusiastic, and I was delighted to accept the invitation.

Now, there is a song I perform in concert that is a real crowd-pleaser, fast and funny: "The Auctioneer." Usually, I pick someone out of the audience and include him or her in the song. Sometimes I pick on the way they're dressed, or the way they look, or I pretend they're an individual with marital problems, working whatever develops from our conversation into the song routine. I never predetermine who that person will be. I choose someone quite spontaneously, and, when I took to the stage that night, the person who caught my attention, for no particular reason, was Frank.

"I thought I'd sing a song that describes Frank a little bit," I said.

The audience seemed to approve.

"Are you married, Frank?"

Frank was sitting off to the side of the stage and didn't seem to mind the attention I was paying him.

"No, boy. Divorced."

"Divorced!" I said, turning to the audience. "Well, then, here's a little song about Frank and his ex-wife," I proclaimed.

They really seemed to like *that* idea. And Frank actually seemed to like it, too.

"Where is she living now?" I asked.

"Well, last I heard, she was in St. John's," he replied.

"I guess you're pretty sad about her getting the house, eh, Frank?"

Again there was great audience reaction. Frank looked over at the audience and shrugged his shoulders, and even that met with response.

"At least you got the dog," I said.

More applause.

"You must find it tough living here all alone in your tiny hotel room, considering how she sold the house and moved to St. John's and all."

Well, the crowd enjoyed that idea, too. Frank was doing a marvellous job playing the audience. With each comment I'd make, he'd look at them as if to say, "Ain't that the truth!" And they would roar.

"You look nervous, Frank. Is the missus back in town?"

He turned to the audience again, nodding empathically up and down. They were loving it.

"I suppose now she's come to take the car!"

"Yes!" he cried. And the audience burst into applause again.

I began to sing "The Auctioneer," improvising the lyrics to suit my fictitious story about Frank:

There was a little boy from Newfoundland,
A Port aux Basques boy named Frank,
Who lost his job
And then he lost his wife . . .

Between the many verses, I would banter with Frank, painting an ever-blacker picture of poor Frank's life and the persecution he was suffering at the hands of his ex-wife. I was very impressed at his ability to respond with all the "right" words. Unrehearsed routines don't always work. This one most certainly did. Too well, as I was soon to find out.

After I'd finished the song, I joined a table of Minnie White fans. Before long a blonde lady wearing glasses approached us and obviously wanted my attention. There was a pained expression on her face.

"Mr. Rostad," she said, quietly and deliberately, "Mr. Rostad, I have been a fan of yours for years. I've hardly ever missed a single "On the Road Again" show. And I've played your music for years, too. I even have one of your tapes."

I was on my feet as she spoke, looking for a chair to offer her. She was obviously upset about something. Exactly what, I had no idea.

"I always thought, sir, that you were a nice man, a kind man, until tonight. I never thought you could be so cruel!"

Now I was really concerned. What had I done?

"I'm terribly sorry, ma'am, but I don't understand. Is it something I said?"

"Something you said? Something you said?" Her voice was rising in pitch. "I have never been hurt more in my entire life. And in front of all my neighbours!" By now, she was in tears. "No one has ever hurt me more than you did tonight, Mr. Rostad. I'm

Frank's ex-wife! And I came up from St. John's yesterday to visit my family for the first time in months. Obviously, you knew that. How could you belittle me like that in front of everybody?"

By now, my cowboy boot was not only in my mouth, it was down my throat about as far as it could go.

"My dear lady, I am so sorry! I had no idea you were Frank's ex-wife. I didn't even know for sure he had a wife!"

"Then how could you know I only came home yesterday? And how did you know about the house?"

Tears were streaming down her cheeks, and I was welling up with a sick kind of feeling.

"It was just a routine," I began to explain. "You have to believe me. My God, I would never do that to anyone. I've used that routine in my stage show for years. You have to believe me. It was only a routine!"

My words were of little use. She wheeled and walked briskly away across the room. Everyone at my table was completely silent. They seemed about as stunned as I was.

"That was just a routine," I said once again. "I had no idea . . . no idea at all. Where did she go? I've got to find her. Excuse me. I have to make her understand."

I found her at the very back of the room, still in tears, sitting on a chair off to the side of the hall. Another woman had her arm around her and was trying to console her.

"I just have to talk to you," I said, kneeling down beside her. "You have to understand that all of this is the wildest coincidence. This is absolutely unbelievable. Never in a million years would I ever intentionally hurt someone like that!"

To my relief, she had settled down a little and was prepared to listen to me now. After a few minutes of conversation, she accepted the fact that I *was* unaware of her presence in the lounge and that the whole thing really was an uncanny coincidence. Finally, a smile.

"Thank goodness," I said, with a great sigh of relief. "I would never have been able to forgive myself if I didn't reach you on this."

"I'm glad, too," she said. "I didn't want to leave here tonight thinking you would do something like that. I'm okay now. I understand. It's almost kind of funny, isn't it?"

It felt so good for both of us to laugh about it.

A few minutes later, I told Malcolm what had happened. He had been as wide-eyed as I was when Frank's ex-wife first approached me at the table. He was equally relieved when I explained that I had straightened everything out with her. For the remainder of the night at the Chignic, I made a point of setting the record straight with everyone I spoke to in the lounge. Word of mouth would make it quite clear in the community that what happened at that poor lady's expense was nothing more than an unfortunate coincidence. I felt that going back on stage and trying to explain to the audience what had happened was not the way to go. It would only put her in the spotlight again.

It has been more than five years since the incident at the Chignic. Needless to say, I have since altered my stage presentation of "The Auctioneer." Once in a while, something is said or something happens that brings the memory of that night in Newfoundland alive again. Like the summer of 1993 when Minnie White, bless her heart, received the Order of Canada for her contribution to the musical heritage of Newfoundland. Receiving an award is an event you never forget. I know. One night at the Chignic Lodge, a lady handed *me* one – the "Foot-in-Mouth" award.

Teapot Mountain

I used to smoke cigarettes. A *lot* of cigarettes. In fact, I was an absolutely compulsive, *two-and-a-half-to-three-packs-a-day* smoker at the time I decided to kick the habit. Quite frankly, I had to quit; I was out of control. I started my day with a smoke in my mouth, even before my eyes opened, even before my feet hit the floor, and I finished each day the same way – in bed, eyes half-closed, drawing on a Rothman's.

Tobacco companies have always been clever. Back in the early years of television, when it was cool to advertise cigarette smoking, they ran appealing campaigns, attracting new smokers into their fold as well as soothing the nicaholic nerves of existing flock members. I remember Canadian singer Bob Goulet appearing on our fledgling national network with a lit filtertip between his fingers singing, "Smoke du Maurier, for real smoking pleasure. Du Maurier, the cigarette of good taste." It was powerful stuff. Television was still kind of new in our house, and when it fired up we were one fixated family. And when good-lookin', blue-eyed Bob went into his du Maurier pitch, it was not uncommon for my mother to sing along, while drawing on a filtertip of her own. Yes, sir, the tobacco companies were very clever. What a great way to advertise their product *and* extol the virtues of smoking. Why, if young Bob could sing as well as he sang and look as good as he looked, smoking was cool!

My father smoked cigarettes, too. No, actually, he ate them. He was a two-pack-a-day man – Player's Plain for many years, Buckingham's (also *sans* asbestos tip) for a decade or so more, and, of course, Rothman's "Red," when he started to cough. He absolutely loved to light up. When he did, there was this *look* that

Vivien Lougheed stops halfway up Teapot Mountain to take a picture

Cameraman André Villeneuve and I, climbing the final "grunt" of Teapot Mountain

always came over him. It fascinated me. How, I wondered, could anything that smelled so bad make him feel so good?

Not surprisingly, by the time I was thirteen, I was a smoker, too. My friend Bob McLoy and I would meet after school, drive our Canadian Tire Super Cycles down to the park where our peers gathered, and suck back Export "A"s till our tongues were black and our brains were fried. Often, we were so "smoked out" by the time we had to pedal home for supper, we weren't legal to drive. Still, we endured the ritual again and again, because it was just such a gosh-darned grown-up thing to do. Little did I know then that I would smoke for the next thirty-three years. And though I would try countless times to quit, I would fail miserably until my travels took me to a mountain in British Columbia that would make me sit up and notice "what condition my condition was in." A mountain called Teapot.

Teapot Mountain is located almost dead centre of the province, near the town of Prince George, about eight hundred kilometres north of Vancouver. Compared to the Rocky Mountains, Teapot is really just a baby of a mountain, less than a kilometre high. But it's steep, a solitary mound of rock that resembles, as its name implies, a teapot. Forested in a coat of ever-greens, this little solitary mountain is a favourite hiking spot of many area residents. A visit to Teapot makes for a healthy day – provided you have strong legs, hearty veins, and *clear* lungs. It's not the kind of climb recommended for couch potatoes.

It was October 1992. I was fairly svelte, with two hundred and thirty pounds draped on a six-foot-four frame. I certainly felt that I looked like someone who could handle the climb. I didn't have a beer belly and I didn't eat a lot of junk food. I *did*, however, have a full carton of cigarettes in my luggage, one package opened in my left shirt pocket (smokers all have a preferred pocket), and a spare package in my backpack – just in case war erupted in the B.C. interior and all the stores shut down. (That's another thing about smokers – they are absolutely terrified by the prospect of running out of cigarettes.)

Janet P. Smith was producing that week, and she had found the perfect companion for my climb.

"Wayne, I want you to meet Vivien Lougheed. She's going to take us to the top of the mountain. Vivien, this is Wayne."

"Hello, Vivien, I've really looked forward to meeting you."

"Nice to meet you, too. Are you ready for Teapot, Wayne?"

"Yes, yes. Let's do it!" I said, in my most manly, hiking-guy voice. (I think Custer attempted the same bravado moments before Little Big Horn erupted.)

"You'll love it!" Vivien replied. "It's just a little hike, but real pretty. Shouldn't take more than an hour."

An hour. Well, an hour didn't sound all that bad. If I had a smoke just before the climb, I could hold off for an hour and have one at the top. A lot of smokers have to think ahead like that. They have to know how far away their next nicotine draw is, lest they suffer severe withdrawal and exhibit unacceptable social behaviour.

Vivien looked great. She was forty-nine years old, and the picture of health. Her skin was deeply tanned by the sun and winds of many treks abroad. She was an exceptionally lively individual, who spent three months every year hiking through one exotic location or another somewhere in the world. She had walked the Great Wall of China and the Inca Trail in Peru, and had climbed to lofty mountain villages in Tibet. I'm sure that, to her, Teapot was just a little hiccup.

"No matter where I go in the world, I love hiking here best," she said, looking off into the distance. "What a great country. I started hiking when I came to B.C. because there was somewhere to go. Know what I mean? I was born in Winnipeg, on the prairies, and I never found that much motivation to put on a pair of boots. Here, you can go out in the wilderness for five or six days and not even see anyone. You can't get that anywhere else. Nowhere!"

That, I understood. So did Janet. A big part of the story we wanted to capture for "On the Road Again" was Vivien's deep appreciation of our country's vast spaces and how very accessible the simple sport of hiking is to all of us. She was an avid promoter. In a column she wrote weekly for the *Prince George Citizen*, Vivien extolled the virtues of strapping on a pair of boots and taking to the great outdoors. And the purpose of our visit today was for me to experience the joys of doing just that.

"Those are pretty nifty boots," she said, glancing down at my feet.

"Not bad, eh?" I replied. "Janet and I found them downtown this morning, just before we picked you up. Size fourteen. I have a heck of time finding anything to fit me in the big city, and look at this – the first store we hit in downtown Prince George had the size I needed. Seventy-nine bucks! What do you think?"

"I think they'll survive Teapot," she laughed.

I couldn't help but notice Vivien's boots. Mine were store-bought new, with crisp green canvas uppers. Vivien's were made of solid leather and had to be a thousand kilometres old.

"Vivien, they tell me you've climbed Mount Robson several times. Now, that's what I call a mountain!"

"Yes, it's quite a climb. As long as you prepare for it, though, it's not really all that tough."

Robson is the highest peak in our Canadian Rockies, an absolutely stunning peak – a *thousand* Teapots.

"Well," I said, "I'll just climb Teapot with you today. I'll do Robson with you on our next visit."

François Pagé, our audio tech, approached us from the truck, microphones in hand.

"Here's your wireless, Wayne. This one's for you, Vivien."

François would have no trouble with this shoot. He was very fit, a man who ran several kilometres daily and never smoked a cigarette in his life. He knew I was a heavy smoker.

"This should be fun," he chortled, slipping the battery pack of my remote microphone on the back of my belt.

"Piece of cake," I replied, butting my pre-climb cigarette. "Just a little stroll in the park."

"Sure, Wayne. We'll see."

André Villeneuve, our cameraman, was just about ready. He would have the toughest climb, because he not only had to carry the camera, he had to strap on a couple of extra battery belts in case we needed to power a portable light or two on the trail to the summit. It can get dark inside a forest canopy, and the last thing André wanted to do halfway up the mountain was run back down to get another belt.

Janet briefed us on how we would shoot the climb: "Wayne, we'll stay a little ahead of you and Vivien all the way up the mountain. Each time we set up, come towards us and make sure you walk past André's camera until you're both out of frame. Then we'll go ahead again, set up, and wait until both of you go out of frame again. We'll do that all the way to the top."

"That works for me," I said. "Let's do it."

"Okay. André, let's position for our first shot."

Operation Teapot was under way.

I remember the first cough coming on. It started as a little tickle in the throat. André was rolling on the scene and it was important that I suppress the cough or we would have to redo the shot.

Vivien called each leg of the ascent a "grunt." Teapot, she said, had *seven* grunts, each one tougher than the one before. We were only ten minutes into the hike, not even through the *second* grunt, and I was ready to erupt.

This is not cool, I thought.

Smokers know when a coughing jag is coming on; it comes from experience. Cold morning air makes them cough. Too many cigarettes in any given hour will do it, too. And running around the yard playing tag with your kid is a really good trigger. But nothing creates a better Hollywood hack scene than a really tough workout. Climb a mountain, and the ensuing eruption is likely to rival Vesuvius.

Gratefully, the tickle held off long enough for Vivien and me to clear the frame. While André repositioned his camera, I had time to catch my breath and clear my pipes with two or three good coughs. Already, my forehead was quite warm.

"Boy, it's not going to get any easier, is it?" I said, looking up at the next leg of our climb.

"Actually, the really tough climb comes after we reach the flats," replied Vivien. "We'll rest there, because the last two legs are going to make you work a bit."

The third grunt was a doozy. It was not a natural incline. God certainly did not create this pathway for the pitter-patter of little human feet. No. It was meant for goats and creatures with wings. And it was definitely not meant for smokers. Did I cough? Of course I coughed. After all, my morning had started with the consumption of three cigarettes by the time I had shaved, four more at breakfast in the restaurant, and two in the hotel lobby while waiting for Janet to go to the boot store. Considering I had only been up ninety minutes at this point, I was firing up the boilers pretty good. I had a couple more on our way to the bootery and another three or four before we picked Vivien up. By eleven o'clock that morning, I had already smoked half a pack. You bet I coughed.

"You want some juice?" Vivien asked, pausing halfway up grunt number four to let me catch my breath.

"No, not yet," I said. "And I'll tell you, I sure don't want a cigarette."

"Can't say that I blame you."

I thought we would never reach the flats. I had been coughing every minute or so during the last two legs. Janet was going to have a field day editing around my hacking. It was embarrassing.

On the flats, I took Vivien up on her offer of juice. I walked over to a rock and sat away from everyone for a few minutes while I hacked myself back to normal. I reminded myself of a sick horse I once had that coughed all the time. She wasn't pretty, either.

"Hey, cowboy!" It was François. "Are you okay?"

"Yes, yes," I said between coughs. "Nothing a new pair of lungs won't fix. I've never coughed so hard in my life."

Of course, François looked his usual fitter-than-most self. André had a bit of a sweat on because of all the gear he was carrying, and Janet, considering she was a smoker, was doing remarkably well. Vivien was nibbling on some homemade dehydrated fruit chews and looked as if she didn't have a care in the world. To her, Teapot was a cakewalk.

The juice felt good going down my throat. It was soothing. For the umpteenth time, I asked myself, Why do I smoke?

Someone else had asked me that same question earlier that summer back home. I received a letter from an eight-year-old fan in my neighbourhood who had seen me perform at a local concert. After the show, I signed an autograph for her. A few days later, she wrote me a very sweet letter, saying how she enjoyed meeting me in person and how it made her birthday extra special – except for one thing. "Mr. Rostad," she asked, "why do you smoke? Love, Heather."

I was moved by her concern. When I wrote back, I apologized for my habit, explaining I was a nicotine addict and found it very difficult to quit. I also told her that her letter really made me sit up and take notice. I thanked her for taking the time to write, and promised I would do everything in my power to quit. Well, her letter stayed with me, because here I was, far from home, with the words of an eight-year-old ringing in my ears.

Another voice interrupted my thoughts. It was Janet's.

"Well, how does everybody feel. Are we ready?"

It was time for the final two grunts, the ones Vivien warned would make me work. She had no idea how much they would really make me do just that. I had nicely settled down in the last few minutes on the flats, but it didn't take long for my lungs to voice their discontent when we started climbing once more. Halfway up the sixth leg, I starting coughing again. It was very persistent, and no matter how hard I coughed to clear my passages, there was no relief. Now, had I been alone, I would have stopped and regained my composure before carrying on. However, there was a degree of pride at stake here. This climb was making a statement, and to ask everyone to stop while Wayne got his physical well-being in order was simply not an acceptable option. I had no choice but to keep up with everyone.

Damn, damn, damn! I thought. This is the last straw. Talk about being out of shape!

My cough was starting to sound more like the chronic, hacking cough my father had in the latter part of his smoking life. I had sworn that, if I ever started to sound like him, I would quit. Listening to him made even the most ardent smoker wonder if it was worth it. What a terrible habit! To think that people have actually smoked themselves into their graves. Why, some people dying of lung cancer have even asked for a cigarette *on their death beds*. Pretty scary stuff!

The final grunt proved *final* for me. I never dreamed my lungs had been so badly affected by smoking until I experienced the coughing jag of my life just before reaching the summit. I thought I would be leaving my liver on Teapot Mountain. Everyone was genuinely concerned for my well-being, particularly André. When we came down the mountain, André took me aside and told me how concerned he was at the summit.

"At one point, right near the top, I started to worry," he began. "I thought, how are we going to get Wayne off the mountain?"

"You're not serious," I said.

"Very serious. Wayne, I thought you were going to die!"

"Come on! It wasn't that bad, was it?"

"Yes, it was. All of us were worried."

That night, back at the hotel in Prince George, I called Leanne at the farm and told her about my climb up Teapot and my story of revelation on the mount.

"Well, it sounds as if you are going to have to make a decision about this smoking business sooner than later," she said.

Leanne never smoked a day in her life and, in hindsight, I

realize she was the most patient person in the world. She always believed I would quit. She never really pushed me to give up the weed. She knew that, if she did, I'd get my back up and go the other way. She chose to silently suffer until I came to my senses.

Eight weeks later, I quit, this time for good. I had my last cigarette on New Year's Eve, 1992, in the kitchen of my sister, Darlene's, home in Jerseyville, Ontario. (She had quit smoking five years earlier and had prayed I would follow suit.) I now walk five kilometres a day – a very *brisk* five kilometres – and have never felt healthier. Best of all, I don't cough any more.

I must confess, though, I have become one of those dreaded *reformed* smokers – the kind who sometimes forget, while chastising people who still have the habit, how *hard* it was to quit in the first place. And if the conversation becomes a little heated, Leanne usually nudges me under the table with her knee to snap my memory to attention.

"Now, darling, remember how tough it was for *you* to quit."
She's absolutely right.

Some people need a mountain of willpower to quit. Some just need a mountain.

Life Is a Railway

ᖘ

I feel a little sad when I look at what's left of the railway in our country. Canadian National no longer owns or operates a single metre of track in Prince Edward Island or in Newfoundland. With the exception of a few privately owned kilometres purchased from CN, those long ribbons of steel are gone forever, and island residents will never see a train rumble through their valleys again.

The rest of the country still has a railway; but, more and more, when I travel now, I notice long, narrow strips of grass-covered gravel beds where railway track once linked towns, communities, and indeed a nation, together. Even the rails that remain seem to be used less and less, and for the most part lie rusting in the rain. I just hope we don't wake up one day and realize we've made a big mistake by not maintaining our rail system.

The Americans have already discovered this. During the 1970s, they tore up thousands of kilometres of track in the Midwest. Well, it didn't take them long to figure out the days of the railroad weren't over. Today, they're putting that track back – at incredible cost.

Europe never made that mistake. There, trains are a key component in the lives of almost everyone who travels. But, in Canada, it has become an exciting event just to see a train go by. Recently, while I was on a shoot in the British Columbia interior, my rental car and a great long train snaked along together for many kilometres through the mountain passes on our way south to Penticton. It was a beautiful sight. A real working train, one hundred cars long, with two big diesels happily straining under the load. A train that was still vital!

Tom Payne in the cab
of one of his big diesel
locomotives

One of Tom's trains
sitting in the station at
Meeting Creek, Alberta

I know I'm not alone in my concern for our once-mighty railway system. Over the years, I have crossed paths with many people who feel as I do. They don't want to see the railway die either. But, while most of us stand around lamenting the demise of our trains, a few individuals have actually gone and done something about it. Each of them, in their own way, is determined to keep the railway – or at least its memory – alive in their part of Canada.

One of those individuals is a big, gregarious, six-foot-four Albertan by the name of Tom Payne. When Tom Payne laughs, he roars! You can hear him clear across the Stettler railway yard. Of course, he's allowed to laugh as loud as he wants. His railway owns the yard. Tom is president and chief operating officer of the Central Western Railway, one of the few privately held railways in Canada. When I first met Tom in 1991, his company owned more than one hundred and sixty kilometres of track, three huge diesel locomotives, and railway yards in ten towns between Camrose and Drumheller. Not bad for someone who just a few years earlier was a train engineer.

Tom Payne loves every single aspect of the railway. If he has to perform his duties as chief operating officer for Central Western, he gladly dons his three-piece pinstriped grey suit, replete with gold fob and chain. When something needs fixing, he isn't afraid to put on a pair of coveralls and slide under an engine, oilcan in hand. More than anything else on earth, though, Tom loves *driving* trains. Heaven, for him, is standing on the deck of an engine, with one hand firmly on the throttle and the wind caressing his beard.

Interestingly, Tom is only forty-seven years old. He started his railway career a scant twenty-three years ago, in 1973, when he joined CP Rail as a brakeman out of Calgary. By 1977, he was an engineer. Some would have been happy with a position like that for the rest of their lives, but not Tom Payne. He decided he wanted to run his own railway line. Since the 1960s, both national railways, Canadian Pacific and Canadian National, had been abandoning their smaller, less-profitable lines. But Tom couldn't understand *why* they were unprofitable. Something had to be wrong with the system, he felt. In 1982, when it was announced that the line from Camrose to Drumheller was going to be shut down, Tom made his move. Somebody had to stop the big guys from tearing up the tracks!

Tom reasoned that this particular hundred and sixty kilometres of track was very important to the grain farmers along its route. If it shut down, they would have to move their grain by truck to the main rail line – a costly arrangement. Farmers, grain-elevator operators, and even some of the smaller towns might be forced to shut down operations completely. Tom knew if he could just buy the line, people along the route would gladly ship their grain on his railway. But how did one go about *buying* a railway? Tom started to look for an answer.

His search quickly led him, not surprisingly, into a bureaucratic maze. It was a nightmare! Everyone he approached passed the buck to someone else. Paper shuffled between Tom, the national railway companies, and the Alberta government, but very little headway was made. The CN told Tom, "Sure, we'll sell you the railway line, but you'll need a charter first. When you get a charter, come and see us." The problem was, no one in the entire country had applied for a charter to run a common carrier railway since well before the First World War. Tom then discovered that nobody in the Alberta government had a clue as to what department was in charge of handling railway charters. And, quite frankly, the government didn't *want* to know! It sounded like a heck of a responsibility. It tried everything in its power to make the big bearded guy go away.

Undaunted, Tom continued his research. After months of relentless digging, he found what he was looking for. Sitting on a dust-laden shelf in a government office was an old archive copy of the Alberta Railway Act, an act that had not been amended since 1919. According to this legislation, the person responsible for the sale of government railways in Alberta was the Minister of Public Utilities. With act in hand, Tom went to the minister and presented him with an application for a charter.

"You should have seen the minister's face!" Tom roared. "He didn't even have a bloody clue a provincial act existed until I walked in the door and applied for a charter! And he sure as hell wasn't going to accept my application unless he bloody well had to!"

But getting a charter was only half of Tom's problem. He still had to come up with $2.7 million before CN would hand over the Stettler line. That was going to be tough, too. His efforts to convince modern-day bankers that it was safe to invest money in a railway went nowhere. They told Tom the last time anyone had successfully invested in a railway was around the time they drove the last spike.

"They all thought I was a few bricks short of a load," he laughed.

Luckily Tom found a friend in Don Mazankowski, then federal minister of Transport in Brian Mulroney's government – and a fellow Albertan. He understood Tom's love for the railway. He knew that all Tom wanted was a chance to prove he could haul freight at a lower cost than the big boys, and Mazankowski believed Tom should be given that chance. The minister began clearing up the bureaucratic mess. It took him two years but, in the end, there was a contract in place and Tom Payne finally had his railway.

"How long did it take to settle the whole business, Tom?" I asked. "I mean, from the very first call you made right up until Mazankowski settled things for you?"

"We finally turned a wheel on the twenty-first of November, 1986, several years later. It was one o'clock in the morning."

"And how have things gone since then?"

"Great! In our first year of operation, three hundred farmers signed on to move their grain on Central Western. In less than five years, my customers have doubled. I've now got over six hundred and fifty shipping on CWR. And CWR is making money! Hell, I might even get out of debt someday!"

It was a heck of a story. When he first started out, Tom had mortgaged his house and everything he owned just to get his diesels. He bought three of them at a used-locomotive sale in St. Thomas, Ontario.

"Think about it. I went shopping for locomotives! My wife was great about it. Can you imagine how most wives would respond if their husband came home and said, 'Honey, I mortgaged the house and bought three big diesels'?"

He had a point.

"They're doing it all wrong in this country," he continued. "There's no reason to lose money and keep closing down railway lines! The railway made this country what it is and can continue to make this country great. We're making the same mistake today the Americans made back in the seventies. We haven't learned what they learned twenty years ago. We're moving backwards here!"

Since our visit in 1991, Tom's railway has grown even larger. Recently, his company bought the Coronation and Lacombe subdivision, the line that runs east from Stettler to the Saskatchewan border. Central Western now has more than four hundred kilometres of track in Alberta. That tells me two things. First, it tells me the little guy hasn't quite finished showing the big boys how to do it right. It also tells me that, as long as Tom Payne is around, there will always be a railway in Alberta.

There is another railway that is growing in Canada, a little railway that is getting bigger and better every year, too. It's called the Prince Edward Island Miniature Railway, the PEIMR, a money-making, passenger-carrying service that boasts of having more on-time departures than Via Rail. Mind you, it doesn't boast of having more track. The miniature railway has only two circuits, for a total of three kilometres of track, but what it lacks in steel rail, it makes up for in pretty scenery. It runs through the countryside of Prince County, the northeast region of Prince Edward Island. This railway's domain is a manicured forty-two-acre property on South Kildare Road, about one kilometre outside the town of Alberton.

The PEIMR is the brainchild and personal obsession of Barry Maloney, now seventy-five, an Englishman who came to Canada in 1954. Back in England he was a fabrication engineer who built truck bodies. When he came to Canada, he got a job working at the same trade with a firm in Montreal.

"I worked that trade for twenty-five years in Montreal. I needed something to relieve the monotony. Trains always fascinated me. I guess that's why I decided to build a locomotive."

The little locomotive Barry built – primarily to see if he could – was beautiful, and authentic in its detail. A small coal furnace was housed in the cab of the locomotive, and the engineer sat on top of the coal car. It was the engineer's job to feed the little furnace with coal, which in turn heated the water and provided steam to power the engine. After many hours of labour, Barry's miniature iron horse was ready for its pioneer run. He fired up the boiler, mounted his little steamer, and opened the throttle. It ran beautifully, and Barry Maloney was filled with a yearning to chug on and on. But the feeling quickly subsided when he ran out of rail. The test track was far too short. Barry felt rather like someone all dressed up with nowhere to go.

Barry had suspected he might feel this way. In the final months of building his engine, he had been thinking a lot about where he was going to run it. "I knew I was hooked. I knew I would have to find a bit of land and lay some track to run it on." And so Barry's dream began. When his vacation came along, he went east to find his personal "Field of Dreams." In 1974, after several "searching-for-location" vacations, he found the perfect acreage on the banks of the picturesque Kildare River in Prince Edward Island. The land was relatively flat and there were several open meadows on the property. That was good. He wouldn't have to remove too many trees in order to build the PEIMR.

For the next four years, Barry continued to travel between his job in Montreal and his little piece of railway heaven in Prince Edward Island. "I'd lay twenty to forty feet of track a year, go back to Montreal, work away, and come back down here. But after four years I decided to quit my job and move down permanently. I was simply taking too long to build my railroad. I needed more than just vacation time to get the job done."

I met Barry in 1993, fifteen years after he and his wife made the big move east.

"What did your friends think about your move?" I asked.

"What did people think? Well, they thought I was a little crazy, quitting a safe job and all. People who knew Prince County couldn't fathom why I wanted to build my railway here. There was little tourism happening in the area, and they were concerned I would never make any money!"

But Barry has proven them wrong. Every summer, the PEIMR carries between four and five thousand paying passengers. It's so busy, in fact, that Barry has to hire several students during the peak summer season to help run the railway.

"I let the students do the actual operating of the trains. I just oversee things now. David, here, primarily does the maintenance."

My producer, Lauren Sawatsky, had told me all about David McLellan. He was Barry's right arm.

"Have you been with Barry a long time?" I asked him.

"I came out here in '83 just to pester him," he said jokingly. "I came out three or four different times and just made a pain of myself. Finally, I guess Barry figured, 'Heck, I might as well pay him.'"

We all laughed. There was an obvious father-son affinity between Barry and David. They even looked as if they were related. Mind you, wearing the same clothes sure enhanced the resemblance; they were both in blue jeans, wool socks and Greb Kodiaks, blue shirts, denim jackets, and matching engineer caps.

These guys were definitely taking their jobs seriously. Minutes into our conversation, I learned that this was a "miniature" railway, not a "toy" railway. The size of the trains had nothing to do with it. It was a real, operating, passenger-carrying railway.

The amount of work that has been done over the years is nothing short of awesome. The train yard alone is a study in miniature detail. The place even *smell*s like a train yard! Several tracks switch off the main lines and run into the maintenance sheds. Two PEIMR engines, painted deep blue with yellow stripes, make daily runs, while Barry's original steam engine, the one that started this whole thing, sits proudly on its own track, prominently on display. Though it still operates superbly, Barry now runs his "baby" only on special occasions. Oilcans, tools, and polishing rags are everywhere. Through the open doors of one of the sheds I could see big metal fabricating tools, spare parts, another engine, and various repair projects on the go. As with all things mechanical, this was a place of never-ending maintenance.

Nearby, there is a smartly built train station for customers, and benches to sit on while waiting to board. When I visited, everything had been painted a light sky-blue, with the locomotive's darker blue paint used as trim. Railway-crossing signs, lights, bells, and whistles were all properly placed and beautifully detailed. I was very impressed.

"The two circuits we have here," Barry explained, "are both quite different. The Tunnel Run features a trip through a sixty-foot tunnel I built in 1980 and a trip through our miniature village. It's very nice, but my favourite is the Bridge Run. It's rather special."

"How's that?" I asked.

"Well, because of the trestle bridge I built, my *pièce de résistance*. It's two hundred feet long, thirteen feet high, and has over six thousand board feet of lumber, enough to build a small house."

"And I'll bet it's built just like the real McCoy," I added.

"Actually, yes. I copied it from photographs."

"How long did it take you to build it?"

Barry Maloney
at the controls of
his PEIMR
locomotive

A few passengers
ride the PEIMR

Frank Rogers poses proudly with his model railroad

"It took me about two years. Every spring I crawl all over that bridge and inspect it to make sure there are no cracked timbers and everything is in place, braces intact and so on. You'll see it when we take our run later this morning."

About one hour later, Barry and I walked over to locomotive number 814. It was a beautiful machine.

"Boy, did you ever do a great job on these diesels," I told him.

"It's the Pacific type of locomotive," he replied. "But, I couldn't use diesel-electric engines like the big machines. You can't duplicate that kind of engine on a small scale and get any kind of efficiency. I had to opt for petrol."

He fired up the little gas engine. All eight horses came to life, straining in the traces, ready to take us on the Tunnel Run.

"All aboard!" Barry called over his shoulder. I eagerly grabbed the first seat behind him. He pushed the throttle ahead, and I was off for a private tour of Barry's railway heaven.

Engine 814 was surprisingly strong, considering it had only eight horses. It was capable of hauling eleven cars at a time, with each miniature car carrying one seated passenger. Since I was the only passenger for this particular run, we were light. In no time at all we were up to speed, clickity-clacking our way through Barry's enchanted forest. It was full of healthy young birch and maple groves that he himself had planted when he first came to the island. There were also several stands of forestry-planted spruce and red pine. Our shoulders literally brushed their outstretched branches as we rumbled along. The entire three kilometres of track running through Barry's property had been lovingly laid by hand. Many tons of gravel, used to build the railway bed, had been carried by wheelbarrow to minimize any damage to the natural setting. Talk about a labour of love!

"This is the miniature village coming up on our right, Wayne."

The village was a gem. Maloney's General Store had a sign on its storefront that read "Horse Collars Sold Here." There were several little farmhouses, typical of the homes found on the island, and an impressive church in miniature.

"The church used to be in Alberton, before it burned down," Barry told me. "I copied it from an old engraving."

A few more turns of track brought us along the banks of the Kildare River, where Barry had erected a pretty little red-trimmed lighthouse. Then, inland again, we left the light of day and rumbled into Blackwall Tunnel. Switching to the other circuit, we soon arrived at Barry's trestle bridge. He was obviously very proud of it.

"There she is. Drove every single one of those support pylons in by hand! Some of them had to go down twelve feet before I hit bottom."

"You did all this by hand?" I exclaimed.

"Had to. Imagine how we would have torn up the ravine getting a machine in here. It was far too pretty to do that."

While the setting was indeed pretty, the bridge was pretty, too. Pretty spectacular. It was a work of art. Not a bolt was out of place, every beam was positioned square and true, built the way railway trestles were meant to be built – to last. Sixty metres – two hundred feet – of strong, solid, post-and-beam construction is a very impressive thing to see, even in miniature. But frankly, my notion of "miniature" was fading quickly. Here in Barry's forest, with only small trees providing a sizing reference, the bridge looked quite . . . well . . . normal.

"You're an amazing man, Barry. I can't believe you did all this alone. How old are you, again?"

"I'm seventy-three."

"Going on what?" I asked.

"Fourteen!" he laughed. "Face it, Wayne. If you lose the little boy in you, you're dead."

The entire trip took about twenty minutes, far too short a time for the little boy in me. I didn't want to get off the train. As a matter of fact, the little guy inside me was even considering throwing himself down and holding his breath till his face turned blue just to keep Barry at the controls for another circuit or two. I wondered how many other "kids" had caught a case of *Miniaturailroaditis* as quickly as I had.

Across the big pond, in Newfoundland, trains were legends. "Carbonear" and the dearly loved "Newfie Bullet" were household names. The Bullet was a big, strong steam locomotive that hauled a long, sleek, black-and-silver passenger train with different names adorning each car – "Avalon," "Fogo," and "Terra Nova," to name a few. It was the pride and joy of the Newfoundland Railway. Her big, bright, single headlight and great, trailing puffs of billowing smoke and glowing cinders were a powerful sight. But, despite its great strength, the Bullet had its share of problems dealing with the harsh Newfoundland climate. It was not uncommon for the great train to be stranded for several hours, even a few days, when the elements unleashed their fury and a blizzard blocked its path. When Newfoundlanders kissed their spouses goodbye at the station, the operative phrase in the dead of winter often was, "See you Friday, if the weather holds." In fact, one stretch of track, about thirty kilometres from Port aux Basques, was notorious year-round for having ungodly high winds that could literally lift train cars from the tracks.

In the old days, the Newfoundland Railway relied on an elderly couple who lived in a house along the stretch of track to signal their trains if the winds were safe for passage at the moment. They called it "Wreckhouse." If a red flag flew from the Wreckhouse mast, the trains waited the wind out until they were given the green. Today, the old couple, like the trains, is gone. Today, anyone entering the Codroy Valley from the east or west while driving the Trans-Canada Highway is given this ominous welcome on huge signs:

CAUTION WIND WARNING: Winds in this area have been recorded to gust up to 200km/hr. If any difficulty is experienced in operating your vehicle you are advised to stop until wind subsides.

With such a rich railway history, it is not surprising there were many heavy hearts in 1991 when the last remaining sections of track in Newfoundland were ripped up and the train yards went silent. In St. John's, Frank Rogers had a heavy heart, too, but he understood and accepted the railroad's passing more readily than most.

"I could see it coming," he said. "I knew it was going to happen. Nobody really wanted to see it go, but you can't keep a train unless people ride it, and nobody was riding the trains any more."

Frank's father, Chesley F. Rogers, had been an engineer on the Newfie Bullet, and Frank grew up in a world that lived and breathed railway. He and his father were great pals, and when they spent time together, which was quite often, they talked railway; when the family ate dinner, the entire clan talked railway. In the Rogers household, the Newfoundland Railway was as vital a way of life as the fishery was to almost everyone else who lived on the Rock.

Frank was in his late sixties when "On the Road Again" paid him a visit in 1992. All the changes the Newfoundland Railway had experienced occurred within his lifetime. He saw steam give way to diesel and Newfoundland Rail change its name to the Canadian National Railway; he witnessed the removal of the narrow-gauge track from Newfoundland soil forever.

His father, Chesley, worked the railway for forty-five years. Chesley first became an engineer back in 1918 and he told his family hundreds of stories over the years about his life "on the road," as Newfoundlanders called railroading in those days. Yet, in spite of Chesley's willingness to share his world with his sons, he never wanted them to work on the railway. He felt it was too hard a life and didn't want his sons going through what he went through.

"Dad simply wouldn't hear of it," Frank told me. "I always wanted to be on the road. It was my sole interest in life, but when the time came that I was old enough to pursue it, I didn't go at it."

"You respected his wishes that much?"

"Yes, yes," he said with a bit of a distant look in his eyes. "That's how we were in those days. I would gladly have gone to work on the road, but Dad didn't want me to and that was that."

So Frank did what his father wanted him to do. He got a good education, and climbed the corporate ladder as an accountant with a highly respected firm in Newfoundland. By the time he retired, he was a general manager. But the lure of the railway never left him. In fact, for the last forty years, Frank has been building a private railway world in the basement of his St. John's home. It is a small world, even smaller than Barry Maloney's in PEI, but it's a vital one, nonetheless.

Frank started living out the life he missed on the road shortly after he married Marjorie, his childhood sweetheart. They had grown up just blocks apart in the east end of St. John's. She understood Frank's world from the beginning and was very supportive of it. When they first built their house, they set aside a room in the basement for Frank to pursue his dream.

"Two or three Christmases after we were married – I think Frank was thirty-three," Marjorie recalled, "he got his first train. He had it running around the Christmas tree. I knew then I was in it for the long term. And since he retired six years ago, we're even more into it than ever."

Frank's railway is contained in one large room in the basement. The table on which it sits is about 9 feet wide by 15 feet long, or 3 metres by 4.5 metres. Obviously, the Rogers' "Memorial" railway operates on a much shorter track than Barry Maloney's, and certainly far shorter than Tom Payne's in Alberta. Barry has three kilometres of rail, Tom operates on well over three hundred kilometres. Frank however, does it all in less than twenty square metres. Of course, if you got down to scale, Frank's railway is actually bigger than Barry's and Tom's. Frank has more than twenty steam and diesel locomotives with about seventy-five railway cars of all types. His railway yard has a working turntable and a great roundhouse to store his engines. There are countless switches, levers, bells, and whistles at Frank's fingertips. When the railways ran in Newfoundland, they were adorned with gaily painted logos. Frank's railway is historically correct. The older Newfoundland Railway logos adorn the steam locomotives, while CN logos flash by on his diesel-electric machines. Two hundred and seventy-five watts of raw Newfoundland power drive the mighty little trains as they rumble through the Newfoundland towns and scenic hillsides that blanket his tabletop railway. A framed photo of Chesley F. Rogers overlooks this domain.

"What was it that fascinated you so much about the trains, Frank?" I asked. "What do you remember most as a boy spending time with Chesley?"

"I think it was the power, more than anything. The feeling that you had control of this big monster, spewing smoke and steam. It had this grand smell about it, that I've known all my life."

"Do you smell it even now, Frank? Here in this model world?"

"Oh, yes! The dirtier I get, the better I smell it."

He pushed back his engineer's cap, which he always wore when he entered "the yard" and reached over to one of his locomotives.

"This is one of my favourites" he said. "The 1024. It was another one of the locomotives my father worked on. You know, he always had a special way of blowing the whistle when he was coming home. My mother would hear that blow and tell us it was time to go pick Dad up at the yard. She always knew if that was him coming home."

Frank started to chuckle a little. "You know, sometimes I think Marjorie knows when I need her, too. If I'm in underneath my table doing a little fixing or wiring and I need a tool or someone to lend a hand, darned if she doesn't show up right on cue, just like Mom did for Dad."

Our crew brought a "pencil-cam" for the shoot at Frank's place. As the name suggests, it's a tiny camera about the size of a pencil. We fastened it to the Bullet locomotive and, with Frank at the levers, the train went through its paces. Staring at the video monitor, I was amazed at how realistic everything looked through such a small lens. Frank got a great charge out of it, too. He hadn't seen this perspective since he and his father sat aboard the real McCoy many years ago.

Frank is helping to keep the memory of the Newfoundland Railway alive in that small room in his basement. School groups have dropped by and been treated to his eloquent stories of the once-mighty railway. In one ninety-day period, more than three hundred people passed through his basement world to learn about the little Newfoundland railway and to listen to a few tales about the "glory days."

But, the crowning glory in Frank's mind happened in 1991 when he rounded up all the old Newfoundland engineers he could find and threw a Newfoundland soirée for them to rekindle old memories and have a go at his trains. Seventeen former engineers showed up, and each one of them had "fired" with his dad. Needless to say, many yarns were told that night as each engineer took his place at Frank's control centre, fired up the boilers, and went on the road one more time.

I left Frank's place that day feeling much as I did leaving Tom's and Barry's. I had a warm feeling inside. That's what's so wonderful about my job: I have this great privilege of meeting people across the country, who so often fill me with their passion and emotion. Mind you, I didn't need a lot of help when it came to doing stories that involved trains. I have loved the railway all my life. The days of the trains are not so distant in my memory. As a boy, I remember hopping a few slow-moving freights for a short ride from the Black Bridge that crossed the Rideau River over to Ottawa's old New Edinburgh district. Even today, I still get a rush hearing a whistle or a horn in the distance.

The Canadian rock singer, Tom Cochrane, once wrote a hit song called "Life Is a Highway." He was close.

Flies and Turpentine

George Schmidt absolutely hates flies. If he had his way, there wouldn't be a single fly on the face of the earth.

"They're filthy little things. I detest them!" he said.

"Why do you hate them so much, George?" I asked.

"Well, I think a fly is a very dangerous thing. People don't realize how dangerous. Three years ago, a fly got caught in my right ear and punctured my eardrum. I can't hear too good now. I'm partially deaf in this ear," he said, tapping the right side of his head with his fingers.

The memory was obviously still very vivid. For a moment, I thought the fly was still in there.

"They're dirty! Very dirty!"

It was June 1993. George had retired from farming near the little town of Leader, Saskatchewan, back in 1979. Luckily for him, when he sold the farm, harvesting grain was still a profitable business, so he had a few dollars stashed away. Not a lot, mind you, but enough to live comfortably. He spent his early retirement years tinkering with a few pet projects and even had a small business on the side repairing farm equipment. Life in Leader, two hundred and fifty kilometres southwest of Saskatoon, near the Alberta border, was pretty idyllic for George. Until 1990, that is, when that fly punctured his eardrum.

"I was determined to do something about this fly problem. I just wasn't sure what. But one day – let me tell you, I had so many flies in my shop you wouldn't believe it! And that's when it hit me!"

What hit him was an idea for an invention that would rid the planet of flies forever: the Schmidt Fly Trap! Three short months

George P. Schimdt, Flycatcher, of Leader, Saskachewan

Preparing to catch a few flies of my own for cameraman Gilles Guttadauria

Caught in my own trap!

later, Schmidt Manufacturing got a patent for a trap that "would last a lifetime." Schmidt further boasted that his fly trap would also catch moths and wasps, that it didn't use chemicals or sprays, and that it wouldn't warp or rust in any weather! Yes, sir! If every family on the face of God's green earth bought one of these beauties for just $39, plus $4 postage and handling, plus 8% PST *and* 7% GST, those hairy little black beasts wouldn't stand a chance.

The idea was pure genius: a simple cylinder, twenty centimetres in diameter and thirty-five centimetres high. The lower half of the cylinder was wrapped in tin and had a bunch of holes punched in it.

"This is where the little buggers go in," George said, pointing at the holes. "That's their first mistake."

The flytrap worked on the same principle as a lobster trap. The upper half of the cylinder was wrapped in plain window-screen. The flies entered the holes punched in the lower half and flew up into the "open-air" section. To get there, though, they had to fly up through an inside passageway shaped in an inverted cone. At the very top was a single hole allowing them access into the upper, screened-in half, where there was no way to escape other than going back down through the hole at the top of the cone. They end up dying there in the upper part.

"Why *don't* they go back down the hole in the cone and out again?" I wondered aloud.

"Because they're too stupid!" George sneered. "That's why I don't hear so good. Same thing with that fly in my ear. It was too stupid to come out!"

"So tell me, George, what makes them enter the trap in the first place?"

"Bananas."

"Bananas?"

"Yes, here . . . I put a banana on the plate in here."

He reached over and lifted a small hook that held a door shut at the base of the trap. Behind the tin door, on the floor of the trap, was a small Styrofoam plate, the kind assorted fast-food outlets like McDonald's and Burger King used to use.

"But only half a banana. The closer to rotten, the better. I just lay it down inside and close the door. Fish is good, too. That's why you hang the trap outside. It smells terrible! It has to be at least ten feet from the nearest door."

"What do the flies think of it?" I asked.

"The flies love it! The more smelly, the better."

George was quite a character. He was of medium height, and appeared to be in his early sixties. His lips curved slightly downward at the sides, making George look as if he wore a perpetual scowl. I wondered if that scowl was directed at flies in general or specifically at the fly that damaged his right ear.

His Schmidt Manufacturing "factory" was actually the third floor of George's house; the entire attic of his home had been converted into a workshop. It was a little tight on space, but large enough to launch his new undertaking. Normally, he worked alone, moving from the tin-cutting area to the woodworking bench and then over to the assembly area. Assembled units were carried over to the far side of the attic and painted near the windows, which provided a little ventilation from the paint fumes. If he got a lot of orders and things became a little hectic, George's two daughters, Josie and Georgina, would pitch in and help. When I visited him, George had sold more than seven hundred traps. It was not enough to cleanse the world of the little buzzers, but there had been enough units sold in the town of Leader alone to make it a true "leader" in the war against flies. At least forty of George's units dangled enticingly from tree limbs and verandah eaves in yards throughout the community. The whole town was a kind of fast-food strip for flies. There were no flies to be seen, probably because they were all out dining on rotting bananas and stinky fish.

"How many flies will each trap hold, George?"

"About a gallon."

I laughed. I had never thought of flies in that kind of measure.

"And how do you empty them once they're full?"

"You just open this little door on the top . . . see, right here. Now, you turn the trap upside down and dump them out. Any live ones stay in the trap because they keep flying up. They're too stupid to fly down."

Once we finished the "interview" portion of our shoot, the crew repositioned outside. My producer, Malcolm Hamilton, wanted me to see, first-hand, the incredible fly-catching quality of George's traps. Our cameraman, Gilles Guttadauria, was in position by the time we walked out, busy shooting close-ups of the fly trap hanging in George's yard.

"Too much!" Gilles exclaimed. "Look at all these dead flies."

Sure enough, the trap was half full. There were hundreds of flies inside. Or, as George would say, at least two quarts full.

"You should see what it looks like through the lens," said Gilles. He was obviously having a great time. "George, come over here and have a look!" he called.

I studied George's face as he looked at flies for the first time in his life through a powerful close-up lens. It was as if he were really meeting the enemy for the first time face-to-face. The captor had his captives *exactly* where he wanted them. How sweet it was!

"Yes," he muttered. "That's them all right. Dirty little things!"

By now, I was sold on his invention. I'd never seen so many dead flies in the same place at one time.

"George, I'd like to buy one of your traps," I said, interrupting his moment of ecstasy.

"Good, good!" he replied. "Yes, I have some ready."

He was absolutely thrilled. Another soul was about to take up arms and help him in his holy crusade against the infernal blue-bottle fly.

I left Leader, Saskatchewan, that June day with a genuine, patent-approved Schmidt Fly Trap. I could hardly wait to get home. My wife, Leanne, was going to be very happy with my homecoming gift. You see, we were undergoing renovations to our kitchen at Indian Creek, and the workers were going in and out of our house like shoppers walking through revolving doors at an Eaton's sale. Needless to say, there were more than a few flies in the house. We had pints and pints of them! And not just everyday suburban houseflies. These were big, Ontario-horse-farm, hey-let's-have-a-party-at-Rostad's-type flies. They were everywhere! So I was pretty happy on my way home. I was about to fix that problem with the greatest fly trap in the world. Those dirty, arrogant flies were about to be "Schmidt-enized!"

When I arrived at Indian Creek, I wasted no time in getting down to business.

"Lee-Lee," I said to my wife, "give me half a banana, please."

"Half a banana?"

"Yes, I need it for the flies."

"So it's not enough we open our doors and invite them in. Now, you want to start feeding them!"

I pulled George's trap out of its shipping box and held it by its hanger in front of Leanne's face.

"Say goodbye to our flies!" I announced, triumphantly.

"And just what is this thing?" she asked.

"It's a fly trap."

"A fly trap?"

"Yes. It catches flies."

"No kidding. And the banana?"

"Well, the banana is going to act as bait. See, you put the banana on the Styrofoam plate behind this little door here, and when the flies get a whiff of it, they go crazy! The flies go through these little holes around the bottom, feast on the banana, fly up the middle of the trap, out the top of that cone-shaped thingy inside, into this screened, open-air penthouse, where they fly till they die! It's brilliant! What do you think?"

Now, my wife is a very expressive woman. She clearly voices her opinion on just about anything. But sometimes, a certain look comes over her and she communicates without uttering a single word. During these moments, her silence is deafening, and it was clear to me that George's trap was going to have to prove itself. You see, Lee was not about to fill herself with false hope. I had done that once to her already. When the renovations to our kitchen began, the workers told me it would be a six-week job, start to finish. And that's what I told Lee. But, I made a few changes in the renovation plans partway through the job, and that led to a few delays. The renovations were now ten weeks old and would not be finished for at least another four weeks. The way my wife saw it was that I was the one who was way behind, not the workers, and she had reached the end of her rope. She had been at *war* with our Indian Creek flies for well over two months and I knew, if I got rid of them, I would be at least partly exonerated. So that night, before going to bed, I cut a well-ripened banana in half, placed the tantalizing morsel on the Styrofoam plate inside the bottom of the unit, and hung the "mother of all fly traps" from a kitchen-ceiling beam, smack dab in the middle of the construction war zone.

Now, I don't know what the difference is between an Ontario fly and a Saskatchewan fly, but I didn't have a lot of luck with George's trap. I knew the trap worked. I had seen how successful it was back at George's place, but at our house, something was wrong. After it had hung in the kitchen for several days, there were only five or six flies in the trap. These Ontario flies were a marvel to watch. They would fly all around the trap, land on it and pass the time of day all over it – then go in *and* out of the little holes leading into the trap! But only five or six flies were stupid enough to get caught!

"Honey, the thing works! I don't know what's wrong with this one. Maybe the banana isn't rotten enough. Maybe we should try a piece of rotten fish."

There was no reply. Only silence.

Finally, I remembered George's instruction sheet (I never read instructions), and there it was, in bold print: FOR BEST RESULTS HANG IN SUNNY PLACE ABOUT TEN FEET FROM HOUSE ENTRANCE. DO NOT HANG INSIDE BUILDINGS.

"Lee, I did it wrong. We have to try this all over again," I said.

Well, that comment went over like a lead balloon. So I took the trap out to the barn, where the flies in June are thicker than rain, and hung it ten feet from the double doors, out in the bright sunshine. I decided that I would wait until it was at least two quarts full before showing it to Leanne again.

Three weeks later, my producer, Malcolm, called to remind me that he and the crew would be arriving at our farm on Wednesday morning to do a few on-cameras for the show. The farm, or Studio R, as we often refer to it, is used as a set for "On the Road Again" every other Wednesday of the month. The house and property provide a rural background for me to say hello or goodbye to our viewers and to introduce some of our stories. Wednesday, we had to do an on-camera for the George Schmidt fly-trap story.

"How has your trap been working?" Malcolm asked.

"To tell you the truth, Malcolm, I haven't checked on it. It's out at the barn. What have you got in mind for the on-camera?"

"Well, nothing at the moment. I haven't been able to think of anything since the monkey idea fell through."

I was quite relieved to hear the monkeys weren't coming.

Malcolm had originally planned to do a closing for the fly-trap show in the kitchen. He envisioned me telling our viewers how beautifully George's trap performed and how successful the banana bait was. So successful, in fact, that, while the bananas got rid of the flies in our house, another problem – an even bigger one – had taken over. Then, Malcolm intended to have the camera pull back to reveal a kitchen full of monkeys, having a banana fight, he hoped.

Incredible? Not really. Our show has always relished doing unusual and outlandish on-cameras. Over the years, I have had litres of water dumped on my head from the front-end loader of our tractor; I've bathed on the CBC network in our tub upstairs with nothing but a little rubber duckie to keep me company; I've been dragged around the farm by an out-of-control track machine; I've had pies thrown in my face and had solid barn walls come down on me. No, the monkey idea was not an unusual proposition – especially coming from Malcolm Hamilton. No one could ever accuse him of lacking imagination! But apparently, there weren't enough monkeys in the region and they would be far too expensive to bring out to the farm, because we'd have to bring their owners and trainers with them. Malcolm needed something else.

"I'll check the trap out first thing in the morning, Malcolm, and I'll try to think of something to say in the on-camera by the time you get here."

On Wednesday, I walked out to the barn and had a look at George's trap. There were only a few dead flies inside. I didn't quite know how to evaluate it. The weather had been cool for several days now, quite uncharacteristic for early July in the Ottawa Valley. I assumed that the million-plus flies lurking in the barn didn't care to venture outdoors when the mercury dropped.

"Still no joy," I told Malcolm after he and the crew arrived. "For some reason, the trap isn't working."

"But it sure worked in Leader," Malcolm reminded me. "George had hundreds of flies in his trap."

"I think our flies are a lot smarter than theirs," I countered. "I'll tell you what, though. If you want flies, just walk into the barn. It's like a fly resort out there."

"What we need are flies in the trap," Malcolm said disappointedly.

"I have another idea that might work," I said. "Supposing I say goodnight to our viewers and explain that I am determined to solve the fly problem at the farm with good old-fashioned fly stickers – not just the little twisters, but the big, six-foot-long barn-type stickers! The ones you yank out by slipping your fingers into the brass grommets and pulling for all you're worth. They're massive stickers! Six inches wide!"

I had Malcolm's undivided attention.

"Now," I continued, "imagine hanging seven or eight of them from the kitchen ceiling, along with a few of the standard little flypaper thingies and a Vapona pest strip or two."

Malcolm's creative juices started flowing.

"Yes! Yes!" he said. "Then you can accidentally get stuck on one of these giant fly-catchers!"

"Precisely!" I replied. "Completely tangled up."

"But do you really want to do this, Wayne?"

"I don't know. What's that glue stuff made of, anyway? And what happens to my clothes after I'm covered in the stuff? Worse than that, what about my hair or my face?"

For a moment, we stopped talking. We were thinking. Then, in typical "On the Road Again" fashion, we agreed to give it a go. Sometimes, creativity overrules caution. Heck, it was only fly-paper!

I phoned our friend, Murray, over at the local feed store in the village of Pakenham, to see if he had any big barn fly-catchers in stock.

"Plenty in stock. How many do you want?" he asked.

"We'll need an assortment. Throw in a half-dozen of those and a dozen of the regular little guys."

"I'll put them aside for you," he said.

"Great, Murray. I'm sending a guy over to pick them up. His name's Malcolm."

A half-hour later, Malcolm returned with a box full of anti-fly artillery. He had little fly-stickie things, giant, roll-out, stick-anything-you-want-to-it things, sprays (thank goodness Leanne was at work), and an assortment of other things that one hangs to attract flies.

We did a quick test on one of the big, roll-out-type catchers. It was horrible! Thin wisps of gooey stuff floated up from the edges as we unravelled it. They lingered in midair for a few moments and then settled on our clothing.

"I don't know about this," I said. "I kinda wish now that you had those monkeys."

"No, you don't," said Gilles. "Have you ever seen a bunch of monkeys in a group? They drop crap all over the place and throw it at each other. You'd be getting it, too . . . in the face, all over!"

"Besides," added Malcolm, "it was cost-prohibitive. One trainer, in Montreal, was willing to bring his monkey only if we paid him eight thousand dollars a day!"

"Eight grand!" I exclaimed. "That's nuts! Let's stick with the paper."

We started hanging the various fly gizmos from the big heavy beams in our kitchen. The plan formed as we went along.

"God, this is sticky stuff," I said.

It was getting harder and harder to move between the ribbons of guck hanging around me.

"We're going to have one crack at it, boys," I cautioned. "Gilles, once I walk into one of these things, that's it. It's 'rock-and-roll' shooting – you get what you get. That okay with you?"

It wasn't the first time Gilles would "rock and roll" it. He was very good at "shooting from the hip."

"Yeah," he said. "I think we'll be okay. All right, I'm rolling."

Moments later, the scene unfolded rapidly – and unexpectedly. I had just finished hanging the final two-metre roll from a nail in the beam overhead. While I was unravelling it, the nail pulled free from the beam. The thing landed right on my head and I was draped in horrible, sticky, fly-catching guck. Instinctively, my hands went to my face, and, much to my dismay, my left eyelid was stuck closed. As I shoved the stuff aside, it felt as if I had pulled the skin off the tip of my nose. But there was no time for any self-concern – this was it, the one take! I fell backwards into another big hanging sticker and twisted my body so it would wrap around me, then, into a third glob of goop, just to make sure Gilles had the shot. I was a human fly! I fell to my knees in the kitchen, looking as if I was in a brown, gooey straitjacket. I couldn't move my left arm; it was glued. Gilles was moving all around me now, getting all the necessary camera angles to help edit the scene together for the show. Finally, I couldn't take it any more.

"That's it! That's it! This stuff is gross. Somebody help me get it off."

There was no way to save my shirt. It was married forever to the flypaper. We literally had to peel the shirt off my body. My face and arms were festooned with dozens of wispy cobweb-like trails of goop. I was very concerned now about my eyes. My left eye had opened again, but something kept trying to close it – probably a strand of goop. And my hair was starting to harden! That's when realization dawned. This was glue! I wasn't sure what kind, but it sure wasn't "gentle to the hands" kind of glue. No, sir. This was good old-fashioned fly glue! Catch 'em, hold 'em, and kill 'em glue! Who knew what chemicals were in this stuff? Had I read the instruction label on the flypaper rolls before I got into this mess? Of course not. Why hadn't I? Well . . . because I never read instructions!

I wanted this stuff *off* me now, but nothing seemed to work. Sunlight dish detergent was useless. Hand soap? Forget it.

"Gas!" I exclaimed. "Gas! Let's go out to the shop. Gas will get this stuff off."

Malcolm came out with me. In the shop, I had a container of gas we used for the chainsaw. I put some on my hands and had some success removing the goop.

"How about this?" said Malcolm as he handed me a container. "This should work."

"Malcolm, this is paint stripper! It'll work all right. It'll probably take my skin off!"

It's amazing how people interact on the verge of total panic. There we were, Malcolm and Wayne, the Laurel and Hardy of the '90s.

"Turpentine!" Malcolm exclaimed. "What about turpentine?"

Malcolm put the paint stripper back on the shelf and handed me the turpentine. By now, my hair was rock hard. I tried a little bit of turpentine on my arm. It worked beautifully. The goop disappeared.

Inside the house, I headed straight for the shower, clutching that bottle of turpentine.

"You're not going to put that in your hair, are you?" asked Malcolm. "Don't put that on your head!"

As if I was going to take advice from a man who just suggested I use paint stripper!

Now, before I explain what happened next, allow me to digress for a moment. I know that only a crazy person would wash their hair in turpentine. I know that *now*. But I was completely oblivious to such logic at that moment. My hair was a mass of rock-hard glue, something was trying to pull my eyelids together and shut out the light of day forever, and there was no doubt in my mind that life-threatening chemicals from the flypaper were leaching through the pores of my skin. In a few minutes I would probably suffer the fate of millions of flies before me: namely, total collapse of the nervous system. This was no time for logic! This was time for action!

Within seconds I was in the shower, bottle in hand. For the first minute or so, I didn't detect anything unusual – except maybe the odour of the stuff. I felt nothing but relief. The turpentine was working. My petrified mass of hair loosened with each application, and the pulling sensation on my left eyelid suddenly ceased. I was grateful for the bountiful flow of water because of all that turpentine flowing about my eyes.

Suddenly, a wave of nausea hit me. The fumes of the turpentine were trapped in the shower stall.

I flew out of the shower. I looked in the mirror. The horrible goop was off me and, mercifully, my hair was no longer a glob of glue. However, I felt a slight tingling sensation on my scalp. Nothing to be alarmed about, I thought at first, just a slight tingling. But then the tingling started to feel more like a burn. Five minutes later I was on the phone talking to a nurse at the hospital in Almonte. Malcolm walked into my office to see how I was doing. The top of my scalp now felt like it was on fire. I was about to spew lava!

"You've got to tell me what's happening, ma'am. My head is burning terribly!"

By now, Gilles was in the office, as was Mike Champagne, our audio man. They had been unaware of what was going on because they had been packing their gear in the truck. Malcolm was telling the boys about my turpentine shower when my son, Josh, who was twenty years old at that time, arrived home from school and entered the office. He was quite upset.

"How could you do that, Dad? You don't put turpentine on your head!"

Josh continued to chastise me as I tried to explain matters to the nurse on the phone. The nurse asked if someone would be able to answer the phone when she called back in a couple of minutes.

"Yes. My son, Josh," I replied.

"Okay. Get right back in the shower and keep rinsing your head. I'll phone the Poison Control Centre and call you right back."

I must say it felt good to get back in the shower. The cool water helped ease the burning sensation on my scalp. Josh came in to tell me the nurse had called again with good news. I would be okay, but I was to stay in the shower for at least another half-hour.

"Well, that's a relief." I said. "Thank you."

Thirty minutes is a long time to stand in a shower. I had a lot of time to think. I rinsed a lot and actually took time to do something I should have done before: I picked up the bottle of turpentine and read the instructions! Yes, sir! Skull and crossbones . . . "DANGER . . . Poison! . . . Harmful or fatal if swallowed . . . Avoid breathing fumes." I didn't die, but I did have a severe case of dandruff for the next two weeks.

It's been three years since that fly trap got me into all that trouble. It now sits out in the barn by the hot-water heater. I've never put bait in it since the summer I brought it home. The cold weather has come now and, once again, there isn't a fly in sight. The little buggers are all in a state of suspended animation. And I'm not about to wake them up.

I'm sure that George P. Schmidt's invention performs admirably. I know for a fact that it works on Saskatchewan flies. It just remains to be proven on my farm. Truth is, I don't really have much desire to find out if it works or not. I've kind of had it with flies. Besides, the renovations are done now, and those pesky *Musca domesticas* are under control. I'm pretty happy about that, because I don't ever want to see one of those sticky flypaper things around the farm again.

You sure learn a lot doing a television show like mine. Thanks to George, I know a lot more about flies now. And, thanks to Malcolm, I know a lot more about turpentine.

A320 Tour Bus

~

Doing a show like "On the Road Again" means a lot of travel. It also means having to deal with all kinds of people in the service industry. So, when a person goes the extra mile to make someone feel special, I don't miss it. And I appreciate when it happens.

The other day, Air Canada did something really nice. Actually, it was one of their captains; he just used one of Air Canada's jets to do it.

I had finished a week of shooting with my crew on the Great Northern Peninsula of Newfoundland and had flown from St. Anthony to St. John's on a beautiful, clear August day. You could see for miles! The weather had been like that all week. It was probably the most beautiful week in the history of the province.

It just doesn't get any better than this, I thought.

That only added to my chagrin. You see, Newfoundland does not get that kind of weather often, and I was perturbed that my own plane was sitting in the hangar back in Ottawa, laid up for maintenance, unable to go winging across the isle. The approach into St. John's was spectacular. Every approach I had ever made with my plane into St. John's was always in lousy weather, and I felt cheated.

After a brief stopover, I boarded one of Air Canada's big A320 Airbuses for the mid-afternoon flight to Halifax, where I would connect with yet another flight to Ottawa.

Oh, to have my own plane! I mused. No security hassles, no waiting around, just keep the blue side up, point the nose, and go.

On the flight from St. Anthony, I had had a window seat, and throughtout the trip was mesmerized by the view of all the icebergs drifting below in the Atlantic. So, after clearing security in

St. John's, I naturally settled into another window seat, well in front of the big A320's wing. Before you could down a glass of orange juice, we were pushing back from the gate.

The Airbus is one of the newer generation of jets flying today, and one of the most powerful in domestic service. Its two huge engines are remarkably quiet, but oh, so strong! I always marvel at how quickly it climbs to altitude. On this particular day, however, we levelled off *very* quickly. The big engine's throttles were pulled back from takeoff power to slow cruise less than a minute after we left the asphalt. Looking out my window, I figured we were only two or three thousand feet up. While this is certainly a legal altitude at which to fly, it is, to say the least, just a little lower than normal for a high-flying Airbus.

"Good afternoon, ladies and gentlemen," said a warm cheerful voice over the intercom. "This is your captain speaking. Because it's such a beautiful day in Newfoundland today, we thought you might like to see how lovely the island is. We don't get too many flying days that are as clear as this, so we thought we'd do a little low-level flying for a few minutes to let you folks have a look before we climb to our assigned altitude en route to Halifax."

What followed was the most remarkable view of the Avalon Peninsula I have ever seen. If you look at a map of Newfoundland, the Avalon is that lower, easternmost portion of the island jutting out into the Atlantic that resembles a four-petalled orchid in full bloom. We travelled completely around the northernmost petal of that orchid in the sea that afternoon.

"Flight deck again, folks. If you look off the left side of the aircraft, you'll see Harbour Grace coming into view. We'll continue north for a couple of minutes up to Carbonear and Baie de Verde, then we'll swing south on the Trinity Bay side. That's Conception Bay underneath us right now. Pretty, isn't it?"

Our flight attendant was tickled by the reaction from the passengers on board. Tired, well-travelled faces suddenly came to attention as it dawned on them that they were being invited to experience more of a flight than the typical, fire-up-the-burners, thunder-down-the-tarmac, and beetle-to-altitude flight. Suddenly, it was as if we had bought tickets for an Air Canada sightseeing tour!

The quaint fishing villages along the shore, with their houses and fishing shacks clinging to the cliffsides, were picture-perfect in the sunlight. I wondered how many faces in those villages lifted skyward that day as our giant tour bus winged overhead.

"This is absolutely wonderful!" I said to the attendant. "I can't believe he's taking the time to do this for your passengers."

"This guy does this when the weather is good," she said. "Some do, some don't. He's very good like that, this captain."

"I'd like to know his name," I said. "Somebody should let Air Canada know how considerate and thoughtful this man is."

"I'll pass on your regards," she replied. "He'll like that. I'll get you his card."

The tour lasted a good ten minutes, with an excellent running commentary from the man with the warm voice in the cockpit. He certainly knew the island well. And he obviously loved his job and cared for people.

"Well, folks, we'll head off for Halifax now. We'd like everyone with their seatbelts securely fastened for the climb. We should be at the ramp in Halifax on time as scheduled. We hope you enjoyed the tour. Thank you for flying Air Canada. Enjoy the rest of the flight."

As the intercom clicked off and the mighty engines throttled up, there was a spontaneous burst of applause from all aboard the Airbus. Our attendant beamed with pride and ran to the cockpit door, pulling it open so the captain could hear our appreciation. We laid on a good round of applause with a few hearty "here, heres!" and "well dones!" thrown in for good measure.

I was doubly appreciative. All week I had wanted to see Newfoundland from the air from that glorious clear sky, and, thanks to one very thoughtful Air Canada captain, I managed to do just that. My disappointment at not having my own plane vanished completely. This was far more special: cruising the skies

over Newfoundland at low level in an A320 Airbus with one of
the best tour guides imaginable. Was he a Newfoundlander by
birth? I don't know. I do know his name though. The card the
flight attendant gave me was a formal Air Canada card that read
"Captain H. W. Brown, Air Canada, Toronto Int'l Airport,
Toronto, Ontario." But when I turned the card over, I caught a
glimpse of the real man at the controls that day. On the back was
a label bearing the logo of the Ontario Federation of Anglers and
Hunters. It read William Brown, General Delivery, South River,
Ontario. A country boy. It all made perfect sense.

JONATHAN CRAVEN

Jim and Gail Henry of Sandspit, B.C. garbage-dump millionaires

MIKE CHAMPAGNE

"Interview" day with the Henrys

MIKE CHAMPAGNE

Jim and Gail, dressed to the nines, toast their good fortune in the Sandspit dump.

The Garbage-Dump Millionaires

There is a dump in the beautiful Queen Charlotte Islands, just off the coast of British Columbia, that is owned and operated by the Henry family. It's ten kilometres down the road from the laid-back little town of Sandspit, on the island of Moresby, second-largest of all the Queen Charlotte Islands, the ancestral home of the Haida nation. Moresby sits out in the Pacific, just about one hundred and thirty kilometres west of Prince Rupert and the same distance south of Alaska. The Sandspit dump is almost as far west as you can go in Canada.

It's really quite a nice dump. The region's garbage, picked up twice a week by Jim and Gail Henry, is neatly separated into burnable and recyclable piles: over here, a great heap of black rubber tires; back there, fridges and stoves; over there, along the entrance road, car and truck bodies; and in the far corner, the huge burning mound, with refuse, ever-smouldering, from yesterday's fire. Overhead, the dump's resident scavengers, big, beautiful bald eagles, circle the site, keeping an eye out for their next meal. Sometimes, it's a rodent, but, more often than not, it's something delivered "à la carte" by the Henrys. Everything in this Queen Charlotte "dumpository" is in perfect order. The Henrys work hard to keep it that way, in spite of the fact they don't need to work at all. You see, the Henrys are millionaires. They won a million-dollar lottery three years ago, and could have retired for life. But they didn't. They still collect interest on their money – and they still collect garbage in Sandspit.

Now, I don't know about you, but if I won a million dollars and worked at the local dump, sorting, raking, and burning all

kinds of smelly trash, I don't imagine it would take me very long
to quit stacking garbage and start stacking bills. And while a
million dollars doesn't go as far as it used to, it can, with proper
handling, mean manageable bills, no mortgage, and a wonderful
sense of security. The trick is not so much having the money
in hand. It's getting it out of your hands and into the bank. Needless to say, as I travelled west to meet the Henrys, I was quite
intrigued about why these garbage-dump millionaires chose not
to dump their jobs.

Jim and Gail Henry are originally from the state of Oregon.
They came to the Queen Charlotte Islands with two young sons
in 1975. A daughter was born shortly after they arrived on
Moresby. For the first seven years, Jim worked with MacMillan
Bloedel, the forestry giant. When he got laid off in 1982, he and
Gail considered leaving Sandspit; however, they finally opted to
tough it out and stay.

After he was laid off, Jim managed to find other work in the
region, as a forestry engineer, and Gail got a job doing the books
for the Sandspit Landfill Site – also known as the dump. In 1990,
when the owner of the dump had a heart attack and wanted out of
the garbage business, Jim and Gail pooled their resources, and
before you could say, "Where do you keep your garbage?" they
bought him out. The Henrys were now the proud owners of the
town dump, the new collectors of Sandspit's community garbage
– five hundred persons' worth!

It's hard, and often smelly, work.

"We see it all," Gail told me. "Diapers broken open, and stuff
like that, are definitely not fun. You earn your money." Talk about
having to deal with disposable income!

Tuesday is Sandspit's main collection day. Saturday is devoted
to picking up glass and metal and sorting it for recycling, since
the community is very environmentally conscious. It is also well
kept and well laid out, with lots of biking and hiking trails.

When I arrived in Sandspit, they were enjoying pretty good

weather. There were a few sunny periods, although late March in the Charlottes is usually quite cool with lots of rain. My first order of the day was to check out the dump.

Jim and Gail gave us the Cook's tour. For Jonathan Craven, our producer that week, it was a review of what he'd seen a few weeks earlier on his research trip. The dump was completely invisible from the main road, tucked in behind a shelter of trees. A couple of rather large eagles were perched on the branches of a big tamarack at the edge of the dump, keeping an eye on us.

"They're like crows," I commented, pulling my camera out of its case.

Gilles Guttadauria, our cameraman, already had his still camera out and was busy framing the eagles in his viewfinder.

"Amazing, eh?" Gilles said. "We never think of eagles as scavengers. They look out of place, hanging around a dump."

"I've got to get a few snaps, too," I said. "No one back home will believe the great bald eagle has come to this."

"Not so unusual, when you think about it," Jim Henry said. "It's the best lunch in town. Lots to eat – and not just rodents."

"And not a lot of competition, either," Gail added. "Not too many crows care to argue with an eagle."

The Henrys were a very nice couple. Jim, in his early fifties, was of medium build, with short, greying hair and a warm, pleasant smile. I think he rather enjoyed our crew's visit. Gail did, too. She was in her mid-forties, very jovial and good-natured. They *both* laughed a lot. I don't know what it is about dump owners and operators. They *all* seem to laugh a lot. Willie Bowes, the man who runs the Pakenham Township dump a few miles from my farm in Ontario, is always chuckling away when he works at the site. And the boys who owned and operated Rump's Dump in Carp, Ontario, for years and years were always in great humour, too. Maybe it's the fumes coming off all that garbage.

"Tell me, Gail, are there any other millionaire dump owners that you know of?" I asked.

"Well, yes. I can think of one or two. But their dumps are bigger than ours – big enough to make them millionaires. Remember, we won our million. You'd never make that kind of money with an operation this size."

Gail bought her winning ticket at the small video-rental store in Sandspit in December 1992. Then, she got so caught up in the festive season, what with Christmas and the bringing in of 1993, that she forgot to check her ticket when the draw took place. In fact, she forgot about the ticket completely until the last Saturday in January. She had just completed her grocery shopping and was trying to find enough money to pay the cashier when she spotted the ticket floating around in the bottom of her purse. It was now a month and a half old. Surely, she thought, someone had claimed the million by then, and almost threw it out, then and there. But she decided, instead, to go next door to the video store and check it out anyway, just in case.

So she and her daughter, Meredith, placed the groceries in their truck, and she asked Meredith to wait while she went to look up the lottery numbers.

"At first, I thought I had won fifty dollars. You know, you never expect to win the million. Then I noticed more and more of the numbers were the same as the ones posted and I started to think I was seeing things. I mean, you never think it can happen to you. I looked at the numbers again and thought, this can't be! So I asked the girl to check it."

"And what was her reaction?" I asked.

"Well, she said, 'Yes . . . you won!' And I said, 'What? Fifty bucks? A hundred?' She said, 'No! You won a million!' I said, 'A million!' She said, 'Yes! Here, look! You just won a million dollars!'"

"You must have gone through the ceiling," I said.

"I was totally shocked! I remember hanging on to the counter. I couldn't breathe! I didn't know if I was going to fall over, or pass out, or what! I was a millionaire! What a way to start the year!"

"Where was Jim? At home?" I asked.

"He was out here at the dump, working. I remember driving out on an empty tank. I was so excited! I wanted to be the one to tell him."

"You must remember that day, Jim," I said.

"Oh, yeah, I remember, all right. She came tearing in here with something on her mind, that's for sure."

"How did you react?"

"Well . . ."

"I'll tell you how he reacted," Gail interrupted. "He said, 'Why me? Why now?' Here we are, married almost twenty years, our kids are almost grown . . . Why now?"

"Weren't you excited?" I asked Jim.

"Oh, sure, I was excited! I just wished it was twenty years earlier, when we were first starting out. But, yeah . . . I was real happy about it! I said, 'Hey, we'll take it.' You bet!"

"So, what did you two do then?" I asked.

"Well," said Gail, "I drove back to town, still on empty. And made it."

"And, Jim, what did you do?"

"I went back, too. I had the afternoon run to do, the glass pickup."

"You didn't take the day off to celebrate?"

"No. This is what we normally do on Saturday. I mean, somebody had to pick it up."

"What happened when Tuesday rolled around?" I asked. "Did you get someone else to pick up the garbage?"

"Not at all," Jim replied. "We did our pickup as usual. It's what we wanted to do. That's what people around here expected us to do. People didn't expect to have to say, 'Where's the garbage man?' Tuesday is pickup day in Sandspit, and that's exactly what we did."

"Speaking of Sandspit," Jonathan said, "we should really head in there now and sit down for the interview."

Having said that, we bid adieu to the eagles and headed for town.

At the Henrys' modest two-storey house on the Beach Road, Gilles and Mike Champagne, our audio man, set up lights in the living room, while Gail and Jim cleaned up in preparation for our sit-down chat. By the time we were ready, so were they. Gone was Gail's ball cap. She'd washed and curled her hair. Gone was her grungy grey sweatshirt, riddled with holes; she was now wearing a lovely plum-coloured silk blouse. She also wore lipstick and makeup. Jim's ball cap had been discarded, too. His hair was neatly combed across his forehead, and he was dressed in clean woollen work socks, a grey flannel shirt, and cotton pants, smartly held up by snappy black suspenders. No trappings of the rich were evident, no heavy jewellery, and no Rolex watches. Not only had the money not gone to their heads – it wasn't on their backs, either.

"Are there any problems that come with winning a million dollars?" I asked. "And if so, what was the first one you had to deal with?"

Gail responded first. "How not to let it change our lives," she replied. "That's the biggest problem with winning so much money. Not letting it change you."

"Did it?"

"I don't think so," Gail said. "We've got that under control. I got awfully sick worrying about it changing us, though. You see, we always felt our lives were rich enough before the money came along. So I worried a lot about that. That was very stressful."

"How do you feel now?"

"I'm fine about it now," Gail said. "We're controlling the money. It's not controlling us."

"Truth is," Jim said, "a million dollars is nice, but it also means a lot more responsibility. Our kids, for example."

"Yeah," Gail laughed. "They immediately expected something from all this."

"So, how did you handle that?"

"Jim and I told the kids, right at the beginning of all this, we would be sharing the money. We didn't tell them with whom or how much, because we needed time to sort that part out."

Jim said, "I've taught my kids there is no such thing as a free lunch. You just don't get something for nothing. You've got to earn what you get."

"They all had paper routes from the time they were nine years old," Gail added. "They understand where their money comes from. When they went back to school after the win, everybody said, 'Hey, wow! Are your folks gonna buy you a car? You don't have to worry about going to school. You've got it made!' That's when my daughter, Meredith, said, 'Whoa! These are *my* parents, you're talking about, remember?'"

"So, I gather they didn't get new cars."

"No," Gail answered, "they didn't. But we did give each of our kids five thousand dollars. And twenty-four of our relatives got five thousand each, as well."

"Boy, that's what, about a hundred and thirty thousand, right there?"

"Yeah, about that," said Jim. "And the Coastal Mission got some, too."

"What is that?"

"A spiritual organization that services all the remote communities up and down the coast. We gave them a hundred thousand."

"That's a heck of a gift!" I said.

"Yes, but it was something we felt we had to do. They do good work."

"And we treated ourselves to a new truck!" Gail added. "A new Ford Explorer."

"What about the old garbage truck?" I asked. "Are you going to replace that one, too?"

"Heck, no!" Jim said. "Whatever for? The old Dodge runs fine. She isn't pretty, but, hey, we're talking garbage, here."

"What have you done about your future?" I asked.

"Well," Jim replied, "we bought the local gas station. It's the only one in town, so we thought it was a good investment to make. We kept the manager on."

"We're also going to invest a little in the house!" Gail said, with a beaming smile.

"Are you going to put on an addition?" I asked.

"No. Don't need an addition," she said. On her fingers, she counted off the five items on her home-improvement list: "New windows, new roof, new siding, a sundeck, and a hot tub."

"Boy, you sound like you know exactly what you want."

"You bet I do. And, I'm going to hire someone to come and do it, so I don't have to wait another fifteen years for it," she added, nudging an elbow, lovingly, into Jim's shoulder.

"What about the dump?" I asked. "You're millionaires. Why continue to pick up garbage and run a dump?"

"It has never crossed our minds to get rid of the dump," Jim replied. "It keeps us busy and pays for itself, as well as providing us with a basic income. So why sell it? We figure we'll run it for at least another ten years."

"Why should our values change," Gail asked, "just because we came into some money?"

"In a lot of ways," Jim added, "*nothing* is going to change a whole lot, except we've told our kids we'll give them interest-free loans to go to university. But, it will have to be paid back once they get jobs."

They remind me of some neighbours back home in Pakenham, who, like the Henrys won a pile of money in a lottery not long ago. I guess a lot of folks wondered what would happen to them under the influence of so much money; but not a heck of a lot changed. They modestly renovated the same house they lived in before the win and continue to live and work in the community.

I wondered how the people of Sandspit felt when the Henrys won their money.

"They've been great," Gail told me. "They have definitely taken it in stride. Everyone treats us just the same. No one has tried to hit us up for money, or anything. Our lives are much the same as they've been here for, what, twenty years now?"

"Do you still buy lottery tickets?" I asked.

"I probably spend fifty to sixty dollars a year on lottery tickets," Gail replied.

"That's all?"

"Yes."

"Can you afford it?"

"No!" Jim interrupted. "We can't!" We all laughed.

When we shot the closing scene for the story of our garbage-dump millionaires, Jonathan Craven's genius came into play. He had the Henrys dress up! Jim donned formal black tails, complete with vest and bow tie, and Gail slipped into a long plum gown and dressy evening jacket. For a crowning touch, Jim wore hightop gumboots – the kind every farmer from St. John's to Sandspit wears in the barnyard – and Gail jumped into big old rain galoshes. The combination was priceless. They popped a bottle of champagne, poured a little bubbly into crystal glasses, and toasted their good fortune. Then, Jim gathered Gail in his arms, and they began to dance. It was quite a sight. There they were, in the heart of the Sandspit dump: the Henrys, garbage-dump millionaires, dancing gracefully among the tires and the recyclable and smouldering garbage, as the bald eagles looked on in silent wonder. In television, we call that a million-dollar scene.

Tamusi Qumak shows off two of his proudest achievements – his dictionary and his Order of Canada medal

Nellie Echaluk and Mary Igaluk throat singing in the Eastern Arctic

My two little wing-walkers

Charlie Adams, of the Inuit Television Network

The Arctic

One by one, our customs change,
New voices teach new ways,
These changes flow as rapidly as the river.

I wonder, as time goes by,
Will we be wise. Will we survive,
Or be swept away by the ever-changing river.

– from the song "The River"

There is so much to say about the north that I find it hard to know where to begin. I have to take a breath before starting to describe the place, because these days things are changing so fast in this part of the world that it boggles the mind.

I have made several trips to the north with "On the Road Again." I have travelled up to the high western Arctic, the Yukon, all the way over to Baffin Island, visiting communities on both sides of the Arctic Circle. Every journey to this vast and beautiful land fills me with a sense of adventure.

While the land itself remains timeless, never changing, our native Inuit, who have lived in the north for centuries, have experienced tremendous change. Over the last fifty years, they have raced through time. I'm just grateful for the opportunity to see the north now, before the few remaining vestiges of the northern life I read about as a child are gone. The truth is, what many of us learned in grade school has nothing to do with the way the north is today. So, before I speak of my travels to the north, let me paint a few pictures of what to expect north of 60.

First of all, everyone – except for maybe a few people in the southern United States – knows there is no chance of finding a community of Inuit in this day and age living in igloos and tents. So forget that picture. It belongs to the 1940s and before, when the Inuit were completely self-reliant, surviving only by the wisdom and knowledge passed down orally from one generation to the next. That was all over by the late 1950s. By then, the Inuit had discontinued their nomadic lifestyle and settled in permanent communities across the Arctic.

Today, the majority of Inuit live in the high Arctic in energy-efficient, well-insulated homes, complete with modern conveniences. Communities like Coppermine, a hamlet of twelve hundred people situated at the edge of the Beaufort Sea in the western Arctic, now have street signs and numbered housing. Holman, a tiny hamlet of three hundred, first established in 1940 as a Hudson's Bay Company trading post on Victoria Island, has taxi service! Yellowknife, in the Northwest Territories, a city of only seventeen thousand people, now has bus service running every hour on the hour, from one end of town to the other. And get this. The "Golden Arches" came to Yellowknife in 1993. They now have not one but *two* McDonald's franchises open daily for business. In isolated communities across the high north, there are snow machines and four-wheel all-terrain vehicles parked outside every door and satellite dishes, in yards and on rooftops, bringing in the outside world.

You can also forget the image of having to travel for days to reach "isolated" communities in the north. Today, if you want to visit the magnificent Pangnirtung Fiord on Baffin Island, once an arduous trek taking several days, it's an easy trip. You simply fly to the community of Pangnirtung. They have an airport with regularly scheduled daily flights. Want to go to the Magnetic North Pole? That's easy, too. There's a strip in the community of Resolute. From there you can travel by land to the Pole.

Today, if you suddenly decided you wanted to spend a few hours with a herd of muskox, out on the barren lands high above the Arctic Circle, you could be doing it in less than twenty-four hours by simply flying into Cambridge Bay on Victoria Island in the high central Arctic. There are thousands of muskox wandering all over Victoria Island, and a good number of them are never more than a few kilometres from Cambridge Bay. All you need to do on arrival is hire a guide and hop on a snow machine. If you're a purist, though, hire a guide who still travels the land by dog team. That's a lot more fun.

Another image of the north I would like to dispel is that of having to do without. If you're the type of person who enjoys the creature comforts of home, don't worry too much about how you're going to keep warm and comfortable when you visit. While "guesting" in most of these "isolated," high-north communities, you'll stay in surprisingly modern hotels and motels, with all the amenities – telephones, remote-controlled televisions, full three-piece washrooms, wake-up calls, and maid service. In many places, you can even have your choice of rental car. The truth is, the day a McDonald's franchise shows up in Iqaluit is not that far off.

One image you will see in the north today, however, is an Inuit society still reeling from so much change in so short a time. They have suffered tremendous upheaval in their transition from a society whose strong traditions dictated their way of life for thousands of years to this new world and its new way of life – and it has not been easy, because the changes occurred far too fast. As a result, problems of alcohol and drug abuse, family and spousal abuse, depression and suicides, plague their society. These problems must be overcome. The new world and its ways are a fact of life. It's here. The Inuit can't fix them by going back to the way of life they once knew, living in igloos and tents, burning whale oil, and following the caribou. They must tackle these problems with the same tenacity it took to survive for thousands of years out on the land, in the harshest and most demanding environment known to humankind, and beat them. And the good news is that they are succeeding. Step by step, the Inuit are finding peace within their social order in spite of the river of change flowing in from the outside world.

All of this is not to say the north is no longer a place filled with wonder and excitement. They are still there, waiting for the adventurous. But, you'll have to go out on the land to find them, away from all the modern-day trappings.

One of my "On the Road Again" trips to the north was in June 1993, during an Arctic spring. It took me to the eastern Arctic to visit three Inuit communities above the tree line on the Ungava Peninsula, the northernmost tip of Quebec, one in Kuujjuaq, at the bottom of Ungava Bay, and two in the coastal communities of Inukjuak and Povungnituk on the shores of Hudson Bay.

If you look at a map, you will see that the Ungava stretches upward to Baffin Island, with Hudson Bay on the left and Ungava Bay on the right. It is a land mass the size of all the Maritime Provinces combined. The Inuit call the peninsula Nunavik, and, considering they have lived there for more than four thousand years, I will call it Nunavik, as well. The tree line runs east and west along the Fifty-fifth Parallel, about halfway down Hudson Bay, and Nunavik is everything on the Ungava to the north of that.

I was particularly excited about that trip to the north, because I had decided to fly my own plane. I had never been that far north piloting my own ship before. I had been to the north, but only to the major centres like Iqaluit – which, when I was in school, was called Frobisher Bay – and to the city of Yellowknife. I had never visited a genuine Inuit hamlet.

The fact that the Inuit communities we were going to visit were in Quebec puzzled me, in that I always associated the Inuit with the Northwest Territories. Only when we flew over the tree line into Nunavik did I realize the Ungava Peninsula was very much like the land of the N.W.T., made up of barren lands. From the air, at twenty-three thousand feet, we had a magnificent view, and could clearly see the change in topography between Nunavik and the rest of Quebec. It looked as if someone had spray-painted a line with an airbrush, east and west along the Fifty-fifth. Everything south of the line was green, and everything north was barren-land grey.

Dave Jadis, a fellow pilot from Ottawa, was co-piloting that trip. Dave was between jobs, waiting to get on with one of the major airlines full-time, and was available to come along with me. He was as excited as I was about flying north, and we had a lot of time for conversation during the flight, so we covered a lot of topics.

"All this talk about Quebec being a distinct society," Dave said, looking down on the scene below, "kinda makes me wonder what Quebecers call the Inuit."

"Well," I replied, "there's no question the Inuit are distinct. Maybe the government should recognize all our distinct societies at the same time. It's kind of hard to say Quebec is distinct and ignore the Inuit."

"Inuit means 'people,' doesn't it?"

"Yep. It's certainly more appropriate than Eskimo."

"'Eaters of meat,' right?"

"'Eaters of *raw* meat,' no less. You know, maybe by choosing to call ourselves multicultural, we've closed the door on recognizing one particular faction as being 'distinct.'"

"Yes, that could be."

"Anyway, the Inuit have made pretty good headway these last few years. Here, let me read you something."

From my bag on the floor behind Dave's co-pilot seat, I pulled out a recent copy of the magazine *This Country Canada*.

"There's an article in here, written by John Amagoalik. He's a real Inuit mover and shaker. He talks here about the formation of Nunavut in 1999."

"Another new word. What does Nunavut mean?"

"It means 'Our land.' In '99 they'll be cutting the Northwest Territories in half, changing the map again."

I found the article I was looking for in the magazine.

"There's one thing in here that got my attention . . . here it is: 'When the map of Canada is changed it will not be by the departure of Quebec but by the birth of Nunavut.'"

"So, is Ungava down there going to be part of Nunavut?" Dave asked.

"No, that's going to remain Nuna*vik*. At least, that's what the Inuit will continue to call it. I don't think Quebec will ever recognize the name. Certainly they will never accept that the Ungava Inuit are distinct enough to give up part of the province."

The article reminded me that changing the map was not exactly a rare thing in Canada. We created new boundaries when the Confederation was founded in 1867. We made changes again around the turn of the century when the Northwest Territories were formed and other provinces joined, and then again in 1949 when Newfoundland joined Confederation.

"So what happens to the rest of the territories?" Dave asked.

"The Northwest Territories will keep Yellowknife as its capital, and Nunavut will be forming its own. Probably Iqaluit."

"Old Frobe. I spent a month up there one week a few years ago."

"I passed through there once on my way to Yellowknife. Cold, huh?"

"Freezing! I've seen January days around 35 below. If they pick Frobe as its capital, it'll be the coldest capital in the country."

"Did you know that Iqaluit means 'place of fish'?"

"No, I didn't. But since you brought it up, we'd better start letting down for fuel or we'll be swimming like fish in the bay down there."

We'd been airborne more than three hours now. We left Ottawa in rain, but for the last hour and a half we had been flying in clear skies and brilliant sunshine. Down below, in the distance, we could see our first fuel stop, the community of Kuujjuarapik, formerly Great Whale, at the edge of the tree line, near the base of Hudson Bay. The ice was just beginning to melt along the shore of the bay.

"It looks warm here," I said, as we started descending into Kuujjuarapik. "What's it like in Povungnituk?"

"In our weather briefing this morning, it was clear and minus-five Celsius."

"Not bad."

"Well, not bad for June in the north, I suppose."

After landing on the big gravel strip, we taxied up beside a Canadian 737 jet. The captain was a man in his fifties, who identified himself as Dave. I introduced him to Dave Jadis and went through the obvious "Dave, meet Dave" thing. "Canadian Dave" had been flying in the north for years, even though he had tons of seniority and could fly just about any route he wanted within the airline, simply because he loved this part of the world. The north can do that if it gets its hooks into you.

Three Inuit teenagers came scrambling across the dusty tarmac to check us out. The one with the biggest smile was on crutches, but very adept at getting around. I marvelled at how quickly he moved. They had heard that the "On the Road Again" guy would be landing around noon. Well, we were right on time – and so were they.

There were actually several families waiting inside the terminal for autographs. That's another thing about the north: word travels quickly in small communities. That morning, before leaving Ottawa, I had placed a call to Kuujjuarapik to ensure that the fuel I needed was going to be waiting for us when we got there. There was no fuel in Povungnituk, where our first story was waiting, and I needed full tanks leaving Kuujjuarapik if I hoped to make it back. Obviously, someone had mentioned we were en route.

Everyone was so friendly. I signed a few autographs and handed out a bunch of pictures, while my Dave went hunting for the fuel guys, who, as luck would have it, were nowhere to be found. It was lunchtime. By the time we found them, another hour had gone by, and I was supposed to meet our "On the Road Again" crew by two-thirty that afternoon. I was late. To add to my woes, I discovered the fuel quotation I had received on the phone was for automobile gas, not aviation gas. Av gas was going to cost me *three times* the quote. That's another thing about the north. Things are expensive.

I called the airport in Povungnituk and left a message for Jonathan Craven, who was the assigned producer for our week in the north, letting him know we wouldn't be landing there until five-thirty that afternoon.

Actually, I wasn't too worried about our shooting schedule, because there was lots of light. It was coming into high summer and the season of the midnight sun, and even in this lower region of the eastern Arctic, it would remain light until nearly midnight.

Airborne again, we set out over the barren lands of the Ungava, towards Povungnituk. After climbing to twenty-three thousand feet, we levelled off, and it didn't take long for the awesomeness of the landscape to set in. As far as the eye could see, endless undulating rock lay before us. Two hours later, we started our descent into Povungnituk. We could see this Inuit community on the edge of Hudson Bay at the mouth of the Povungnituk River, a cluster of buildings huddled together along the shore, the only sign of humanity for miles.

"What a sight, eh, Dave? Can you imagine living so far from everything and everyone?"

"Not exactly my cup of tea. I suppose when the ice is melted, they're not so isolated."

"Water is their link with the outside, all right. That or air. There isn't a single Inuit settlement that doesn't lead to the sea and to each other, except for one."

"Which one?"

"Baker Lake, in the Keewatin District, over there on the other side of Hudson Bay, smack dab at the geographic centre of Canada. It's a freshwater lake, the only Inuit community without access to the sea."

The Inuit call the month of June "the season of caribou calves," because that's when female caribous deliver their young.

In the same month snow geese arrive, the main flock taking as long as two days to fly by overhead, and Arctic char migrate downstream to the sea. In the old north, the Inuit would have had plenty of food at this time of year, as they pulled lake trout with fishing hooks from holes in the melting ice to supplement their summer diet of caribou, char, and summer berries. I wondered how much of that lifestyle I was going to see this trip.

As in Kuujjuarapik, it had not taken long for word to get around Povungnituk about our arrival. Dozens of families were standing behind the plate-glass windows of the terminal, waving as we pulled up and shut our engines down. Talk about making someone feel welcome! There was a lot of handshaking waiting for us inside, too. It made me realize the power of television. They certainly knew our show; one Inuk even sang a couple of lines of our theme song for me.

Jonathan was there, too, right on time.

"Wayne, this is Tamusi Qumak, our guest. He came out just to welcome you."

I was flattered. Tamusi was a very respected elder in the north. What touched me even more was that I knew the frail gentleman was dying of cancer and had postponed a radiation treatment at a hospital in the south to accommodate our shooting schedule. To see him at the airport, extending such a warm welcome, was very humbling. He wore a dark blue parka with a bright orange-lined hood and a sky-blue baseball cap.

Tamusi was seventy-nine years old, small and bent, with dark skin. He wore little half-glasses, which really should have been full, because he needed to tilt his head up to see clearly when he looked at something or someone. He had a thin face and a lovely, boyish smile, which revealed that he had no teeth left.

"I'm honoured to meet you, sir," I said. "We're very happy to be here to tell your story to the rest of Canada."

Tamusi was an Inuk historian, the recipient of many awards, including the Order of Canada, honouring him for humanitarian work on behalf of his people. His greatest achievement, the thing

he was most proud of, was single-handedly compiling the first
Inuit dictionary, a six-hundred-page, thirty-thousand-word dictionary of the Inuktitut language – an amazing feat, considering
Tamusi didn't go to school a day in his life. What surprised me
as well was that no one had ever come up with a dictionary
before Tamusi published his in 1991. Throughout history, the
Inuit had been an oral society. They spoke a common language
known as Inuktitut, or Inuttituut, which was divided into six different dialects, from Greenland across Canada to the western
Mackenzie area. Then one hundred and fifty years ago, mission-
aries began to interpret the Inuit language, using shorthand
symbols for each letter of the alphabet, with each symbol repre-
senting a sound. Tamusi used these symbols to put his dictionary
together, a task that took him six long years.

Povungnituk was quite modern, a town of about a thousand
people. There was a big, brand-new school, powder-blue with
white trim, a lot of government financial assistance was in
evidence. All the houses were recently built – warm houses,
mounted on screw jacks that allowed adjustment if the ground
heaved in the spring.

House construction in the north is, to say the least, expensive.
I don't know about places in the Ungava, but in the high north,
up by the Beaufort, even modest houses can cost as much as
$150,000 to $200,000. Water is transported into homes in tanker
trucks, and there is no underground sewage. Everything is
drained by tankers as well. And if you live somewhere like Grise
Fiord on Ellesmere Island, heating can cost as much as $15,000
per house, per year, since residents have to get their electricity
from huge generators fired by gas or oil. Utility companies
simply don't run hydro poles that far north from generating
plants in the sunny south. The more time one spends in the
Arctic, the more one realizes how different things have to be.
Constant adaptation is required to beat the elements.

At Tamusi's house later that afternoon, I sat and conversed
with him through an interpreter by the name of Rynee Oqaituk.

She was a young woman, probably not much more than thirty years old, whose father had been a close friend of Tamusi's. When Rynee's father died, Tamusi became her adopted father. He loved kids. He had several children of his own and no less than thirty-four grandchildren, to whom he loved to sit and tell stories about the old ways, about Inuit life as it once was, out on the land. Tamusi grew up near Povungnituk, and lived most of his life out on the land, as a hunter and gatherer, moving seasonally from camp to camp with groups of a hundred or so in the winter and as few as a dozen in the summer. In recent years, he lived alone in a little bungalow in town. His wife had died several years before.

He was very proud of his medals, especially the Order of Canada, which had just been awarded to him earlier that spring.

"If you wore all these medals at once, they would be very heavy," I quipped.

Rynee interpreted my words, and Tamusi laughed a big wide-eyed laugh, making a tumbling motion with his hands towards the floor as he replied in Inuktitut to my comment.

"He says he would fall to his knees under all that weight and never be able to get up," Rynee translated, chuckling at Tamusi's antics.

On a more serious note, I asked him about the dictionary and why he undertook such a big project.

"I was afraid," he replied, "that our traditional Inuit language would die. I wanted to do something to keep it alive. I thought a lot about it and decided that the best way would be to write a dictionary in Inuktitut."

In spite of his lack of eduction, Tamusi was considered a scholar in the greater Inuit community. He was also highly regarded all over the Ungava Peninsula as a social adviser to the people and, for several years, was a member of the Justice Task Force. But the dictionary was his crowning achievement. He showed me the book, entitled *True Inuit Words*, with great pride. Rynee explained how happy Tamusi was about his book now being in all the schools and used by teachers to teach the Inuit children how to read and write in their Mother tongue, helping to preserve the language. He was very concerned about the future of the Inuit, deeply saddened by the effects all the change in the north was having on his people.

"I wish there was more I could do," he told me, through Rynee. "But I'm getting too old. I'm scared what might happen to our people. At least, when I die, my dictionary will be there to help."

"How do you feel when you see an Inuit youngster reading your dictionary?" I asked.

"When I was making the dictionary, I wasn't sure how useful it was going to be. Now, I am very happy and proud when I see children reading it. Before I wrote the dictionary, the most difficult thing in my life was hunting in bad weather. Writing the dictionary was even harder than that."

Later that afternoon, we shot footage of Tamusi reading to a few of his grandchildren out in the back yard, overlooking the barren lands. And we needed one last shot of Tamusi before we left for the day, a shot of the wise elder sitting on a rock looking out over the land he loved so much.

"What do they want me to do on the rock?" he asked.

Our producer, Jonathan, asked Rynee to explain to Tamusi that we wanted a pensive shot of him, and suggested he think about how life used to be living on the land or to think about his people today and their future. When we rolled tape, Tamusi wept openly, so deep were his feelings and concerns for his people.

The next day, Jonathan and I got together to talk about what we were going to say in the on-camera introduction of Tamusi.

"We're going to have to do two different openings," Jonathan said.

"I've been thinking about that. He's quite ill, isn't he?"

"Apparently his cancer is really serious. He just might not be around when we go to air in the fall. I feel kind of funny doing one that talks about him as 'the late,' but it's a reality we have to face."

"Not to mention the fact he's seventy-nine years old."

"Exactly."

So, we did two introductions for Tamusi. One spoke of the grand elder still living, the other, of his recent passing. Tamusi died of cancer a few months after our visit, and, when we went to air in October with our new season, we used the on-camera we hoped we wouldn't have to use. The one consolation was that "On the Road Again" got there in time to document the man's achievements and share his story with the rest of Canada. He deserved the recognition.

After taping Tamusi's introductions, we spent the afternoon shooting activities around Povungnituk, returning that evening to our modest, but comfortable, two-storey hotel, where, much to everyone's delight, Dave Jadis informed us we had all been invited to a gourmet meal at the coffee shop in town. A former Montrealer by the name of Denis Brasseau ran the place, with his Inuit wife, Lucy. Denis, who had been in the north for twenty-five years now, was reputed to be quite a cook. The night before, he had bet on the Stanley Cup finals, which Montreal won, and to celebrate Canada keeping the cup, Denis invited a whole whack of people, including the "On the Road Again" gang, for a true gourmet meal. He didn't disappoint anyone, especially us.

That night, in the isolated little town of Povungnituk, hours by air from anywhere, we sat and had the mother of all meals in the north. Course number one was a tomato-based soup with vegetables and noodles. That was followed by smoked char with lemon seasoning on a bed of crisp lettuce. Course number three was baked char with a wonderful rice side dish filled with shrimp and red and green peppers in an avocado shell. Course number four was dessert – a large orange, which was scooped out and stuffed with large, red, ripe strawberries, kiwi slices, and pieces of orange, covered in a thick, creamy custard sauce. I remember wondering what people down south were having for dinner that night. Who says all you eat in the north is seal meat?

Friday morning, the hotel manager, Matuisi Tulugak, a very helpful fellow and a devoted fan of our television show, helped us load the van with our gear before we headed out to the airport. He brought his daughter along for the ride, as well as the cleaning girl from the hotel. He had already been out to the airport to drop off Jonathan, Mike Champagne, and Paul Morisset, who was shooting camera that week.

It was quite foggy on the ground as we took off, but just six hundred feet in the air we broke through into clear sunshine. In less than an hour, we would be in the eastern Arctic community of Inukjuak, a little further to the south.

Our arrival at the airport in Inukjuak was one of the most memorable I have experienced in all my years of hosting "On the Road Again." When we pulled up in front of the airport terminal, I noticed a lot of people with big smiles inside waving at us. No sooner had the propellers stopped turning than one hundred and fifty people, pretty well all Inuit, *poured* out of the small terminal and surrounded our plane. They were swarming like bees – mothers, fathers, and children. They had still cameras clicking and video cameras rolling. Two young children, about three or four years old, had managed to get up on my left wing and were running from one end to the other.

"We'd better open the hatch, quick," I said to Dave, "before somebody gets hurt."

"That, or somebody breaks something on the airplane," Dave replied.

Well, about the last thing you want happening to an airplane is someone using the wings for a trampoline, and it sure didn't take us long to climb out of the cockpit. People were singing our theme song, snapping pictures, and thrusting children into my arms for snapshots.

"Hi, friend!" said one.

"We're on the road again," sang another.

I was very touched. And the first fan I had in my arms for a picture? You guessed it: one of the little guys who had been on my wing. Dave was holding the other wing-walker. Better safe than sorry.

After a lot of glad-handing, when things had settled down, we were driven into town to the local Co-op hotel. Ninety-five bucks a night gave us a clean room and no charge for the taxi. Inukjuak was as nice, if not nicer, than Povungnituk. There was a lot of government money assisting this community, too, because there were new subsidized housing and lots of new trucks in town – obviously shipped in by boat during the summer thaw on Hudson Bay – even though there were certainly no roads leading out of town except the one leading to the airport. Come to think of it, those trucks would be great vehicles to advertise for sale. "One used pickup. Only three thousand kilometres. Never taken out of second gear. No highway miles. Best offer."

The man we came to meet in Inukjuak, Charlie Adams, knew both the old and the new north. He was born in an igloo forty-six years ago, out on the land. After his father died when Charlie was only a year old, he was raised by his mother. She became the hunter, and she and Charlie travelled by dog sled and lived in igloos in the winter and in sealskin tents in the summer for the first few years of his life.

"My mom and I travelled by dog team for five years from place to place," he told me, "following the caribou for food. She was a great hunter."

I was interviewing Charlie on a bluff overlooking Inukjuak the afternoon of our arrival. He sat with the sun shining on his deep-brown face, dressed in a modern nylon windbreaker, with high-tech sneakers on his feet. He had a thick black moustache and a deeply recessed hairline. His hair was also jet black.

Charlie worked for the Inuit Television Network and had found a way to use the magic of television to keep the age-old tradition of storytelling alive in today's Inuit culture. Charlie had been troubled that the young people were not listening to the elders any more, but had found a new teacher, television. Charlie reasoned that, if he recorded the elders on tape and played them talking about earlier times and surviving on the land, the Inuit youth might just listen.

"Charlie, what is the importance of reaching the young with stories of the elders?"

"We don't have many elders left now that can tell their side of the story, how to go hunting, how to hunt seal, what to do in case you meet polar bears – certain things they know that we don't."

"You're using television as a tool, then?"

"Yes. We have to, because, if we don't, were gonna lose our culture and our language. Using it this way, I think television's good for us."

"Lots of changes, huh?"

"Yes. It's like a tug of war between the old ways and new, the elders and the young people. It's kind of a mix-up, you know? I have seen the frustrations of our young Inuit. The more they seem to know about the values of the south, the more unreachable they become. We have seen many changes here on the Arctic coast. If you follow the history way back to the beginning of the century, the changes begin with the white man coming here to hunt whales. Those were the first changes – nothing like the changes we have seen in the last few years, though."

"That really wasn't all that long ago, when you think about it," I said.

"Well, certainly it was before my time, but I can remember, back in the fifties, when I was just a kid, Inuit people hiding under rocks when the planes came overhead. They were so loud and noisy."

"And no houses to hide in, either, I gather."

"No houses. Until the fifties, the only wooden buildings in our communities were the churches or the Hudson's Bay trading buildings. The Inuit were still in igloos or sealskin tents, like the ones my mom and I lived in."

The next morning, bright and early, I was out on the tundra with my crew and two Inuit women to learn how to perform the ancient art of throat singing. Charlie was there with his camera, too, to record our visit for the Inuit Television Network. The Inuit call throat singing *katajaq*. Two people stand together, tummy to tummy, holding each other by the forearms and placing their mouths inches apart from one another. Then, with eyes closed, they release guttural sounds in wonderful, rhythmic syncopation, while swaying back and forth like dancers. It began in Inuit culture as a game for women, to occupy their time while their men were away hunting. The first one to laugh and break the rhythm, lost.

My throat-singing partners, Mary Iqaluk and Nellie Echaluk, were in full Inuit dress, right down to their sealskin boots, creating a beautiful silhouette on the high bluff overlooking the rapids on the river below.

"A sure sign of spring," I yelled over to Charlie. "Must be nice to see the water running."

"Yes. People are starting now to get out on the land for the summer."

Mary and Nellie, wind-weathered Inuit women in their late fifties, looked as if they had lived on the land all their lives. They were very good at throat singing, and had performed all over North America and in many countries in Europe. I will never forget the sounds that came from their throats that day on the bluff. They were amazing. The Inuit believe that they have a close relationship with all of nature, and that animals have the magical power to hear and understand the human word. Well, those two ladies uttered every animal sound imaginable. And talk about rhythm!

Like Charlie, they too were doing their bit to keep ancient Inuit customs alive. Just ten years ago, throat singing came close to being lost forever. The young people simply were not interested in learning the art from their elders. But now, thanks to people like Mary and Nellie, who perform their art everywhere they can, more and more young people are beginning to learn how to do it.

When it was my turn to sing with the two experts, I lasted a minute or so before breaking up in stitches. It was so unlike anything I had ever tried before. What an experience, standing out on the tundra of the eastern Arctic, eyes closed, face to face with two Inuit women, singing a song the way the Inuit have sung for centuries, with the sound of the rapids in the river below providing rhythm. I was filled with such a sense of good fortune at being in the north in time to experience this ancient custom, in case it, too, disappears forever.

The following year, in April 1994, I travelled to the Arctic again, to Baffin Island. This time, I spent several unforgettable days out on the land with a five-foot-three dynamo of a woman by the name of Matty McNair. Matty doesn't weigh much more than a hundred and fifteen pounds, but she handles a dog team and a five-metre Inuit sled, or *qomatiq*, in a fashion that puts most men to shame. Matty is forty-five years old, but you'd never believe it to see her, for she absolutely brims over with energy and enthusiasm. She has long, brown curly hair and fiery eyes that sparkle when she speaks of her life in the north.

Matty was originally from Philadelphia. She is married to a French Canadian from northern Ontario, Paul Landry, a strapping six-footer with a broad smile and an easygoing manner. Together, Matty and Paul work full time in an outdoor wilderness-adventure company called North Winds, which they run from their home along the shoreline of Frobisher Bay in Iqaluit. They alternate weeks taking adventurers out on the land, so that one of them is always at home with their children. Paul is also a volunteer, helping develop a French First Language Program for the Baffin Divisional Board of Education in Iqaluit. They are kept pretty busy, because things are booming in what will soon be the new capital of Nunavut. The city now has three fifty-bed hotels with full dining facilities, and daily air service which leaves Ottawa and Montreal early in the morning and arrives in Iqaluit at noon.

But some of the people who come to Iqaluit these days come for adventure. Matty and Paul introduce novices to the "old" North, taking them out of modern Iqaluit, onto the frozen land by dog team, staying out for periods of time ranging from half a day to twelve full days. People learn how to stay overnight on the land in winter, how to set up tents in the snow, how to set up stoves for cooking, and what foods to eat in order to stay warm.

In the summer, they take visiting adventurers from the south hiking and white-water canoeing. Both of them are certainly qualified. Matty's father, Robert McNair, was the first person to introduce white-water canoeing to North America, back in 1950. In 1985, Matty and Paul revised the book her father wrote on the sport.

Matty spent her entire youth with her father in the great outdoors, which explains why she grew up so connected to the land. She and Paul met at an Outward Bound Adventure School sixteen years ago, in 1980, and they spent a lot of time together travelling to places like South America, where they frequently did high-altitude climbing, tackling some of the highest mountains in that part of the world. They have also paddled some of the wildest white water in North America.

When they decided to raise a family, however, common sense dictated that they give up that high-risk sport in the best interests of their children. So, they ended up settling in Thunder Bay, Ontario, where Matty worked for the Outward Bound School at nearby Black Sturgeon Lake, running a team of husky dogs, teaching others the art of dog mushing and outdoor winter-survival techniques.

Matty McNair and I, with her team of Inuit dogs, stop for a break during our trek out on Frobisher Bay

Giving Matty a polar-bear hug in the magnificent caribou outfit that, sadly, did not fit

It was Matty who first fell in love with the north. She had always felt the lure of the wide-open spaces above the tree line, and it took one trip to Baffin Island to hook her forever. She made that first trip to Baffin in 1987, and when she returned home to Paul in Thunder Bay, she couldn't shake the memories. She convinced Paul to visit Baffin, and after he did, he fell in love with it, too. Soon, they were both dreaming of living in the north. Most people would have simply moved in, and that would be the end of it. But Matty and Paul did it with flair. They started working on a plan to circumnavigate Baffin Island by dog sled, a trip of approximately four thousand kilometres, which had never been done before. But, in February 1990, after two years of planning, they set out to do just that.

Matty and Paul began the four-month journey around Baffin Island with thirteen of their strongest Inuit dogs to pull their eight-hundred-pound *qomatiq*. They left with another couple who never completed the trip, giving up after twenty-five hundred kilometres, too tired and weak to continue. Matty and Paul, however, pressed on, finishing the last fifteen hundred kilometres alone, travelling with their dog team, battling days of whiteouts and high winds, and sleeping at night in canvas tents. It was a journey filled with adventure. For the last thousand kilometres or so, they didn't pass a single community along the way. One night, they were attacked by polar bears and, luckily, were able to scare them off.

When I met Matty in 1994, I asked her about that incredible trip and whether she was, in fact, the first woman to travel around the entire island by dog team.

"As far as I know, yes, I am the first one. There were certainly Inuit women who, with their husbands, did different lengths of that trip, and many of them have done very long dog-sledding trips, but probably there was no reason for them to ever go all the way around the island."

"Why did you do it?"

"Well, it just seemed like a wonderful trip to do, to see the land, to visit all the communities, and to meet Inuit people and to do it through a medium which they could relate to."

"Did doing a trip like that help solidify your place in the community?"

"Oh, I'm sure it helped place us in the community. I mean, word spread about our trip around Baffin, and, when we finally moved in, it no doubt gave us a sense of credibility as new residents in the north. We didn't just move into a new home and set up a business. In a sense, we proved our worth, not just as residents, but our worth in terms of the kind of business we were offering as adventure-tour guides."

Their home, built on the quiet side of Iqaluit, overlooks Frobisher Bay. It is very modern, with brand-new maple floors which Matty and Paul are very proud of. They live there with their two children, Eric and Sarah, now twelve and ten. By purchasing a home in Iqaluit, it sent out a signal to the local people they were serious about living in the north. Most people who come up from the south don't buy homes, because they usually come up on short-term work contracts. Matty and Paul came to stay, determined to share the north with people from away, to bring adventure into visitors' lives by taking them out on the land to experience and appreciate the beauty and splendour of the Arctic environment.

Between them, Matty and Paul have more than thirty-five years of experience in outdoor survival and tour-leading. Matty has lived in Canada since 1976, and, although she has landed-immigrant status, she has never bothered to seek Canadian citizenship, because whether she is Canadian or American has never been important to her. All that matters is her connection to Baffin Island.

"I feel when I'm up here, I'm part of the earth. I'm such a tiny, tiny, insignificant part, and yet I re-energize by being out on the land and being out with the dogs. That fills me up. When you start to feel good about where you're living, you start to take better care of it. Whether it's your own back yard or your neighbourhood or your whole country or the whole earth, it all starts right where you stand."

The day I arrived, I sat in Matty and Paul's home and talked with Matty about their life since moving to Iqaluit.

"How do the kids like living here?" I asked.

"They absolutely love it. Paul and I spend a lot of time taking the kids out on the land. They always want to go camping on the weekends, and it doesn't bother them if there's a storm out there. They still want to go out."

"I gather you really like getting out on the land."

"Well, you know, I've never been an observer. I don't like to watch sports or sit on the sidelines. I've gotta go do it."

Matty's Inuit dogs were much fiercer and much stronger than the ones she worked with in the south. There was certainly some resemblance to huskies, the breed of sled dog most of us are familiar with; however, there was an element of the wild evident in the Inuit dogs. Their hair bristled in the wind, and their eyes cut through you. They were much stockier than Huskies, too.

Matty explained that southern dogs can pull about thirty pounds each. However, Inuit dogs, what we used to call Eskimo dogs, have no trouble at all hauling a hundred pounds. Without those tough, trail-hardened dogs, the same ones used by the Inuit for over two thousand years, the same ones that pulled Peary to the North Pole and Amundsen to the South Pole, she and Paul might not have successfully circumnavigated Baffin Island.

I got a chance to experience travelling over the land with Matty's dogs the next morning. She kept nineteen of them, and, as we walked out to where the dogs were tied, we were greeted with much barking and anticipation. Matty slipped a sealskin harness over her lead dog, Raven, giving the big dog a hearty pat before moving on to the next one.

For the excursion, Matty wore a pair of grey sealskin boots, a maroon parka with a fur-lined hood, a woollen tuque, and big furry mittens. Much to my disappointment, the wonderful caribou parka Matty wanted me to wear on the land didn't fit. I ended up dressing in layers: Polar-fleece shells and a Gore-Tex jacket. She looked like she belonged in the north; I looked like I was visiting.

Matty finished hitching the team for our excursion out on Frobisher Bay. She had them hooked up in fan formation, not two by two, and at first glance I wondered how she ever kept them from tangling their lines. But there was no problem. The dogs ran along silently, at a slow-but-steady clip, tongues lolling, seeming quite content pulling the great, long *qomatiq* with its two passengers. Everything was so clean. The air had no smell to it, just a clean crispness that filled our nostrils. There was no sound, save the sound of the dogs' feet, the sound of the *qomatiq*'s runners, and the occasional barking command from Matty.

"Hike!" Matty would call out, cracking a long, sealskin whip on either side of the fanned-out dog formation. "Come on, Raven, lead on!"

Frobisher Bay was a mass of giant, frozen chunks of sea ice, thrown up by the surging tides of the sea. It's called pressure ice. When the tide comes in under the ice, the pressure of the incoming tide from the sea heaves the ice of the bay upwards, leaving in its wake large pieces of ice along the shoreline of the bay, ranging in size from a metre to several metres high, that quickly freeze in place. As formidable as they looked, we were safe to travel. It was still early spring, weeks before break-up.

Matty steered her sled around with great ease, in total command of her dogs, jumping off to assist them turning the sled around some of the jutting pressure ice in our path. Then she would run alongside the gliding *qomatiq* for minutes at a time, before jumping back aboard the sled. I marvelled at the strength of this diminutive woman, especially when the dogs came upon the remains of a caribou kill left out on the ice by some hunters. They went crazy, and converged on the carcass, hauling the sixteen-foot *qomatiq* with them like it was a Dinky toy, and began a feeding frenzy on the remains, snarling and snapping their jaws viciously at one another. Matty was off the sled and into the midst of the snarling mass in seconds, yelling at her dogs to back off, fearlessly grabbing one, then another, by the scruff of the neck and literally tossing them aside. I was stunned. And amazingly, the dogs actually listened to her orders. In the time it took for me to catch my breath, we were under way again, as if nothing had happened.

"That makes me so mad!" Matty said quietly. "Some of these hunters on Ski-doos forget there are still a whole bunch of us out here with dog teams. They have absolutely no consideration."

Out on a flat section of the bay, Matty settled in for a well-deserved rest as her dogs pulled us along, their feet silently padding in the snow. Paul Bélanger, another of our premier cameramen, was busy taping the event, while François Pagé captured the sound of the dogs and the gliding of the sleigh out on the frozen bay. Janet P. Smith, who, like me, is thrilled with every northern assignment given her, was producing Matty McNair's story. Janet's design was to have Matty take me out to the far side of the bay so I could experience the herds of caribou roaming on the rolling tundra.

"Did you ever wonder, Matty, why you decided to come here?" I asked.

"Well, I'm not here to conquer the wilderness or the Arctic. I came here to be a part of it, to flow through it. I have lots of energy, and it needs lots of space, because it's always bouncing off things. Up here, it's like I'm on a different planet. There's space, open space. I can look across the bay and I think it looks really close and it's twenty-five miles across the bay. Illusions like that remind me that everything I think is supposed to be isn't necessarily. It's silent and peaceful. That's what makes this part of the world very special."

Matty's lifestyle in the north and the adventure tours she and her husband offered continued to fill me with questions.

"What do you tell people who are interested in coming to visit?"

"If someone is interested in coming on a dog-sledding trip, I need to find out how adventuresome a spirit they have. I don't care if maybe you've never dog-sledded or you've never been camping in your life before. That doesn't make any difference. What makes a difference is your attitude on life. You don't need to be in excellent shape, but in good enough shape that, when it's very cold, you can just get off and run for two minutes and get on the sled again. Now, you think, oh, anybody can run two minutes. But when you've got a lot of clothes on, that's a little bit harder."

"Is all this still fun for you, Matty?"

"If it wasn't fun, I wouldn't do it. Paul did confront me one time about whether I'd ever had a nine-to-five job, and I said, 'Sure. Well, I probably did. Well, I must have.' But I really couldn't think of one. And the type of work I've always done is what's been more play to me and fun. And it's combining my love for the out-of-doors with liking to share that with other people and bringing those two together."

All that day, we travelled, spotting herds of caribou on the rolling slopes of the two-thousand-foot Meta Incognita Peninsula as often as people are accustomed to spotting cattle grazing in fields on a drive in the country. We stopped for lunch, sitting on the *qomatiq* while the dogs lay curled in circles on the snow, napping in their harnesses. We downed sandwiches and hot tea, and listened to the silence. It was a memorable day – the kind of day Inuit elders lament not having enough of since all the changes came. I liked that day. I liked it a lot.

I have made two more trips to the north since my visit to Matty McNair's in 1994. In 1995, I again flew my plane north, this time to the little hamlet of Pangnirtung, nestled deep in its giant Baffin Island fiord, northeast of Iqaluit, where, in order to land, you first fly over the airstrip which divides the town in half, so that people who use the runway as a walkway to get from one side to the other know enough to stay off until the plane has landed. They actually have a flashing red light that is turned on by the airport operator until the engines are shut down.

In 1996, I spent a day with helicopter pilot Bob O'Connor, lifting cars with his big chopper from one side of the Mackenzie River to the other – cars belonging to people who had had enough of winter for one year and didn't want to wait another six weeks for the ferry to start running. They wanted to head south *now*, and were willing to pay any price to do it. Well, Bob, enterprising soul that he is, accommodates them for a mere two hundred and seventy-five dollars. He'll even heli-lift your dog.

I could go on and on about the Arctic. But the place is just too big to be contained in one chapter. I'll have to save Bob's story and my visit to Pangnirtung for another time.

I do have one final note to make, though, one that fills me with a great sense of privilege. When I returned from doing the Mackenzie River story, I met a man walking his dog on York Street in downtown Ottawa. He recognized me and told me he was a great fan of "On the Road Again."

"You've gotta have the greatest job in the world!" he said.

He was absolutely right. I do.

Don Goguen (left)
with his helmet-
mounted camera

Gil, Clint,
and Greg –
the Flying
MacBeths

Thumbs up and
ready to go with
my lifeline,
Dave Williamson

Skydive!

~

About the only thing I have ever refused to do as the host of "On the Road Again" is eat bugs. Other than that, I have pretty well felt, tasted, and experienced the principle element of every story I've ever covered. Whether it was handling a two-and-a-half-metre boa constrictor at a reptile hospital in Ontario, balancing backwards on a cantering horse, dancing the flamenco out on the windswept prairies, or playing golf with a llama on a golf course in Quebec, for the most part, I've done it. I even rode a camel at Woodlawn Farm in Nova Scotia and found out all about that soft cushion which supposedly exists between the two humps. I discovered that there's no such thing. It hurt! But such is the nature of "On the Road Again." Our mandate is to go forth, taste, touch, and experience, bring it home, and share that experience with our viewers.

So, it was not surprising I had a lot on my mind preceding my arrival in Moncton, New Brunswick, in September of 1995. It was the beginning of our ninth season on the network, and one story had come finally, and inevitably, to the forefront. Skydiving! Since our television series had begun years earlier, this topic had been broached – usually in jest – at many of our production meetings, but none of my producers ever actually got around to putting such a story in place. I'm sure part of the reason was that they knew that if the topic did materialize, I might be crazy enough to try it, and, being caring souls, concerned about my future, they steered away from it like the plague. (At least, that's what I like to *think*.)

In reality, the skydiving story we were about to cover was irresistible. It involved three generations of a single family who jumped out of airplanes as a unit almost every weekend of the summer. They called themselves the Flying MacBeths: seventy-three-year-old Gil MacBeth, a retired automotive-shop operator, his thirty-nine-year-old son, Greg, a veteran of sixteen hundred jumps and a certified instructor, and Greg's seventeen-year-old son, Clint, who had been skydiving with his father and grand-father for about a year now. What a story!

I was written out of the script as an active participant – a fact that was painfully obvious. My story-outline papers called for me to do nothing more than interview the three men, and then talk to them as they landed, fresh from a jump. I hadn't been approached by anyone on the matter. Executive producer Paul Harrington had taken this particular shooting assignment under his belt and, when I tried to talk to him a week prior to departure about the notion of my actually doing a jump with the Flying MacBeths, he turned a rather sickening ashen-white and refused to discuss the matter. He chose instead to walk into his office, where, I imagined, he called someone at head office for insurance advice or sought out a quiet place to recite the rosary.

Mind you, I was hardly adamant about it myself. It wasn't as if I were champing at the bit to skydive. After all, who in their right mind would ever want to leave a perfectly safe airplane in the first place? So, when Paul walked away, mercifully, so did I. But his reaction made one fundamental thing very clear: if there was going to be a jump, the decision would be mine and mine alone. Except for that brief encounter with Paul, I can't remember a single comment from any individual on our team in the days preceding that shoot about whether I should or should not attempt one.

My flight from Ottawa to Moncton in my own twin-engine air-plane, a Beech Duke, had been a good one, smooth and clear, with only a few scattered clouds. Steve Spencer, a fellow pilot from Ottawa, was with me for the trip. As I approached the Moncton area, I heard an aircraft over McEwen Airfield report to Moncton Centre that "the jumpers were away."

"I guess that'll be them," I said.

Steve nodded. He knew a dive was on my mind. Throughout the flight he had noticed I was looking down at the ground from the cockpit a little more often than I normally do.

"What's so important outside?" he asked.

"Nothing," I replied. "I'm just looking at all the beautiful shades of green down there!"

"You gonna do it?" he asked.

"I still haven't a clue, Steve. I won't know till I meet everyone and get a feel for this whole skydiving business. Let's get this one down on the ground first and take it from there."

I flew the approach into McEwen, a small three-thousand-foot family-owned airfield north of Moncton's main airport, and landed. As I taxied to the end of the runway, I noticed a small, high-winged Cessna airplane, the kind generally used for sky-diving, and a whole whack of people off on the grass. This was the Moncton Sport Parachute Club's annual gathering of sky-divers, and people from all over Atlantic Canada had gathered for several days of camping out – and *jumping* out. Two young lads began waving, beckoning us to park my Duke near the Cessna.

"Looks like this is the place, Steve. There's one of their planes. Nice logo, 'Atlantic School of Skydiving.' What a gang of people."

When we shut down, a dozen or more very excited individuals rounded the wing and stood waiting at our cabin door.

"Wow! What a plane! Imagine diving out of *this* baby. Can you take the door off?" one enthused individual asked.

"How fast is she?" asked another.

"Bet ya this bird'll get us to altitude quick," said yet another.

"Hi, I'm Wayne Rostad. Are you *all* skydivers?"

"You bet!" said one.

"Greatest sport in the world," said another, thrusting a hand out.

"Welcome to Moncton!"

"Thank you," I replied. "This is Steve Spencer. He's piloting with me this trip. Tell me, where is Paul, my producer, and the crew?"

A hand pointed in the direction of the skydiving office. By now, Steve and I were out of my plane, and two or three members of the excited throng had their heads inside the cabin.

"Wouldn't take much to get those seats out."

"There's room here for six of us!"

"Cool!"

I spotted Paul making his way over to us from the club office.

"Better lock your plane before you lose it," he laughed.

"You're telling me. I think they're trying to figure out how to remove the seats! Where are Gil and his boys?"

"They should be jumping any minute now. We're just getting ready to shoot them landing."

"Well, they certainly have a beautiful day for it. It's smooth as silk upstairs."

From the ground, the clouds looked like great scattered cotton balls suspended in the blue. I could hear the drone of a single engine labouring high above those clouds to reach altitude.

"You'll hear the engine cut any minute now," said Paul. "That's when they jump. You won't see them, though, till they open their chutes, about a minute or so later. That's how long they freefall before they pull the cord."

"A whole minute!" I exclaimed. I felt my pucker factor rise about ten points.

Paul tilted his head, looking skyward.

"See that hole in the clouds right above us? They should be coming through there any minute now. The three of them are jumping together. Tom's over there by the touchdown zone ready to shoot when they land."

Tom Sharina, our cameraman, looked as if he were really enjoying himself. He loves action, and this story certainly had lots of it. He'd already been up shooting pictures of the jump plane from another aircraft flying in formation. Mike Champagne, our audio man, was with him, tied as usual by the ever-present umbilical cord that connected his audio mixer to Tom's camera.

"Hello, Tom! G'day, Mike!" I called out. "Looks like a good one!"

"Hey, Wayne! You're just in time," replied Tom. "They should be jumping any minute now."

"I'm thinking about doing it too, Tom. What do you think? Would I be a crazy man to try it?"

If I was looking for an answer, Tom wasn't about to give me one.

"You're actually thinking of doing it?" Mike said, surprised.

"No, he isn't!" Paul quickly interrupted.

"We'll see," I said. "We'll see."

The engine cut was quite noticeable, and we knew they were away. Right on cue, about sixty seconds later, we heard the distant slap of nylon catching the wind.

"There they are!" Paul exclaimed.

Three colourful rectangular shapes came into focus high above us. Three jumpers, three chutes. I wondered if, like me, the first thing people on the ground did every time they watched people jump was count chutes.

"Is that them yelling?" I asked.

"Yes," said Paul. "They're higher than kites."

"No kidding," I laughed.

Minutes later, my guests literally dropped in on their waiting host. I was most impressed with the manoeuvrability of their chutes; they all landed within fifteen metres of each other. Not only that, they each touched down as light as a feather, landing on both feet and simply walking casually away. Forget the Hollywood hit the ground, dump, and roll routine.

Paul was right. They *were* higher than kites. *Naturally* high! They were laughing and hugging each other and carrying on like people who hadn't seen each other for years. Well, I thought, if this is what skydiving is all about, how am I going to resist trying it? There isn't a pill known to humankind that makes anybody feel that good!

When I first laid eyes on Gil, my immediate thought was that we'd all be wise to take up skydiving when we retire. His appearance defied his years; he looked lean and fit and chock-full of energy. Of course, how many seventy-three-year-old grandfathers do you lay eyes on for the first time fresh out of the sky from two miles high, dressed in a fancy nylon jumping suit with canvas harness and macho metal clasps spanning the body from shoulders to groin? Add a helmet, goggles, and the ear-to-ear grin of a big ecstatic kid, and you've got a picture of Gil MacBeth having the time of his life.

Gil made his first jump when he was sixty. That was thirteen years and close to four hundred jumps ago, after his son, Greg, suggested Gil try it, too. It took only one jump, and Gil was hooked.

Then last year, Greg's son, Clint, turned sixteen and was finally of legal age to skydive. After years of watching from the ground as his father and grandfather dove through the sky, Clint joined them upstairs, and the Flying MacBeths were born.

"Hello, Gil. I'm Wayne Rostad. Greg, Clint, nice to meet all of you."

A warm welcome and hearty handshakes ensued. The MacBeths were most anxious to know if I was going to skydive; they knew my television show and had noticed that I tried a lot of the subject matter on for size.

"You gonna try it?" Gil asked.

"I'm working on it, boys. I don't know just yet."

"There's nothing like it!" Gil continued with that big boyish grin of his. "Words can't describe it!"

"You want to know what part of my problem is?" I said. "Now, don't laugh. But what if the chute doesn't open? I think that's my main fear."

"It's everybody's," said Greg. "But technology in parachuting over the last twenty years has just gone crazy. Parachutes today are almost malfunction-proof."

"Almost? What do you mean, almost?" I exclaimed, eyes widening.

A laugh erupted from the gathering.

"Seriously though, guys, what do you get out of it?"

Clint was quick to respond. "The adrenalin. The rush."

"It's a natural high," Greg added. "You can't get it anyplace else. This is something everyone should try at least once."

"*Everyone?*"

"Everyone! So, what do you think? Want to try it?"

I felt myself starting to bend. If I don't do it now, I thought, I'll never do it. Before I had time to answer, Paul turned and walked away, choosing not to participate in the decision-making process, pretending instead to be terribly captivated by the beautiful cloud formations drifting across New Brunswick.

"Boys, I just don't know. I've been thinking a lot about it, but I can't make a decision. I really need to know a lot more about this business of throwing yourself out of an airplane."

They more than understood my indecision. They too had once been in my boots, standing on the threshold where sanity and insanity meet.

"I'll tell you what might help you make up your mind," Greg continued. "Go over and talk to Dave Williamson. He's here for the weekend meet, and he just happens to be one of the best tandem jumpers in the country."

"What do you mean, *tandem* jumper?" I asked.

"It's the best way for anyone to do their first jump," Greg explained. "Safer, too. Two people come down on the same chute. Dave is one of the few people around qualified to do that. The chute he uses is much bigger than the ones we use, because it has to carry the weight of two people hooked together. Best of all, it gives first-timers a chance to experience freefall on their very first jumps. It takes a lot of training before you can freefall solo."

"Wait a minute. Nobody told me anything about first-timers *freefalling*!" I exclaimed.

"That's the best part of the whole dive," Greg continued. "That's what we live for. The parachute is just a way to get us back to the ground safely."

"This freefall lasts a whole minute?" My stomach moved my liver over.

"Usually forty-five seconds to a minute. It depends whether you jump from ten thousand feet or twelve thousand feet. Dave can tell you all about it. We've already spoken with him and he's more than willing to take you up for your first jump. He's over there where that big tent is."

"What's Dave's last name again?"

"Williamson. Dave Williamson."

"And he's that good, eh?"

"One of the best!" Gil reiterated. "If you're ever going to sky-dive in your lifetime, this is the time to do it, and Dave is the guy to do it with."

I glanced over Gil's shoulder at Paul, who was standing off near the parachuters' landing zone, just out of ear's reach. He now appeared to be totally engrossed in the indigenous bird sounds wafting across McEwen Airfield.

"I don't think Paul wants me to try this," I whispered.

"No," said Greg. "He doesn't."

I found Dave over by the big tent that the Moncton Sport Parachute Club had set up as a chute-packing area. Dave was on his knees, a huge chute stretched out on the ground in front of him. He was reeling in great lengths of white parachute cord, folding the strands securely in the chute's backpack.

"Hello, Dave. How's it going?"

"Wayne! I've been looking forward to meeting you. I've been a fan of your show for years!"

"Nice to hear. Thank you."

"In fact, I've wanted to be on your show for a long time. I always wanted to introduce you to skydiving. Here, have a look at what I'm doing. This is how you pack a chute. It's a bit of a pain sometimes, 'cause it takes a few minutes to do right, but you have to. After all, this *is* the most important part of the whole business."

"You're telling me! Looks like quite a process."

"Not as complicated as you might think. This one is a little more labour-intensive than most, because it's a little bigger than most."

"Then this is the tandem chute?"

"Right. It's bulky and not as manoeuvrable as the smaller chutes, but it allows us to do a double."

"Greg has already told me a little bit about it," I said.

"We've all been waiting," Dave continued, "wondering if you might want to try it."

"Well, to tell you the truth, Dave, I can't make up my bloody mind! One minute it's yes, the next minute it's no. I'm like a yo-yo on a string."

"That's natural. Take your time; it's a big decision. I'm going up for a tandem jump now with someone else. You'll be able to have a look at how it's done, and maybe you'll feel better about it. It's really quite safe. This chute is a particularly good one, state-of-the-art. If the main chute fails for *any* reason, an altimeter inside the chute automatically releases the safety chute.

"How do you actually hook up to each other?" I asked.

"See these metal clasps on the front of my harness? I connect them to the clips on the backside of the harness of the person I'm jumping with. It's almost like I'm riding piggyback. I give the rip cord to the first-time jumper, and they actually release the chute, which I carry on my back. The nice thing about tandem jumping is that it allows a first-time jumper a way to legally . . ."

"I know," I interrupted. "To freefall – without having to take hours of training."

"Exactly! We freefall for about a minute before pulling the cord."

"How fast do we fall?"

"We freefall for the first seven thousand feet or so at a little over one hundred and twenty miles an hour."

My stomach was now lodged in my esophagus.

"A hundred and twenty! Are you serious?"

"For sure. But your mind adjusts quickly. Two or three seconds after you leave the airplane, there's nothing to it. You will absolutely enjoy the fall. It never lasts long enough. There's nothing in the world like it."

Dave continued to explain the business of skydiving to me as he finished packing the tandem chute, and the longer we talked, the more confident I became about the notion of jumping with him. His hands were experienced, deftly pushing, prodding, and packing every little piece of that chute into the pack exactly the way he wanted it. I liked him. He looked fit and strong and exuded great confidence in his ability. He'd been jumping for more than twenty years and had more than twenty-four hundred jumps to his credit. And it certainly boosted my confidence to know that several hundred of those were tandem jumps.

By suppertime that Monday, only four hours after first arriving at McEwen Airfield, I had made up and unmade my mind four thousand three hundred and ninety-eight times. I was a creature of total indecision, a master of procrastination, a man-wimp, half sinew and bone, half quivering jelly. A hundred voices were chanting, "Go for it! Go for it!" when one voice suddenly spoke in front of my face, interrupting the cacophony.

"Well, what are we doing?"

It was Paul.

"What do you mean, 'What are we doing?'"

"If you're going to do this thing, we've got to do it now. We won't have the light much longer."

"Right. You're absolutely right, Paul. We need light. We need light."

"Well?"

"Well, what? I thought you didn't want me to jump."

"I don't."

"Well?"

"Well, what?"

"Well, then, what are asking me that question for?"

The last decision Paul had heard on the grapevine was that I was going to do it. An hour earlier I had even done the necessary thirty minutes of ground instruction with Dave. He simply needed to know what he was going to have Tom shoot next. Had God not have intervened, chances are we would have probed and dodged one another till the moon came up. But we were spared that ordeal when a cloud drifted quickly from the west and came to rest over McEwen Airfield. The base of the cloud was at about five thousand feet, with no holes in it. While high enough to allow a legal jump, it was not high enough to allow freefall. Paul and I both knew that if I was going to jump at all, it had to include freefall. I wasn't about to do it without getting those magic shots on tape. When God's little saviour rolled in over us, we knew today's elusive jump was off.

"Too bad," I said in my manliest voice. "I was really looking forward to this. Oh, well, guess we'll have to wait till tomorrow and see what the weather brings."

I don't think anybody was really listening.

That night back at the Hotel Beauséjour in Moncton I told Paul, Tom, and Mike that I wanted to do the jump and needed all the help I could get from them. I didn't want any more negatives in my mind. I wanted their support. Paul nodded his head and continued to choke on his soup.

"I'm sure about my decision now," I said. "There is no way I can leave Moncton tomorrow without trying this."

Tuesday morning found us back at McEwen Airfield, the weather was fantastic. Besides, Dave Williamson, bless his heart, had returned to Moncton from Waterville, Nova Scotia, after taking his son home overnight, just to do my tandem jump. In fact, a *lot* of the skydiving group was still hanging around.

The morning was spent doing an interview with the MacBeths. It was wonderful sitting in the sunshine, listening to the boys speak about their love of skydiving.

"You don't see a lot of families, especially nowadays, hanging around together," Greg said. "That's what we do, we hang around together. The three of us *live* together in the summertime. We're buddies. We look after each other and make sure we stay safe and have fun."

"Me, being the grandaddy and the daddy," said Gil, "to see my flesh and blood flying through the air up there and playing with them, what a sweet thrill. It's so beautiful; it really is."

"What about you, Clint?" I asked. "As a teenager, tell me how it feels hanging around on the weekends with your father and grandfather?"

"It's really cool. All my friends think my grandpa's kinda neat and they like to walk up to us in the malls and stuff and meet him. It even helps me get dates – the girls really like him."

"Yeah," Gil piped in. "Sometimes I even get a date with the mother!"

"Aren't you married, Gil?" I asked.

"No, I've been divorced more than twenty years. This is what I'm married to now – skydiving."

By lunchtime, everyone's attention turned to me. There was only one thing that could possibly save me now – a phone call. You see, earlier that morning it had dawned on me that it might be wise to check my insurance companies out to see how they felt about my jumping out of a plane. Were my bank loans and chattel mortgages insured if I risked life and limb wilfully? What was the CBC's position on all this? Was my wife going to be husbandless and penniless? Was my son going to forever remember his father as the dummy who threw himself out of a plane one day over McEwen Airfield in New Brunswick and implanted himself six feet deep in *terra firma*?

When I ran these notions by Paul, he really wasn't sure, either. What we *knew* for sure was that the shuttle was about to launch and, if I was going to be on board, I needed to go to the parachute club's office and make a few phone calls. I phoned everybody! The first call was to my bank manager.

"Rennie, it's Rostad. Tell me, are my bank loans insured if I jump out of an airplane?"

"Not if it's suicide," he replied. Rennie's funny like that.

"No, no. I mean, if I do a parachute jump and the worst happens . . . ?"

"Your policies are fine. Go ahead, jump."

Great. Some friend. Next, I called my insurance agent.

"Hello, Bill, it's Rostad. I'm in New Brunswick with my television show and I'm in a bit of a situation. I'm about to skydive for the show and I just realized my life-insurance policies probably won't allow it. Would you find that clause and read it to me?"

I knew the ears outside the club office were tuned in like radar.

"What do you mean, it's okay, Bill? You haven't even taken time to read the policy! Thanks, Bill. Yes, I'll call you next week."

Nice guy. What if there *is* no next week? Next, I called my wife, Leanne.

"Hi, honey. It's me. Tell me, what would you think if your husband jumped out of an airplane with a parachute?"

"Well, darling, a lot would depend, I guess, on whether or not the parachute opened."

"Lee-Lee, I'm serious. I'm about to go two miles high in an airplane and throw our marriage and our future out to the heavens. I need to know how you feel about this."

"Probably the same way you'd feel if I told you I was about to jump out of an airplane. I trust your judgement. But if you climb out there on the strut and have a change of heart, promise me you'll climb back in."

The ball was still in my court! I thought of calling my mother, but knew that would be futile, too. She always let me do whatever I wanted to do anyway. The jump was on.

Things started happening rather quickly after I emerged from the office. Tom checked to make sure he had lots of videotape at hand. Mike put fresh batteries in everything that took batteries. Paul went into the office and started calling everyone he knew at the CBC. I slipped into my coveralls, and Dave helped me strap on my harness. Then I started to pace like a thoroughbred ready to enter the gate. I could feel my adrenalin begin to pump.

"Here're your hat and goggles," Dave said, handing them to me. The hat was made of rubber and had very little padding.

"Not much head protection," I said.

"The hat's really designed to help with air flow," Dave replied. "The goggles will keep the wind out of your eyes and let you see."

Great! If anything went wrong, I'd be able to see the ground rushing up as I performed a head plant with my little rubber helmet.

"All right. If you're ready, Wayne, let's do it!"

Dave and I climbed aboard the Cessna for the ascent to altitude. Greg MacBeth was also on board. He had a special helmet-mounted camera to shoot my jump from one point of view. Another club member, Don Goguen, was jumping, too. He had a helmet-cam mounted on his head as well, with which he would shoot the freefall, close up. Before the pilot started the engine, all kinds of people took pictures, and I sat, smiling bravely for the cameras, at the same time *pleading* with my eyes for a way out. But it was too late; we were committed.

They tell me the climb to twelve thousand five hundred feet took about thirty minutes, but it felt more like five. The little Cessna strained for altitude under the heavy load. Dave and I alone had a combined weight of four hundred and forty pounds, or two hundred kilograms, which would test the tandem chute to its limits. As we went through one of the big holes at cloud level, Dave told me we were at about eight thousand feet, and would soon have to start hooking up to each other.

Here's how things were going to work out. Once at altitude, Don Goguen would climb out of the airplane first and literally hang off the wing, training his helmet-cam in towards the cockpit as Dave and I climbed out. He would then jump with us, shooting our entire freefall. Meanwhile, Greg would stay in the airplane and shoot us leaving the wing, then immediately jump himself and follow us down, shooting our descent. I was warned to expect a bit of a rush when the door first opened, because of the wind and increased noise level in the cockpit. I was also told to summon up every ounce of bravado for the step out of the cockpit *into* the wind. I would feel a fair amount of buffeting against my body once I was out there, hanging off the strut. Dave would tap my hand when it was time to let go, and we were to count three and throw ourselves prostrate *on* the wind. We would fall, not perpendicular to the ground as you would jumping off a fence and landing on your feet, but flat, as if we were doing belly flops in a pool, with our bodies parallel to the earth, using our outstretched arms and legs as wind deflectors to literally *fly*.

At ten thousand feet, Dave had me move forward and he began the process of hooking us together. There was a clicking sound at each shoulder as the big metal clasps connected. Then at my waist, first on the left, then right.

"I'll tighten them up a lot more as we get closer to altitude," Dave said. "How are you feeling?"

"I'm still trying to figure out what I'm doing here!" I replied, adding a little laugh for comic relief. "I'm all right. I just have this terrible case of dry mouth. I sure wish I had brought something to drink."

"You'll be just fine. We're getting close to the drop zone. We're going to open the door now. Don't worry, you're not going to fall out. Remember, I'm hooked up to you, and you won't be going anywhere without me."

When the door opened, the noise, as promised, was loud. Without question, it caught my attention. So did the ground.

My God! I thought. This is madness!

I had flown my airplane many times at this altitude, but never with a door wide open and never with a totally unobstructed view *straight down*. It felt higher than I'd ever been before.

"I'm going to tighten us up now!" Dave yelled over the din.

I felt a firm tug on my shoulders and waistline as he cinched us together. Then he shifted his body weight against mine, first left, then right, to check the security of the hookup and made one final adjustment at the waist before tapping me on the shoulder.

"We're ready!" he shouted. "We're coming up over the drop zone. When I tap you again, put your foot out on the wheel platform and grab hold of the wing strut like I told you downstairs. Remember?"

I nodded. I couldn't speak because my mouth was bone-dry. I couldn't move my tongue. I watched as Don stepped out of the cockpit and positioned himself with his helmet-cam in our direction. He looked like Spiderman hanging off the wing.

Seconds later, I felt the dreaded tap on my shoulder.

"Let's go!" Dave yelled. "Foot out. That's it. Now, grab the strut and step out. Good, good! I'm right with you. That's it. Don't worry. Hold on."

The sensation of climbing out of a moving airplane three kilometres above the earth was incredible. There I was in a crouched position, being buffeted by the wind, hanging on a wing strut, high above the clouds, right over a big hole in the clouds that clearly showed Mother Earth waiting below. In fact, the whole city of Moncton was waiting for us down there. So was every farmer's field for miles. And somewhere down there was McEwen Airfield. I couldn't see it, but I wasn't about to argue about that right now. I didn't know my name at this point.

Then, I felt the slap of Dave's hand on mine. It was time to let go. Whether it was too soon or not didn't mean a hill of beans. A second slap, followed by an eerie sense of resignation, a count in unison, *one, two, three*, and we were away.

What a rush! The flow of adrenalin I felt in the first few moments after leaving that airplane surpasses anything I have ever experienced. We were flying! The drop speed was absolutely exhilarating! I could feel my cheeks fluttering as we approached two hundred kilometres an hour. Then, the realization hit me. I had done it! There was no more dry mouth, no more fear. This is incredible! I thought. A great yell began erupting deep inside me.

"Yeeeess!!!!!" I screamed. "Yeeeeess!!! Yeess!!"

I yelled! I hooted! I hollered! I was a kid on the greatest ride in the world, and I was deliriously, deliciously, out of my mind! At one point, Don was no more than a metre from my face with the lens on his helmet-cam capturing my every expression. He had this great, outlandish grin from ear to ear that made me roar with laughter. What a place to have a mental communion with someone. I gave him two thumbs up, and let go another primal scream. Dave was hollering, too. After all these jumps, he still sounded like a kid enjoying the greatest ride on earth.

All too soon, Dave's hand grabbed my wrist, reminding me to check my altimeter. It was just about time to pull the rip cord. We were now falling through 5,500 feet. How could that be? I thought. A minute can't possibly go by that fast! But in freefall, unfortunately, it does. As I had been instructed the day before, I placed the handle of the rip cord firmly in my right hand, flashed Dave five fingers three times, and pulled.

There was a sudden, jarring snap against my shoulders as the harness straps took the full impact of our combined body weight. The tandem chute had indeed opened, and four hundred and forty pounds were brought from a two-hundred-kilometre-an-hour fall to an apparent dead stop in the blink of an eye. The freefall ended with one huge grunt, and silence suddenly filled our ears. The wind was gone. It felt as if we were in a state of suspension high above the ground, not moving at all. Of course, we *were* moving; it's just that after falling so fast for as long as I had, my brain had not caught up yet. My first few seconds were spent taking stock of this particular phase of the whole experience. We've stopped! Thank God, the chute's open. Holy smoke, what a snap! My shoulders hurt! Where the heck am I?

I didn't like the feeling of hanging in midair as much as I had enjoyed freefalling. It felt as if my whole life was being supported by nothing more than two strips of canvas and four metal clasps. At that very moment, of course, it was.

"Wayne!" a voice called out. "Wayne! Are you okay?"

It was Dave. He sounded as if he were calling down from some distance above me, which I found momentarily frightening. He was directly above me, of course; he just seemed a lot farther away because I couldn't turn my head up enough to see him and we were, after all, descending through rushing air at a pretty good clip.

"Dave, are we okay? Is everything okay?"

"Yes, yes," he reassured me. "Are you all right?"

"I'm fine. Is this harness secure? Nothing's gonna slip or anything, is it?"

"No, no. I just want to loosen up our connectors. Stand on the tops of my running shoes with your feet and push yourself up. Can you do that?"

"I'll try." I had to pull my legs up about half a metre in order to place them on top of his shoes. It was awkward, but I managed to get my feet on top of his.

"That's it. Now try to stand up. Push against my feet and try to hold yourself there."

All this was very well for Dave; he knew what he was doing. But it was not at all clear to me. When I pushed up, I thought that he simply intended to relieve some of the pressure on his groin – mine was killing me! – but what Dave intended to do was introduce some slack into the lines holding me to him. So, when I heard two quick clicks and felt the clasps at my waist suddenly loosen, I just about had a bird. It scared me so much that my feet slipped off the top of his runners. That sense of falling, coupled with the feeling of being disconnected at the waist, was the scariest part of the whole ride. In that split-second, I thought Dave had done something wrong and I was about to rendezvous with the devil.

"Dave!" I called out in a voice bordering on hysteria. "What's going on? Am I disconnected?"

No answer.

"Dave!"

"No, no, Wayne. Eveything's okay. I was just trying to get this darned harness straightened out."

"You scared me. I didn't know you were going to loosen our connections. I thought I was going to fall."

"Sorry, sorry. I guess you didn't understand what I meant. Everything is perfect."

What a relief. Paul would no doubt be happy about that, too.

"Here, Wayne, I'm going to hand you the steering handles to practice a landing in midair, just like we talked about yesterday. Remember?"

"Yes, I remember. Pull the left handle to turn left and pull the right to go right."

"And pull 'em both just before we touch down for a 'walk-on' landing."

Throw away that other Hollywood fallacy about parachuters always crashing into trees. These babies steer better than Volkswagens!

The rest of the descent was a breeze. Talk about feeling like a bird! In no time at all, McEwen Airfield was directly below us. About a thousand feet from touchdown, Dave and I started whooping and hollering again – and didn't stop until our feet hit the ground.

The first people on the scene were Gil and Clint. Gil walked over as if I had just joined the family and gave me a hug. I was so high from the experience I was hyperventilating. I turned and gave Dave a great big hug.

"My brother, for life!" I exclaimed.

Paul was beaming. I found out later that he didn't stop pacing the field from the time our jump plane started its engine till he counted three chutes overhead.

"Congratulations!" Paul said with a highly relieved smile. "I can't believe you did it."

"Neither can I, Paul. Neither can I."

"So I guess next month's shoot about the cannon guy is on, then?"

"What shoot is that, Paul?"

"The stunt guy in Alberta who wants to shoot you out of a cannon."

"Get out of here!" I said, as Paul broke into laughter.

Nice joke. He knew darn well the only thing I've ever refused to do on our show was eat bugs.

Gas Leak at Bow Valley

❧

I get a real kick out of elevators. What a marvellous invention! When I was a kid growing up in Ottawa, my favourite elevator in the whole world was the one in the old Frieman's department store down on Rideau Street. It had an operator, dressed in uniform, who barked out the floor number and what was on that floor as the elevator arrived.

"Second floor," the operator would say. "Ladies' cosmetics, boys' and girls' wear. Next stop, third floor, furnishings and housewares." It was as if you were being taken on a bit of a tour, or taking a ride at the fair. I remember my stomach rising and falling, much to my delight, as we started and stopped at each floor. I loved the sense of body lightness brought on by sudden descent, and the heavy-body sensation when they put the brakes on at the bottom. I also enjoyed the fact that people talked to each other on the Frieman's elevator. They appreciated not having to take the stairs, and they talked about it.

The big doors on each floor where the elevator stopped to let off and pick up passengers were made of solid steel, with plate-glass windows in them. When you pushed the button calling for the elevator, you could hear the machinery hard at work in the shaft. Through the plate-glass windows you could see the cables straining as the elevator rose and fell away. Pulleys would creak and groan as the transport box made its way between floors. Then the elevator finally magically appeared, filling the dark windows of the doors with light. The operator would open the scissor-like inner screen of the elevator box, drawing it back like a curtain, then would haul down hard on the big handle of the floor doors, opening them. There was a lovely rhythmic quality to all that. It brought delight to anyone intrigued by mechanical wonders of the day. It certainly brought me delight. There was such a wonderful sound and smell to it all.

Frieman's elevator travelled only six floors; today, the sky's the limit. Twenty- and thirty-storey elevators are commonplace in the city-centre hotels I stay in when I'm on the road. The Sheraton in Toronto is forty-two storeys high! These modern-day monoliths have jet elevators that are incredibly fast! Not only that, they're smooth and quiet – *real* smooth and quiet. They have computer-controlled starts and stops that make you wonder if you're even moving at all. But what they don't have today are operators, someone to break the ice with a "Good Morning!" or "Which floor would you like?" A lot of people who get in elevators today share rather long moments with total strangers, ascending and descending in silence. The routine for the most part is: face the door, look at the floor, raise the eyes, follow the light going through the numbers, look back at the door, and wonder why it's taking so long to get where you're going.

I'm the kind of person, though, who loves to break the silence, an elevator extrovert. I've made a habit of talking to people in elevators. I figure if I'm going to spend half my life in elevators going down to meet the crew in the lobby or going up at day's end to my room, I can at least make it a social moment rather than a silent one. Nothing heavy mind you; after all, it's a very short ride.

"It certainly is a lovely morning out there," or "Nice city, isn't it?" are usually socially correct comments to make in elevators. For the most part, even the most paranoid of elevator non-conversationalists can muster up single-word responses to them.

On the other hand, "Tell me, do you think free love is running rampant in our society today?" is sure to induce instant hysteria and frantic button-pushing.

Let's face it. We all like our space. These elevator transit boxes will always be too small and confined for most people, and no matter how fast they travel, it will always take forever to get where they want to go. I don't have that problem, though. I still love elevators. Usually I don't want to get off. But one elevator ride I took made me wish I had never gotten on. It was the longest elevator ride of my life.

It happened in Calgary in the fall of 1994. The crew and I had booked in at the twenty-five-storey Delta Bow Valley, and I was given a room on the twenty-third floor. After performing my arrival routine of hanging my clothes in the closet, putting my shaving gear on the bathroom counter, and placing my shampoo in the shower, I headed for the elevator to meet the crew down-stairs for supper. I hit the call button on the wall and, almost instantly, the jet wonder arrived at my level and the doors opened. I entered, hit the "lobby" button, and the doors closed. That's when it hit me. The elevator was filled with the most foul odour I have ever experienced. It filled my nostrils. Something must have died. Someone had the audacity, the nerve, to pass *gas* only moments ago in that elevator – and then leave! I knew Alberta was big on gas, but *this* was too much! And it wasn't just the smell of it. It was the *volume*. You could cut the air in that elevator with a knife. It wasn't some little "sneaker" that someone silently let go. Someone thought about this one and gave it a conscious effort. We *all* pass gas on occasion but, please, not in a public place, in an enclosed space, in a vessel of public transit!

I reached for the "open door" button. I wanted off. Too late! We started down – me, the elevator, and the gaseous remains. My God, I thought, what am I going to say if this thing stops and someone gets on? They'll think it's me!

Floor 22 went whizzing by.

What if a woman, for example, got on? How would I address the situation with a woman? Most women seem uncomfortable when it comes to discussing flatulence.

Floor 21. No stoppage.

I mean, at least with a man I could be one of the boys and talk about it man to man, something like: "Somebody just cut a hell of a beer fart in here, buddy, and I gotta tell ya, it wasn't me!"

Floor 20 passed by.

But with a woman, let's say an older woman, I'd have to say: "Excuse me. Is there a pulp-and-paper mill in Calgary? I do believe I detect a trace of sulphur in the air. Tell me, ma'am, can you . . . *smell* . . . it?"

Floor 19. Still nobody.

Of course she would smell it! She'd pass out from it!

Floor 18.

So far so good.

17 . . . 16 . . . 15.

It was taking forever. Who am I kidding? I thought. I'll never make it. It's suppertime, and this is a big hotel. People have to eat to live.

Floor 14 went whishing by.

What if this thing stops and a cleanliness nut gets on. They'll gag!

Floor 12. Thank goodness they don't have floor 13 . . . one less floor to worry about.

Who could have done such a thing? Someone with a complete disregard for all living things, that's who. Someone who's probably done it before.

Floor 11 went by.

Holy Smoke! What if someone gets on and recognizes me from my television show? "You'll never guess who I got on the elevator with in Calgary, Martha. That 'On the Road Again' guy, and, boy, did he stink!" What if a group of Girl Guides got on? They'd die. I'd be that decrepit old guy on TV they met in the elevator at the Western Canada Girl Guide Conference!

Floor 10. No Girl Guides! Thank heaven.

You know, there really is a God. Incredibly, I made that entire twenty-three-floor descent, at a busy time of day, with no stops. Not only that, no one was even standing in the lobby when the doors opened! Either everyone was already seated for supper, or no one eats supper in Calgary any more. I stepped out of the transit box, hung a quick left, and walked out into the crisp, *fresh* fall air. The whole ride lasted just a few seconds, but it felt like an eternity. To this day, I wonder who poisoned the air in that elevator at the Bow Valley. Was it a lawyer? A judge? One of the maids? Who knows? The only thing I know for sure is this: no one would ever have done that at Frieman's.

Wilma

Slapping the water to make Wilma come closer to the boat

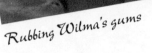

Rubbing Wilma's gums

Captain John Morgan

Wilma

Whales have always fascinated me. As a kid, I read *Moby-Dick* two or three times, and, each time, I was held spellbound by the images that leapt off the pages depicting Captain Ahab's confrontations with the great whale. Likewise, the biblical tale of Jonah being swallowed alive by a whale intrigued me no end in catechism class. The notion of sliding down the innards of a giant whale and living to tell about it was incredible. What made Jonah's story so very vivid was that the Bible said it was true, and, being a good catechism student, I never questioned it. So, for several years, I actually believed that whales swallowed people.

Other large creatures of the deep caught my attention over the years, too, like the giant squid that enveloped the ocean-going submarine *Nautilus* in the epic *20,000 Leagues under the Sea*. I also struggled mightily with Spencer Tracy when he hooked the giant marlin in *The Old Man and the Sea* and, more recently, was held spellbound by Steven Spielberg's tale of the great white shark in the movie *Jaws*. But, of all the critters in the sea, it is the mention of whales that turns my head around. So, when Lauren Sawatsky, one of my "On the Road Again" producers, asked if I would like to go swimming in the ocean with a whale on our next trip to Nova Scotia, she had my undivided attention.

"What do you mean, go swimming with a whale?" I asked, incredulously.

"I mean *you*, in the ocean, with a real live whale," Lauren replied. "A beluga whale named Wilma."

That made me chuckle.

"Wilma? Her name is Wilma? What is she, a pet whale?"

"Nope. She's a St. Lawrence beluga. She shouldn't even be that far south."

"So, why is she there?" I asked.

"Nobody's really sure. All they know is she just showed up in Chedabucto Bay a while ago, all by herself, swam into the harbour by the town of Guysborough, and never left. Some people think it has something to do with the bay's terrific food supply."

"Who found her to begin with?" I asked.

"The guy you're going to interview, John Morgan. He's claiming to be one of the first to lay hands on her. He'll also be taking us out in his boat to meet her."

"What do you mean, 'lay hands' on her?" I asked.

"People actually touch her!" Lauren explained. "They get in the water with her and play with her. It's wonderful! She just kind of *adopted* the whole community, and the community, in turn, has adopted her."

It really was an exciting thought. Imagine, not only swimming in the ocean with a whale, but actually *touching* one.

"So," I asked, "what will I need, besides a swimsuit? Flippers, maybe?"

"Actually, we've rented a wetsuit for you," Lauren said. "It's the biggest one we could find."

"Cute. Very cute," I replied.

"You're going to *need* a wetsuit. The Atlantic in May is no picnic. It's bloody cold!"

For a moment, my mind flashed back to catechism class. Jonah was going down, big time.

"If you don't mind my asking, Lauren, just how big is this whale anyway?"

"This one isn't very big. She's young, only about four metres long, and very friendly. You're going to love her!"

I thought about the upcoming trip for days. While four metres didn't seem big in my mind's eye, compared to the gigantic child-hood images of Moby-Dick which were indelibly etched in my brain, the thought of being in the water with anything bigger than me stirred up some trepidation. I knew a little bit about belugas from an "On the Road Again" story we did three seasons before. It involved a group of people from Quebec who were studying the beluga population that summered annually in the St. Lawrence. Unfortunately, I was unable to be on location for that story and had to settle for watching the whales on video while sitting in the voice booth narrating the script. So this new beluga story was great news. I was thrilled at the prospect of finally seeing a real live beluga, and very excited about possibly getting in the water with one.

Chedabucto Bay is thirty minutes by car due south of the Canso Causeway, the man-made, sea-rock roadway connecting mainland Nova Scotia to Cape Breton Island. The town of Guysborough, with its beautiful sheltered harbour, is tucked deeply in the westernmost nook of the bay, more than a thousand kilometres from the beluga's nearest known summer habitat in the Gulf of St. Lawrence. Wilma was a long way from home. Though not unheard of, it was unusual for a beluga to be that far from its pod. Even more unusual was the fact that Wilma decided to stay in Chedabucto Bay. Good food supply notwithstanding, there was nothing holding her there except her own free will.

The shoot took place during the last week of May, and it got off to a bit of a shaky start when Keith Whelan, the cameraman assigned to the Wilma story, was rushed to hospital with a ruptured appendix. He was going to be out of action for a couple of weeks. Luckily, on very short we-need-you-now notice, we were able to pull Tom Sharina away from his news assignments with CBC Ottawa for the week, and he arrived Sunday to join Lauren and Mike Champagne, our audio man. I landed my Duke late Monday night at the airport in Port Hawkesbury, just a few miles from the Canso Causeway, and Steve Spencer, my co-pilot, and I drove down to Guysborough, arriving at our motel around midnight. Everyone was sacked in by then, but there was a note in my room from Lauren asking me to join them around eight-thirty in the morning for breakfast to go over a few details with John Morgan before heading out into the bay to meet Wilma. I couldn't think of a nicer way to spend the day.

The next morning, I met John for the first time. He was a very personable fellow, a forty-year-old former undercover agent for the RCMP, who had decided to take early retirement and start a charter-boat business in Guysborough called The Captain's Luxury Tours. Originally, John intended to take tourists shark fishing. However, that endeavour didn't last long once he discovered Wilma in Chedabucto Bay. Over breakfast, he told me how it all started.

"On my very first shark-fishing tour, about two and a half kilometres outside Chedabucto Bay, we picked her up. She came alongside of us. This gentleman on board, who was from Alberta, said, 'Look at this, isn't it beautiful?' I said, 'Yeah, it's a dolphin.' He said, 'No. It's a whale, a beluga whale!' 'Well,' I said, 'to tell you the truth, I wouldn't even know a beluga if I saw one.' 'Well, buddy,' he said, 'I've seen a lot of whales in my day, and that's a beluga. You're not *supposed* to have a beluga down here, but you sure do now!' That was the end of my shark-fishing tours. I've been taking people whale-watching ever since."

"John," I asked, "what would bring her to Guysborough County to begin with?"

"Nobody that I've ever talked to could answer that one. She came here, and she made this her home. How she got here, I have no idea. Why she stays I have no idea, either. It's her game. She's in control. She could leave even as we speak, but I know she won't. She'll be here tomorrow."

"Do you see her every single time you go out in your boat? I mean, that's a pretty big ocean out there."

"I'm pretty sure she'll be there. She hardly ever misses. You'll see."

John absolutely bubbled when he talked about Wilma. He delighted in introducing people to her, never ceasing to marvel at her ongoing communion with humans, and at how quickly she bonded with everyone.

John's story had Tom Sharina all excited. He wanted to start shooting.

"So, Wayne," Tom challenged, "are you ready to get in the water with her?"

"You bet I'm ready!" I replied.

"It's gonna be cold!" he warned. "I hope you brought some woollies."

"I'll just borrow yours, if that's okay," I replied. "They tell me you always wear nice warm woollies."

"Well, boys," Lauren interrupted. "We really shouldn't keep Wilma waiting much longer. Shall we go?"

She didn't have to ask twice. We were all really looking forward to meeting Willma, and, after fighting my way into my wetsuit, I drove down to join everyone dockside. Naturally, there was a little good-natured heckling about the fit of my suit.

"Not bad, considering he's well into his forties," said one.

"What did you do, *pour* that on?" said another.

"Go ahead," I called back. "Get it out of your system."

"Wilma really likes rubber!" John yelled from the boat. "It has the same texture as the skin of a beluga. When she tastes you, she'll think you're one, too."

"What do you mean, when she *tastes* me? I'm not letting anything that big taste me!"

Jonah was *really* going down, big time, now.

"C'mon, hurry up," John chuckled, continuing his good-natured ribbing. "Wilma's waiting. And she's hungry! Let's go!"

Once our gear was loaded aboard the boat, John fired up the Johnson and, moments later, we were motoring out into Chedabucto Bay for a much-anticipated morning rendezvous with Wilma.

Belugas are fascinating creatures. They resemble dolphins, except they have no dorsal fin. They swim much like a seal – up, down, sideways, even upside-down. They have broad shoulders that taper sharply to a slender neck, which is highly flexible; all other whales have necks that are more rigidly attached to the rest of the body. Young belugas are slate-grey to brown in colour and slowly turn white by the time they reach maturity at age six or seven. Nobody is sure why. These beautiful white whales choose to live in the high Arctic nine months of the year, enduring pack ice, weeks on end without food, and months of total darkness. Because they are surface breathers, they travel where the sheet ice meets open water, allowing them to poke their heads up between the ice packs to breathe. Our Inuit people of the north have hunted them for centuries. About the only time people other than the Inuit get a chance to see a beluga is from June to September, when they migrate from offshore into river estuaries like the St. Lawrence, where warmer waters suit the fancy of nursing mothers and their calves.

In spite of their harsh Arctic habitat, they have adapted well. According to Dr. Paul Brodie, a Canadian research scientist who lived, travelled, and hunted with the Inuit while researching the biology and behaviour of the beluga, there are up to sixty thousand belugas alive today. An article by Dr. Brodie in the December 1985 issue of BBC *Wildlife* revealed a wealth of information about belugas, including the fact they are capable of diving over six hundred metres, almost two thousand feet, allowing them to feed on the bottom-dwelling fauna in most of the Arctic waters. This is one tough whale! When Wilma first showed up in Chedabucto Bay, Guysborough residents, concerned that Wilma might have been sick, stranded, or disoriented, invited Dr. Brodie down to have a look at her. After examining her, he confirmed she was indeed from a Gulf of St. Lawrence pod – and pronounced her to be a perfectly healthy and happy whale.

Belugas have a life span of about thirty years. John told us Wilma was probably around five or six. She was still a little grey.

"Wait till you see her turn her head for the first time," John chortled. "Belugas are the only whales that can turn their heads from side to side. If she comes up outta the water and she's sideways to you, that old head just swivels around like it's on a socket. It's almost human. Kinda eerie, too. You'll see."

John motored to a point where the sheltered bay began opening to the sea and then stopped the engine.

"All right," he announced. "This is where Wilma usually is around this time of the mornin'. Here's the drill, and I've seen it a number of times now. First thing, when she comes, she's very cautious. She checks you out first, circles around, then gradually makes her way in to where she's comfortable, and then she starts to nuzzle you and brush you. Then she'll move right in as if you were long-lost friends. The important thing, when you get in the water, is just to float there, real still, and she'll come to you."

I passed a leg over the stern of the boat and slowly slipped myself into the water. Lauren was right. The Atlantic in May is still very cold. I felt the water seep into my wetsuit at the neckline, and run down my back and chest. This was natural. Wetsuits are designed to allow a thin layer of water to enter and surround the body. It doesn't stay cold long, though. Body heat warms that layer of water up in a couple of minutes, and one is quite comfortable after that.

"How is it?" Tom asked. "Do you want my woollies?"

"Not bad, actually," I replied. "Keep your woollies. The suit's great! Should have brought a weight belt, though. Look how buoyant I am. It's hard to stay upright. I feel like an inner tube."

There was another problem Tom noted. The tide was going out, and I was drifting with it, away from the boat. In order for him to properly shoot the meeting between Wilma and me, we would have to be fairly close to the boat.

"Here," John said, grabbing a black hand line. "You can hang on to this."

John tossed the hand line over the side and I wrapped it around my wrist. The drift problem was solved. Everyone was happy. We were ready. All we needed now was Wilma.

"Wilma!" John called. "C'mon, Wilma!"

This is crazy, I thought. Here I am in the Atlantic, and Captain John is calling a whale to come like you'd call a dog. It's like a cartoon.

"I feel like a piece of bait," I yelled out.

John didn't answer. He had spotted Wilma.

"There she is!" he exclaimed. "Look! Right off the stern. C'mon, Wilma!"

"Where?" I asked, in a voice rising slightly in pitch. "Where did you say she is?"

"She's coming around the stern now. She sees you. Just stay still. She's coming right at you. She knows you're in there with her."

I couldn't see her. I didn't have the high vantage point everyone on the boat deck had. They could see her clearly.

"She's starting to circle you now," John continued. "Just stay still. Let her get used to you."

Easy for you to say, I thought.

I felt Wilma before I saw her. All four metres of her slithered along the left side of my body.

"Oh, God!" I called out, my voice rising again. "Did that ever feel weird! Where did she go?"

"She's right behind you. She's still sizing you up. Turn this way and you'll see her."

I turned around as John suggested and caught my first glimpse of Wilma. She was about three metres in front of me, sort of hovering in the water just below the surface, much as a helicopter would hover in air. I watched, in total fascination, as she slowly came closer. I could see her quite clearly now. She was swimming directly towards me. When she reached my legs, Wilma's mouth opened and clamped down momentarily on my left knee – not hard, but enough to get my attention.

"John, she just grabbed my knee! Is she trying to bite me? She just put my whole knee in her mouth. What's happening?"

"She's not biting you, she's feeling you. Her mouth is her hands. Don't worry, she doesn't have big teeth, anyway."

Just then, the arched top of Wilma's back surfaced a short distance from me. There was a sudden sound of water being cleared from her blowhole, much like a snorkler clearing a snorkel after a dive, followed by a very large human-like gasp as Wilma replenished her lungs with fresh air. It took about three seconds. Then the blowhole closed, and Wilma submerged to continue her inspection of this new playmate in her back yard.

"She's underneath you now," John advised me. "Looking straight up at you."

"Why underneath me?" I didn't like not being able to see her.

"She's still trying to figure you out. Relax, there's nothing to worry about."

No sooner had he said those words than I felt Wilma's mouth clamp onto my foot. Nothing to worry about! I'm dangling in three hundred metres of ocean with a whale hanging off my left foot, and I have nothing to worry about? What if Wilma suddenly decided to take me down to meet her friends who lived on the ocean floor. "Hey, everybody, look what I found! Isn't he cute? He's got skin kinda like mine. And just look at all the pretty bubbles he's blowing. I wonder if I should let him go? Do you think he needs air?" Nothing to worry about, my foot!

Obviously, John hadn't heard the recent true story of a woman diver who almost lost her life doing research on great grey whales. She was in the ocean videotaping one, when she apparently did something to annoy the big brute. I think she tried to grab onto the whale and videotape the ride or something. I'm not sure. Anyway, the whale took great objection to being touched, grabbed the diver with its mouth, underwater camera and all, and plunged hundreds of feet down into the ocean before letting the petrified woman go. All of this was caught on tape. The footage was absolutely terrifying to watch. It was a miracle the diver survived. In my books, that story was right up there with Jonah's tale. So, when Wilma clamped down on my foot, needless to say, I had a moment. Thank goodness, she only held on for a moment.

"Oh boy, did that ever feel strange!" I shouted, as Wilma let go. "It's almost as if she's checking what I'm made of."

"Exactly," John replied. "Now, slap the water right in front of you three or four times with the palm of your hand and watch what happens."

I cupped my hand and slapped the water as requested, calling out to Wilma as I did so. "C'mon, Wilma. Come see me, honey. Come on."

Wilma suddenly appeared in front of me, no more than an arm's length away. She was only a few centimetres under the surface. I could see her eyes – big soft eyes – staring intently at mine. It was magical.

"Try to touch her, Wayne. Move slowly. Try patting her head."

I reached forward, still in awe of what was happening. As my hand came to rest on her forehead, Wilma lifted her face out of the water. She was beautiful! She had the most wonderful smiling face. And those eyes weren't just big and soft, they were intelligent. She crinkled her forehead as she laughed, mouth open, obviously enjoying the encounter with her new-found friend.

"Rub her teeth and gums," John said. "She loves to have her gums rubbed."

It was almost as if John were directing a play. Lauren loved it. She was not only pleased that Wilma showed up for us, she was thrilled at the footage we were getting. When you deal with animals, you don't always get a second take. Tom was ecstatic. He hadn't stopped rolling tape for a moment. He wanted to get every inch of footage he could while she was here.

Even John was beside himself. Wilma was performing as he said she would, and more. From the beginning he knew there was always the possibly of having a dud day – we had to get footage of

Wilma. Well, we were having a *whale* of a day! In our dreams, we had hoped for a few lucky minutes with Wilma. I thought that touching her would be a bonus. Little did we know I would be in the water with her for nearly two hours that morning.

Wilma was also having a ball. It was playtime. I rubbed her head, massaged her gums, and stroked her body over and over again. We had bonded. There was no fear. At one point she passed between my legs and, for one brave moment, I considered clamping my legs around her for a ride. I'm not sure if it was common sense or visions of the lady diver going down with the great grey whale that prevailed; however, I didn't try it. Besides, I didn't want to scare her off.

There were times in the water that Wilma seemed almost human. That smiling face would surface and she would make the most fascinating noises with her mouth, cute little squeaks, chirps, jaw claps, and whistles. I almost expected her to speak. But it was that flexible neck of hers that really gave her a human quality. Depending on what captured her interest, she was constantly posturing, moving her head to and fro. She'd stare at my face with that big happy smile of hers and suddenly rotate her head over to John in the boat, before swinging back to me again, announcing to all who were gathered that she was no ordinary denizen of the deep. She was Wilma, Queen of Chedabucto Bay, and she was holding court at sea, Sir John of Guysborough to the left of her, Sir Wayne of the Road to the right.

The most magical and spontaneous thing of all happened when it was time to say goodbye and leave the water. I can't remember if I was cold or not. Quite frankly, I was so enamoured with Wilma, I didn't feel the Atlantic at all. Lauren was far more worried about me than I was. I sure hated leaving this special moment, because I knew it might be a few lifetimes before I swam in the ocean with a whale again. By now I knew how to attract Wilma's attention. I slapped my hand on the water, several times in succession, and called out her name.

"C'mon, Wilma. Come say goodbye. Gotta go, Wilma."

Wilma came right up to me and lifted her head out of the water right next to mine. Without even thinking about it, I wrapped my arms around her neck and kissed Wilma on the forehead.

"I don't believe it!" I exclaimed. "I just kissed a whale! In the ocean!" It was an absolutely spiritual moment for me.

John was almost moved to tears. He was so happy we caught that moment on tape. "Now I'll have something to show people who have a hard time believing this thing is really happening here in Guysborough. That was incredible! Today Wilma did everything I hoped she would do and more. But that kiss was too much!"

Wilma followed our boat for most of the return trip to Guysborough. It was fascinating to watch her from the deck; it was completely different looking at her from this angle. She swam effortlessly, sometimes on her side, keeping up with the boat, even at speed.

"This is the only time I worry about her," John said. "It's when propellers are turning in the water. She seems captivated by them. I think it has something to do with the bubbles they create, hot water or turbulence, I guess. You've got to know how to handle a boat around her."

"Has she ever been hurt?" I asked.

"No, knock wood. We're trying to educate the public to use caution when they approach this whale, to shut their motors off. And when they leave, to leave slowly and watch out for her."

Guysborough was coming into view now. It certainly was a pretty town, nestled in the hills and shorelines of Chedabucto Bay.

"Wilma will be leaving us about now," John announced. No sooner had the words left his lips than she was gone.

I think about Wilma often, wondering if she'll stay in Chedabucto Bay now that she's reaching maturity. I hope to visit her again before she leaves. In another year or two, she'll be pure white, an adult, and might follow the call of nature to the frozen sheet ice of the high Arctic to be with others of her own kind. In the meantime, it's reassuring to know that John and the community of Guysborough are watching out for her.

MIKE CHAMPAGNE

Getting ready to "interview" Harry in his tinsmith shop

WAYNE ROSTAD

Producer Malcolm Hamilton with Harry

WAYNE ROSTAD

Audioman Mike Champagne chats with Harry during a break in shooting

Shubenacadie Tinsmith Man

〜

Harry is a quiet man.
All of his life, he's been using his hands,
tinkering in tin,
making things like his daddy did.
A hardware store and tin-shop home
is the only life Harry's ever known,
But it keeps him alive
and keeps him going strong.

– from the song "Shubenacadie Tinsmith Man"

In April 1996, an amazing thing happened. I picked up the phone and called an old friend, ninety-two-year-old Harry Smith in Shubenacadie, Nova Scotia. Harry was on my mind. I hadn't spoken with him in four years, and I wanted to find out how he was doing. I had just been down in my basement rummaging through my files to find a letter Harry had written me back in 1991. I wanted Harry's story to be included in this book, and was determined to find it, because it was filled with information about Harry's life – and it was such a sweet letter.

The phone rang only twice before Harry answered.

"Hello, Harry?"

"Yes . . ."

"It's Wayne Rostad, 'On the Road Again.'"

"Yes . . . Oh, hello, Wayne," Harry replied, in a slow, but steady, voice. "Isn't this a surprise."

"How are you doing, Harry?"

"I just finished hanging your picture on the wall."

"What picture is that, Harry?"

"The picture you sent me a while back . . . two or three years ago, I think. I just put it in a frame about an hour ago and hung it on the wall."

"Harry, I don't believe this. Do you know what *I* was doing an hour ago? I was reading the letter you sent me back in 1991. I pulled it out of my files an hour ago . . . you know, the one you sent me after we did our 'On the Road Again' show on you."

"Oh, yes. Now, that's quite a coincidence, isn't it?"

It felt like more than just a coincidence to me. It gave me the shivers.

"The reason I went down and got that letter, Harry, was I needed information, because I'm writing a book, and one of the chapters is about you, the tinsmith man!"

"Oh, well, that's nice . . . don't go painting too high a picture of me, now."

"How have you been, Harry?"

"Oh, not too bad. Not too bad."

It was so nice to hear Harry's voice again. It had been far too long between telephone calls. I was happy he sounded so good. After all, he was ninety-two.

Harry was a tinsmith. All his life he had made milk cans for farmers, out of tin.

"How's the shop, Harry? Do you still work in the shop?"

"Yes. A little bit. I'm just getting ready to open up again for the summer. I open up when people want to see my little museum."

That was *really* good news. Harry was still at it.

I first met Harry in 1989, when "On the Road Again" paid a visit to his tinsmith shop in the small town of Shubenacadie, fifty kilometres north of Halifax. Harry was eighty-six then. He was a very sweet man, who wore black-rimmed glasses and still had a good shock of white hair flowing back from his temples.

The shop was in the back of a fairly large building on the main street in Shubenacadie. The front part of the building, painted red with white trim, housed a hardware store, which Harry also operated. In recent years it had supported the dwindling tin-shop business. Both were started by Harry's father, Watson, back in 1895. Watson Smith & Sons Retail Hardware & Tin Shop offered just about everything anyone in the community needed. Out front, there were hardware, china, guns and ammunition, nuts and bolts, fishing gear – everything right down to the kitchen sink – and, in the back of the building, all kinds of custom-made tinware, not the least of which were creamer and milk cans.

When you stepped into the tin shop, it was like entering a place where time stood still. It was built back before the turn of the twentieth century and, except for the addition of electric light, nothing had changed. One set of cutting wheels on a circular shearing machine was made of special steel that would be difficult to find today. The wheels were so strong that, in spite of having cut close to a million pieces of sheet metal, they had never needed a single sharpening. Almost a hundred years after the shop first opened, Harry was still using the very same machinery – right down to the last hand crank and foot lever his dad had used – to make milk cans.

"There was a lot of demand for milk cans in those days," Harry told me during that visit to his shop. "I used to make a dozen a day. By the time my father died in 1953, the two of us had made over sixty thousand milk and cream cans. And I can't tell you how many I've made on my own since then."

The tin milk cans and cream cans were the mainstay of the tin shop until well into the 1950s. Harry and his father supplied every farmer for miles around with the ten-quart and sixteen-quart cans they needed for their dairy operations. About the time Harry's father died, though, stainless-steel tanker trucks began taking over the job of collecting the bulk of the milk from the farmers, and, as a consequence, the tin-shop business began to dwindle. By the 1960s, milk cans went out of style and started to become collectors' items. Harry had to rely more and more on the hardware store to earn a living.

But his heart was really in the tin shop. Except for five years spent overseas during the Second World War, Harry had lived his whole life above that shop. He was born upstairs in one of the small rooms back in 1903. Many times, as a child, Harry sat and watched his father at work. He knew every nook and cranny of that old building by heart, and, in all the years since his father had died, Harry left things pretty much the same as they always were. He wasn't interested in keeping up with the times.

When our show did the profile on Harry's tin shop, very few people knew you could actually buy a brand-spanking-new milk can made like they made them in the old days. And because no one knew about it, business at Harry's shop was not exactly brisk. The hardware business wasn't the way it had once been, either. There was a big new Home Hardware store directly across the street from Harry's place, and the writing was on the wall. Harry's one hope for his building was to turn everything in it into a museum; that way, the tin shop and hardware store would stand forever. He figured the days of working in a tin shop were over anyway, and, being well into his eighties, he figured his days would soon be over, too. There was a look of resignation in his eyes that saddened me. I remember him reminiscing fondly about the past.

"Shubenacadie was a thriving little town back then," he told me, "and every farmer in the area used our cans. I made a lot of cans in those days. I was always making something. If I got an idea to make something, I'd just go ahead and do it. Everything was here for me to use. I loved to tinker with tin."

Well, the most wonderful thing happened when the story of the Shubenacadie Tinsmith Man went to air on national television. Harry was flooded with letters, phone calls, and visits from people all over Canada wanting him to make them a milk can. It gave

Harry's life a whole new meaning. The museum, if it was meant to be, would have to be a working museum.

The letter I retrieved from my files the morning I called Harry was written two years after that story aired.

"This is really a lovely letter, Harry," I told him. "Do you remember what you said in that letter?"

"Oh, yes," he told me. "I told you your program really put me to work again."

In that January letter of 1991, Harry wrote:

Since you had the story of my business on your show in February 1989, I was swamped with letters from all over Canada, and one from the Northwest Territories. With the help of my Remington Rand portable typewriter that I have had for more than fifty years, I have been able to acknowledge all of them. I received many wonderful letters. I get a great deal of pleasure reading them over. Many of the letters I received, and the hundreds of people who have been in here since, speak of your show "On the Road Again." I am deeply indebted to you for what you have done for me.

So many people wanted one of my milk cans, as they are collectors' items now. I made quite a few in 1989 and they have gone all over Canada. The first one went to Manitoba. I have had tourists from Victoria, Vancouver, Edmonton and even Oregon and Washington. They all saw it on TV. The ones from Edmonton and Oregon each got a milk can. I am unable to supply the demand now. I am still having people call, wanting a milk can. I hate to disappoint them . . . I only wish I had five hundred cans in stock, as we had at one time.

I had lots of questions for Harry that day on the phone.

"Are people *still* asking you for milk cans, Harry? Even today?"

"I'm still being asked for them, yes. But I get tired now. I make the odd one. Not as many as I used to. I'm not as young as I used to be, you know. I'll be ninety-three in September."

"But are you feeling okay, other than that?" I asked.

"Oh, yes. All in all, I'm feeling pretty good. Not bad for a young fella, you know."

"So the old shop's still keeping you busy? It still keeps you going?"

"Too much, sometimes. But I guess that's good. It keeps me out of mischief."

"Do you still call it a museum, Harry?"

"It's a museum, yes. I only open in the summer, you know. It's a fine museum, and people love to visit, but it's a lot of work."

"Harry, part of the reason I called was to ask you a question about the time you went overseas."

"Yes. Well, I went over in '39. Came home in '44."

"What I need to know, Harry, for my chapter in the book, is whether you actually became a pilot or not? You said you wanted to be a pilot. Did you get to fly during the war?"

"Not during the war, no. I did fly with the Halifax Flying Club in the thirties. When the war broke out, I went overseas hoping to fly a Spitfire or Hurricane, but they said I was too old to fly. You see, when I went overseas in '39, I was thirty-six years old. At the beginning of the war they were pretty fussy, and they said I was too old."

"So what did you do overseas?"

"Well, I worked as part of the maintenance crew on airplanes. I was an airframe mechanic. I got to test-fly a Halifax bomber once while I was over there, but I never flew a plane in a mission."

"How long did you say you were overseas?"

"I was over there nearly five years. I was released in '44. They sent me to Ottawa for five months until I got my discharge, and then I went home."

"You didn't want a change of lifestyle?" I asked

"No. Dad had been keeping the business going while I was away, and he needed me to help him. He was getting old, you know. So I went home and started making milk cans again."

"By the way, Harry, I still sing the song I wrote for you whenever I perform at concerts across the country. I tell everybody about the Shubenacadie Tinsmith Man."

"I know. That's very nice. People tell me they hear it sometimes. They tell me you say some nice things about me in that song. Don't go putting me up too high, now."

"How is Pearl doing, Harry. Are you and Pearl still seeing one another?"

"Pearl's fine. In fact, she's visiting today. She's here now."

Pearl Robinson is a wonderful lady Harry has known for twenty-nine years now. She lives down the street from Harry's tin-shop home. She used to work in Harry's hardware store until it became a museum. Pearl's husband had died in 1986, and we heard on the grapevine a few months after we paid Harry a visit in 1989 that, as a result of all the national attention and the sudden upswing in Harry's milk-can production, there was a renewed gleam in his eye for Pearl. Rumour had it he was about to pop the big question.

"Did you not marry her yet, Harry?" I teased.

"No. We're not married," he laughed. "You asked me that question before, years ago. I explained it all in that letter you have."

Indeed he had explained not being married. On his Remington Rand portable, he wrote:

You asked me why I never married. I worked hard back in those early days, making a dozen milk cans during the day and in the evenings I worked building things I had never made before. We installed a good many wood furnaces back in the cold winter nights. I made a dozen milk cans during the day and after supper drove in the Chev truck, twenty miles, more or less, and installed a wood furnace in their house as they needed the heat. I got home around three o'clock in the morning. I did have some wonderful girl friends before the

war and would have married if the war hadn't happened when
it did. I stayed over there too long and they all got married.
Now they are all widows but one, and we are all still good
friends. They write to me, even the one who is down in Florida
for the winter with her husband. They are both good friends
of mine. Bessie Reid, who worked for my brother in the front
store years ago, is also a widow and she calls me every week on
the phone after I go to bed, as I have a phone by my bed. She
was always cheerful and jolly and it helps. There are a lot of
widows in Shubenacadie – perhaps it is just as well I never
married.

"The only problem with your letter, Harry, is you didn't
address why you never married Pearl," I bantered. "You talked
about everybody *but* Pearl. We heard you were thinking of asking
her. Is it true?"

"Well, I thought of it, yes."

"Well, what happened?"

"I was just too shy . . . I was too shy."

"God love you, Harry. Let me know if you ever pop the
question."

"Well, the way I see it . . . we get along so well, if we got
married, we might *not* get along so well," he laughed.

"I imagine she's pretty special," I said.

"Oh, yes!" he exclaimed. "I couldn't live without her. On top
of that she helps out here, at the shop, all the time, you know. Oh,
I couldn't get by without her."

"Well, Harry, I'll let you get back to your work now. Please
give my love to Pearl."

"Yes. You must come visit, if you're in the neighbourhood."

"I promise. Harry, it was good talking to you. I'll see you
soon."

"Well, bye for now."

"'Bye, Harry."

Harry's in his nineties now. He still lives in that same old town.
He's got a girl named Pearl and, someday, he just might marry her.
They'll probably live in that tin-shop home,
It's the only life Harry's ever known; but, it will keep them alive
And keep them going strong.

Shubenacadie Tinsmith Man, a genuine old time artisan
Working in his tin shop using his hands like his daddy did.
Everything stays pretty much the same;
The truth is, things rarely change
In the world of the Shubenacadie Tinsmith Man.

– from the song "Shubenacadie Tinsmith Man"

Quintin, Emard, and Veard Court

The newlyweds, Alice and Vance

"Captain" Emard at work

The Promise

As far as anyone on Prince Edward Island was concerned, the Court brothers of North Rustico were going to be bachelors till the day they died. There were four of them – Quintin, Veard, Emard, and Vance – all champions of bachelorhood. A fifth brother, Myron, was the only son of Oscar "Beecher" Court and Ella Beatrice Affleck who had ever dared succumb to matrimony, marrying Marilyn Douglas of Alberta twenty-two years ago and moving west with her, leaving his bachelor brothers to fend for themselves. Well, for over two decades they did just that. No way was a second Court going down for the count. No, sir. The Court brothers of North Rustico, fishermen who were very good at hooking fish, were not about to allow *themselves* to get hooked, ever. Then, in September of 1993, the unthinkable happened. Vance Court married.

I had first met the Court Brothers back in 1988 when "On the Road Again" paid a visit to their fishing operation on the north shore of Prince Edward Island, about thirty minutes northwest of Charlottetown. The Court family, I was told, had been established in the Rustico area for more than one hundred and fifty years, first as farmers when they landed on Prince Edward Island from Warwickshire, England, then as fishermen on the point of land they now occupy beside the lighthouse at the end of North Rustico harbour, where the Court brothers' domain looks out on the Gulf of St. Lawrence.

Beecher Court, the father of the present Court brothers, was rumoured to have been a domineering man, who did not want his sons to marry, but I'm not sure that was true. You see, Beecher died in 1980. If he was all that stood between the Court boys and the altar, I imagine one or two of the boys would have at least *thought* about taking a bride. But not one of the remaining four bachelor brothers took that long walk down the aisle in the nine years between Beecher's passing and our meeting in 1989. I think Beecher was just a good excuse.

The Court brothers are, to say the least, four of the most refreshing people I have ever met in my travels. Quintin is the eldest. He was sixty-eight when I first met him in 1988 on their wharf in North Rustico, and he appeared a little stern-faced at first. I think maybe older brothers are supposed to be like that – especially when they have to look after their little brothers by constantly being on the lookout for marauding women in search of husbands. But I knew that, deep down, he was a sweetheart. And, sure enough, once we got to know him, he was as tender a soul as any bachelor in his late sixties could be. Quintin was a man of average height and build, with a full, thick moustache and a dark head of hair. He cut a dapper figure in his blue plaid shirt, brown plaid jacket and trousers, with suspenders. The crowning touch was the ball cap he wore, which had his name, Quintin Court, in big black letters on the front above the peak.

The second-eldest, Emard, was sixty-six back then, a lean man who sported a lovely salt-and-pepper beard, about fifteen to twenty centimetres long, combed straight down. He had wonderful dancing eyes. He wore coveralls and great yellow rubber boots, which he was very proud of, and his ball cap, in white letters, read "Capt. Emard Court."

Veard was sixty-four. He not only loved a good joke, he liked to tell one, too. He was a little more heavy-set than Quintin and Emard, and his red golf shirt had his name emblazoned in white across the chest, framed perfectly between his red-white-and-blue-striped suspenders.

Vance, the youngest at age fifty-five, was a cheerful good-looking "kid," the baby brother, who had a shock of black hair and an easygoing disposition.

When the four of them stood together in front of you, there was an aura of freedom about them. I didn't detect any sense of lonely longing in their eyes, no casting of nets upon the seas of love, no "Will I ever find her?" vibes whatsoever. Just four happy-go-lucky brothers, who, like the famed musketeers, lived by the credo, "All for one, and one for all!"

The present "Fish House," used for salting fish, is painted bright yellow and trimmed in white. Like all the other Court buildings at the wharf's end, it dates back to the 1800s. Life in North Rustico has always been one of harmonious accord with the seasons. The Courts spend May and June lobster fishing. The balance of the summer is spent taking tourists on deep-sea-fishing excursions – three tours daily, at 8:00 a.m., 1:00 p.m., and 6:00 p.m. In the fall, the brothers fish for mackerel, and over the winter they clean and repair their gear for the next season.

That's the way things were for years – and the way everyone thought they always would be. So, the year I promised the Courts I would sing at the wedding if one of them ever decided to get married, I felt I was making a promise I would never have to keep. A Court getting hitched was as likely as someone hitching a hay wagon to a team of hamsters. No doubt about it. This was one safe promise.

I made that promise in front of eleven hundred fans at the Crapaud Exhibition. Crapaud, which translated from French means "toad," is the name of a small hamlet exactly thirty kilometres due south of North Rustico. For years in the month of July, I have performed in concert and entertained people in the big curling rink, singing songs and telling stories about my travels. It is one of my all-time favourite stages to perform on in the country.

My first show at the Crapaud Exhibition was in 1991, and it didn't take me very long to realize just how small Prince Edward Island is. In my audience was just about every Islander we had ever profiled on our television show.

Art Peters, the "fish man" of Oyster Bed Bridge, who sold his fish door to door, was there, boisterously calling out, "Tamarack 'er down, Wayne!", an expression born at a thank-you party Art and his wife, Zeta, threw for "On the Road Again" at their home the year we told his story.

Teresa Wilson of St. Peter's Bay and Jenny McQuaid of Charlottetown, two P.E.I. women who have a comedy act called Bridget and Cicily, which we featured on our television show, were there as my opening act on stage that night. They do a great portrayal of two elderly island women with strong dialects, who carry on about their make-believe husbands, Angus and Johnnie, and all the ailments and problems associated with everyday life.

Bill Acorn – the host of the longest-running cable-TV show on the island – was there. "Wild Bill's Jamboree" has been on the air for twenty years now, putting him right up there with Fred Davis's "Front Page Challenge" and "Don Messer's Jubilee" for the title of longest-running show in Canadian television – though Bill is still on the air. When I heard Bill's voice call out from the audience, I got him to come up on stage to sing a song with me, expecting him to be dressed in his trademark country-and-western garb – cowboy hat, boots, and sequinned silk shirt. When a hatless fellow made his way up the stairs to the stage in a short-sleeved shirt, Bermuda shorts, and knee-length black stockings in a pair of loafers, I wondered for a moment who he was. Well, it was Bill, all right. I'd just never seen him outside the studio, as an Islander.

My friend Eric MacEwen was there, with his wife, Nancy. Eric was a North Rustico native who had left the island to make his fortune as a rock-and-roll disc jockey. But, unhappy with the trappings of the big rock world, and unable to get fiddles and accordions and waltzes and jigs out of his head and his heart, Eric had returned to his roots, bought a small farm outside North Rustico, and started up the highly successful "Eric MacEwen Radio Show," a wonderful syndicated show featuring the music of the East Coast.

The North River Fire Brigade was also in the audience. At my Crapaud concert in 1993, Fire Chief Norman MacPhee would swear me in as an honorary member of the North River Fire Department, presenting me with a genuine firefighter's hat, which I treasure to this day.

But of all the people who filled me with gladness by their presence at my concert, it was the Court brothers that made my heart sing. Elmer MacDonald, the concert organizer, told me that Quintin had heard me say, in a CBC Radio interview in Charlottetown, how I was hoping the Court brothers would be in attendance when I took to the stage in Crapaud. Well, according to Elmer, Quintin took that comment as a request for them to be there, and promptly marched over to the local ticket outlet in North Rustico and bought tickets for all of them to attend my show. They have never missed one of my shows at Crapaud since.

Nineteen ninety-three was the third year in a row I had been booked to appear in Crapaud, and, for the third year in a row, the Court brothers were there. They were at the doors of the Crapaud curling rink fully two hours before they opened, and were sitting front-row centre when I entered the rink for my performance.

Now, it was one thing to see the Courts dressed up in suits and ties, out on the town, away from the wharf in North Rustico. They were a handsome-looking lot. But, what was mind-boggling that particular year in Crapaud was that three of the Courts were sitting with women! Emard was sitting with a woman. Quintin had a beauty beside him, and Vance had a woman sitting perilously close to his left shoulder. Veard was the only Court giving any sign of bachelorhood whatsoever. When I called attention to the presence of the Courts, as I had done in the preceding two years in Crapaud, the audience loved it. At the preceding concerts, I had played the Courts up as the last bastions of bachelorhood on the island and had pointed out that history would be made the day one of them fell prey to the wiles of the opposite sex. Well, that night in Crapaud, when I announced the Courts were in the audience with women, the audience roared its approval. There was a great ovation, which the Courts stood to acknowledge.

"What an incredible sight this is to see!" I gleefully announced over the sound system. "I can't believe there are women sitting with you guys. This is better than seeing Halley's comet!"

The Courts were enjoying the fun. It was all good-natured, and very affectionate. There was no doubt in anyone's mind that Prince Edward Islanders loved the Court brothers.

"Ladies and gentlemen," I said from the mike at centre stage. "I have something I would like to say. If one of the Court brothers ever ties the knot, I promise, here and now, in front of all of you, that, no matter what it takes, I will sing at his wedding."

Well, the audience approved that thought, breaking out in spontaneous applause and cheering. The Courts chuckled. They, and everyone in that arena, including me, knew it wasn't going to happen – any more than the missing city of Atlantis was going to rise from the sea in the Northumberland Strait. But we all enjoyed the image of a Court marrying, and had fun with it.

Three months later, I received a call at my farm in Ontario from Eric MacEwen in North Rustico.

"Wayne, are you sitting down?"

"Yes. Who died?"

"Nobody died. Something bigger than that has happened."

"What?"

I was dying for him to get to the point. Eric was taking forever to make it, as if savouring every moment of his call.

"Remember when you made that promise in Crapaud to sing at the wedding if a Court brother ever got married?"

"Holy smoke! Do you mean to tell me a Court is getting married?"

"They already got married. Vance, the youngest one, married Alice Roberts, the woman you met in Crapaud!"

"The one from Burlington, Ontario?"

"Yes, the lady from Burlington. She and Vance just got married on the Island in West Cove Head, and there's a big wedding reception being held for them in November here in North Rustico."

"I don't believe it!" I said.

"Neither does half the Island. We're all in shock."

"What date is the reception?" I asked, hoping my schedule wasn't going to conflict.

"Would you actually consider coming?" Eric asked.

"Of course, Eric. I promised, didn't I? Not only that, I made that promise in front of more than a thousand people. How could I not come?"

"That will blow their minds. It's the first weekend in November, at the North Rustico Lion's Club. Can you make it?"

"I'm in Saskatchewan that week, but I land in Ottawa at four-thirty Friday afternoon. I think there's an Air Canada departure for Halifax that connects to Charlottetown. I could be there somewhere around eight-thirty that evening."

"Perfect!" Eric exclaimed. "They've asked me to be the master of ceremonies. I won't say a word. I'll have you picked up at the airport. Will you and Leanne be able to stay a day? We have lots of room at the house."

"I'd love to Eric. According to my calender, Leanne is working weekends next month. I'll check it out and let you know."

"Good. Nancy and I will wait to hear from you."

"I can't believe it," I said. "They got one."

"Yes, sir. One down, three to go."

There were no snags or delays the day I arrived at Charlottetown airport. I arrived alone, since Leanne, who also works in television, did in fact have to work in Ottawa that weekend. I was whisked to the Lion's Club in North Rustico by a friend of Eric's and was brought around to the back of the building, where another person, who was on lookout, unlocked the

rear door. I went into the kitchen, where I was to stay until sum-
moned by Eric. While he conducted events in the main hall, I
tuned my guitar for the wedding song.

There were more than a hundred people gathered in the hall
for Vance and Alice's wedding reception. After Mona Clay finished reading cards of congratulation from everyone, Eric walked
to a microphone set up on a small stage and addressed the audience. Vance, dressed in a handsome black suit and tie, and Alice,
in a pretty floral suit, sat in a couple of chairs adorned with
helium-filled balloons and colourful ribbons, listening as Eric
told them how hard pressed he had been to find someone who
would sing their wedding song.

"In the end," Eric told them, "there was one person who
agreed to come here and sing, just for you."

On that note, I wandered out of the kitchen into the hall and
over to Vance and Alice. It was a memorable moment. There
were tears and hugs and a lot of applause.

"Alice," I said, "you have to agree that life is a wonderful thing.
Three years ago you came here to catch some lobster. I'll bet you
never knew then you'd end up catching a Court."

Everyone laughed and applauded Vance's good fortune. In
their eyes, Vance was the lucky one who caught Alice. She's a
lovely lady, and the community welcomed her to North Rustico
that night with open and loving arms.

"We are witnessing the eighth wonder of the world," I said as
I began strumming my guitar. "One of the Court brothers got
married."

I sang a song made popular by Anne Murray, filled with wonderful lyrics like, "Could I have this dance for the rest of my life?"
Then I walked to the stage Eric had prepared for me and sang a
bunch of songs for everyone gathered in the hall. The party went
on for a good while; it was a great night. All the Courts were
there, including Quintin, who was with Florence Rae, the woman
he brought to Crapaud the night I made my promise. I confirmed

my ongoing commitment to the Courts, telling their friends at the shower that, if Quintin and Florence ever tied the knot, I would sing at their wedding, too.

"You have to be next, Quintin," I said. "You, being the oldest, should have led the charge in the first place."

Well, last time I checked, in the fall of 1996, it still hadn't happened. Veard and Emard were still single. Quintin was still on the block, but I think he's going to be next. Meanwhile, Vance and Alice continue to be happily married, living with the three remaining bachelor brothers in the little house by the sea that the Courts have lived in all their lives. Mind you, the house is a lot cleaner these days, and Alice keeps the boys pretty well in line, making sure they all do their part around the place, picking up after themselves and leading good Christian lives.

Other than that, not a lot has changed. The Courts continue to live in harmony with the seasons. They do a little lobster fishing in the early summer and deep-sea fishing in the late summer; they search for mackerel in the fall and clean their gear when winter comes to the Island.

I received a letter from Eric after the reception in North Rustico, telling me how, for days following the event, Vance and Alice bubbled about it. He said the couple were simply overwhelmed by the kindness and generosity shown by everyone. Eric's postscript gave me a chuckle. He wrote: "P.S. Vance was so appreciative he delivered a truckload of manure up here on Monday. I don't know exactly what that says, but I'm sure it's good."

There is one postscript I would like to add to this story, something that happened in May of 1996, just as I was completing this chapter on the Courts. I was working in my office at my farm in Ontario, looking at a file which contained the newspaper clippings from two Island newspapers that carried the story of the special trip I made to the island to sing at Vance and Alice's wedding. In Summerside, the *Journal-Pioneer*'s headline read: "WAYNE ROSTAD MAKES SURPRISE APPEARANCE AT RUSTICO WEDDING – SERENADES VANCE AND ALICE COURT." The *Charlottetown Guardian* had a headline that read: "ROSTAD HONOURS PROMISE."

I had just put the clippings down on my desk, when our doorbell rang. I went to the side door, wondering who was paying us a visit, and there, standing in my yard, were Vance, Alice, and Emard! I let out a scream of delight, spiked with amazement. I thought I was seeing things. This was too incredible a coincidence to be real. I had just finished reading the headlines of the newspaper clippings that Eric MacEwen had sent me years earlier, and here I was looking at the Courts in my yard. Never in my wildest dreams would I have ever imagined seeing them anywhere other than on the wharf in North Rustico or front-row centre at a concert on the Island.

There were two other people with them. Turns out the Courts have two sisters, which I never knew till that day in my yard. I met sixty-seven-year-old Linda Court; she and her husband, Alex, were accompanying Vance, Alice, and Veard to Toronto. Vance was going to a specialist to have his eyes looked at, and they were all making a bit of a "time" of it. The other sister, Una, is well into her seventies, and she and Linda both live in Bedeque, Prince Edward Island, about forty kilometres from North Rustico.

"Now, tell me this," I said. "Because I'm on the hook to sing for all the Courts when they marry, are there any more of you out there that I don't know about?"

"No," they assured me. Just the three boys.

Naturally, they stayed for a visit. I made coffee and they brought doughnuts in from the car. I showed them the clippings I was reading the very moment my doorbell rang, and they were as amazed at the coincidence as I was.

As the years go by and I continue to host "On the Road Again," my friendships with people in all parts of the country continue to grow. I visit the Courts whenever I'm in the neighbourhood, and I trust they will again visit me. And if my phone should ever ring and Eric MacEwen asks if I'm sitting down, I know I'll be "on the road again" to Prince Edward Island. And I know I will have bells on my toes and a guitar in my hand. After all, a promise is a promise.